CW01335784

GROWTH, EMPLOYMENT AND SOCIAL CHANGE IN BANGLADESH

Growth, Employment and Social Change in Bangladesh

Rushidan Islam Rahman

University Press Limited

The University Press Limited
Red Crescent House, Level 6
61 Motijheel C/A
Dhaka 1000, Bangladesh
Phones: (+8802) 9565441, 01917733741
E-mail: info@uplbooks.com.bd
Website: www.uplbooks.com

First published, December 2016

Copyright © The University Press Limited, 2016

All rights are reserved. No part of this publication may be reproduced or transmitted in any form or by any means without prior permission in writing from the publisher. Any person who does any unauthorized act in relation to this publication may be liable to criminal prosecution and civil claims for damages.

Cover designed by Mafia Sultana

ISBN 978 984 506 241 1

Published by Mohiuddin Ahmed, The University Press Limited, Red Crescent House, 61 Motijheel C/A (Level 6), Dhaka 1000. Book design by Md. Nazmul Haque and produced by Abarton, 354 Dilu Road, New Eskaton, Dhaka. Printed at the Akota Offset Press, 119 Fakirapool, Dhaka 1000, Bangladesh.

Contents

List of Tables, Figures and Boxes	xi
List of Acronyms	xxi
Preface	xxiii

PART 1
ECONOMIC GROWTH: AGGREGATE AND SECTORAL

CHAPTER 1
GDP Growth and Its Structural Change — 3

1.1 GDP Growth Scenario: Sustained Progress?	3
1.2 Factors behind the Downturn: Role of Public and Private Investment	5
1.3 Structural Change of GDP	8
1.4 Complementarities of Sectoral Growth	10
1.5 Growth Performance, Middle Income Status and Lost Potential: International Comparison	12

CHAPTER 2
Pattern of Manufacturing Sector Growth: Prospects and Challenges — 17

2.1 Growth of Manufacturing Sector: 1980-2014	17
2.2 Composition of Medium and Large Manufacturing	20
2.3 Labour Intensity and Labour Productivity	22
2.4 A Special Constraint to Industrial Growth: Land Availability for Non-farm Use	23
2.5 Future Strategies of Industrial Growth in the Face of Land Constraint	26

Chapter 3
Resource Constraints and Agricultural Growth: Availability of Arable Land and Irrigation 29
3.1 Agricultural GDP: Share and Growth 29
3.2 Availability of Arable Land 31
3.3 Irrigation 35
3.4 Cropping Intensity and Modern Variety Seeds 36
3.5 Policy Recommendations 38

Chapter 4
Factors Affecting Adoption of Modern Agricultural Technology: Evidence from Early Phase 41
4.1 Introduction 41
4.2 Role of Knowledge 42
4.3 Role of Irrigation 45
4.4 Cash Availability and Credit Facilities 49
4.5 Labour Availability 51
4.6 Summary of Findings and Conclusion 53

Chapter 5
Agricultural Productivity: Role of Farm Size, Tenancy and District Level Variations 55
5.1 Introduction 55
5.2 Notes on Data 56
5.3 Differences in Agricultural Productivity across Districts 57
5.4 Growth of Agriculture: Performance of Districts 59
5.5 Determinants of the Use of Modern Inputs: Role of Farm Size and Tenancy 60
5.6 Is Irrigation the "Leading Input"? 65
5.7 Determinants of the Use of Farm Machinery 67
5.8 Importance and Efficiency of Very Small Farms: Evidence from the HIES 2010 69
5.9 Concluding Observations 72

PART 2
EMPLOYMENT, UNDEREMPLOYMENT AND LABOUR MARKET

CHAPTER 6
Unemployment, Underemployment and Structural Change in the Labour Market — 81
  6.1 Introduction — 81
  6.2 Unemployment and Underemployment — 82
  6.3 Quality of Employment: Type (Formal/Informal), Status and Sector — 89
  6.4 Real Wage — 96
  6.5 Employment in Readymade Garment and Overseas Labour Market — 99
  6.6 Concluding Observations — 103

CHAPTER 7
Seasonal Underemployment and Its Implications — 107
  7.1 Introduction — 107
  7.2 Nature of Seasonality of Labour Use in Agriculture — 108
  7.3 Seasonal Underemployment and Food Inadequacy — 111
  7.4 Seasonality and Labour Allocation — 117
  7.5 Allocation of Labour in Non-Agriculture — 120
  7.6 Seasonality of Food Insecurity and Employment: Recent Evidence — 122
  7.7 Monthly Variation of Wage — 124
  7.8 Monthly Variation of Rice Price — 126
  7.9 Summary and Conclusions — 126

CHAPTER 8
Modern Irrigation and Equity: Do Wage Labourers Share the Benefits? — 129
  8.1 Introduction — 129
  8.2 Modern Crop Varieties, Irrigation and Labour Use — 130

- 8.3 Impact of Irrigation on Wage Rate, Employment and Income: A Framework for Analysis and the Hypotheses ... 134
- 8.4 Findings from Wage, Employment and Income Equations ... 138
- 8.5 Concluding Observations ... 146

CHAPTER 9
Youth Unemployment and Demographic Dividend — 149

- 9.1 Introduction ... 149
- 9.2 Growth of Youth Labour Force and Size of Potential Demographic Dividend ... 151
- 9.3 Youth Labour Force Under-enumeration: Missing Female Youth ... 152
- 9.4 Youth Labour Force Participation: Trends and Implication ... 153
- 9.5 Education of Youth Labour Force ... 156
- 9.6 Unemployment Rate among Youth ... 158
- 9.7 Views of Unemployed Youth ... 160
- 9.8 Major Findings and Policy Recommendations ... 165

CHAPTER 10
Inequality in Access to Education and Employment — 173

- 10.1 Introduction ... 173
- 10.2 Access to Education and Employment: How the Vicious Cycle Works ... 176
- 10.3 Access to Education: Impact of Household Income ... 177
- 10.4 Inequality in Education among Top Income Group ... 181
- 10.5 Multiple Regression Results: Factors Affecting School Enrolment and Secondary Completion ... 182
- 10.6 Rural-Urban and Regional Difference ... 183
- 10.7 Impact of Education on Labour Market ... 184
- 10.8 Summary of Findings and Policy Suggestions ... 186

PART 3
POVERTY, EMPOWERMENT AND SOCIAL CHANGE

CHAPTER 11
Poverty Reduction Experience: Hidden Questions — 197

11.1 Regional Poverty Decline: Fluctuations During 1996 to 2010 — 197
11.2 Poverty Reduction through Reduced Savings Rate? — 201
11.3 Rural-Urban Differences in Calorie Intake: Implications for Poverty Line — 206
11.4 Concluding Remarks — 209

CHAPTER 12
Children's Employment and Its Link with Schooling: Role of Poverty and Social Attitude — 211

12.1 Objectives and Rationale of the Analysis — 211
12.2 Children's Employment: Types and Trends — 213
12.3 A Framework for Analysis of Children's Participation in Economic Activity — 218
12.4 Factors Affecting Children's Participation in Paid and Family Employment — 222
12.5 Attitude towards Poor Working Children's Education: Parents' and Children's Views — 225
12.6 Policy Suggestions — 231

CHAPTER 13
Microfinance and Development: Emerging Issues — 235

13.1 Introduction — 235
13.2 Return from Economic Activities Financed by Microcredit — 235
13.3 Rate of Interest — 243

13.4 Gender Dimension of Targeting and Women's Empowerment	246
13.5 Concluding Observations	248

Chapter 14
Women's Economic Empowerment: Gender Inequality in Poverty, Labour Market and Decision Making — 251

14.1 Introduction	251
14.2 Poverty among Female-headed Households: Results Based on Conventional Definition	253
14.3 Income, Asset and Human Capital of Effective and Nominal Female-headed Households	254
14.4 Gender Inequality in Labour Market, Type of Employment and Wage	257
14.5 Determinants of Women's Employment	267
14.6 Prospects of Employment of Women from Poorer Households	271
14.7 Women's Role in Decision-Making	276
14.8 Policy Suggestion for Economic Empowerment of Women	278

Chapter 15
Linkages between Population Growth and Socio-economic Factors — 283

15.1 Introduction	283
15.2 Pattern of Fertility Decline: Difference among Socio-Economic Groups	285
15.3 Determinants of Fertility Decline during Early Years	287
15.4 Demand-Side Factors behind Fertility Choice: Difference among Socio-Economic Groups	288
15.5 Adoption of Family Planning: Link between Poverty and Supply Side of Inputs	294
15.6 Concluding Observations and Policy Implications	296
References	301
Index	309

List of Tables, Figures and Boxes

Tables

1.1	Bangladesh's GDP Growth Rate: 1981-2014	4
1.2	Private and Public Investment–GDP Ratio: 2001-2013	6
1.3	Share of Agriculture and Non-Agriculture in Bangladesh's GDP: 1990-2014	9
1.4	GDP Growth in Agriculture and Manufacturing: 1995-2014	11
1.5	GDP Per Capita in Selected Asian Countries: 1980, 2013	13
1.6	Growth Rate of GDP in Selected Asian Countries: 2000-2013	14
2.1	Growth of Small and Large & Medium Scale Manufacturing: 1980-2014	18
2.2	Rank of Manufacturing Sub-sectors in terms of Total Value Added/Quantum Index of Production (QIP)	20
2.3	Capital Intensity of Major Sub-sectors of Manufacturing	22
2.4	Productivity of Labour and Capital in Manufacturing Sub-Sectors	23
3.1	Share of Agriculture in GDP: 1974-2014	30
3.2	Rate of Growth of GDP from Agriculture: 1970-2014	31
3.3	Use of Land in Rural Areas of Bangladesh and Changes during 1984-2008	32
3.4	Use of Irrigation on Agricultural Land: 1986-2011	35
3.5	Cropping Intensity: 1972-2012	37
3.6	Coverage of High Yielding Variety (HYV) Paddy: 1980-2013	38
4.1	Distribution of Households by Causes of Not Growing High Yielding Variety (HYV)	43
4.2	Causes of Not Growing HYV Earlier than the Year Reported	43
4.3	Source of Knowledge of HYV Cultivation	44
4.4	Reasons of Not Growing HYV in Aus and Aman Season	44
4.5	Reasons of Not using Adequate Fertiliser	45
4.6	Pattern of Adoption of HYV by Different Size of Farms	47

4.7	Reasons of Not Growing HYV on More Land by Different Farm Size	48
4.8	Reasons of Not Adopting HYV by Farm Size	48
4.9	Amount Borrowed by Households with Different Farm Size	50
4.10	Willingness of Households of Different Farm Sizes to Borrow More Money	51
5.1	Gross Value Added in Agriculture and Rank of Districts	58
5.2	Growth Rates of Value Added in Agriculture (Crop Plus Non-Crop) Crop, Non-Crop, Cereal Crop and Non-Cereal Crop	59
5.3	Rank of Districts in terms of Value Added Per Capita and Population Density	64
5.4	Adoption Rate of High Yielding Variety (HYV)/Irrigation by Farm Size	71
5.5	Paddy Production and Family Labour Days Per Acre by Farm Size	71
5.1A	Determinants of the Area under HYV in Different Seasons: Results of Ordinary Least Square (OLS) Regression	75
5.2A	Determinants of Irrigation, Fertiliser Use and Cropping Intensity: Results of OLS Regression	75
5.3A	Determinants of the Number of Farm Machinery: OLS Regression Results	76
5.4A	Regression of Per Cent of Area under HYV, Fertiliser Use and Cropping Intensity on Per Cent of Area Irrigated	76
5.5A	Regression of Per Cent of Area under HYV, Fertiliser Use and Cropping Intensity on Per Cent of Area Irrigated and Rainfall	77
5.6A	Regression Results from Other Studies on the Impact of Irrigation on Inputs Use	77
6.1	Unemployment Rates in Bangladesh: 1995-2013	83
6.2	Underemployment Rates in Bangladesh: 1996-2013	86
6.3	Rural and Urban Underemployment Rate in Bangladesh	87
6.4	Growth Rates of Labour Force: 2000-2013	89
6.5	Distribution of Male and Female Labour Force by Broad Economic Sector: 1995-2013	90

6.6	Distribution of Employed Persons by Industry and Sex: 2000-2013	91
6.7	Number of Employed Persons by Industry: 1996-2013	92
6.8	Distribution of Employed Persons by Status of Employment: 1995-2013	93
6.9	Distribution of Status of Employment by Sex: 1999-2013	94
6.10	Number of Male and Female Labour Force by Status of Employment: 2006-2010	95
6.11	Size and Share of Labour Force in Formal and Informal Sector: 2000-2013	96
6.12	Growth of Nominal Wage Index and Inflation Rate	97
6.13	Employment in RMG Sector	100
6.14	Overseas Employment: 2000-2013	103
7.1	Monthly Pattern of Labour Use in Crop Production in two Villages in Savar	109
7.2	Pattern of Labour Use in Different Crop Seasons	109
7.3	Seasonal Labour Use in Bangladesh Agriculture	110
7.4	Comparison of Hypothetical and Potential Surplus Labour in Agriculture in two Villages in Savar	112
7.5	Monthly Underemployment Rate among Workers in two Villages in Savar	113
7.6	Extent of Underemployment due to Seasonality	114
7.7	Monthly Pattern of Agricultural Employment for Wage-Work and Self-Employment	115
7.8	Monthly Employment of Landless Workers in two Villages in Savar	115
7.9	Wage Rates in Harvesting Season	119
7.10	Monthly Pattern of Non-Agricultural Wage Employment and Self-Employment	121
7.11	Monthly Employment and Food Insecurity in Villages of Mymensingh	123
7.12	Monthly Wage Rates in Agriculture and Rice Price in Mymensingh and National Average	125
8.1	Use of Labour in Different Crops in Irrigated and Non-Irrigated Areas	131

8.2	Labour Input in Crop Production Per Hectare in Irrigated and Non-Irrigated Villages	132
8.3	Hired Labour Input in Crop Production Per Hectare in Irrigated and Non-Irrigated Villages	133
8.4	Employment Per Worker in Irrigated and Non-Irrigated Villages	134
8.5	Determinants of Agricultural Wage	139
8.6	Determinants of Employment of Rural Households	142
8.7	Determinants of Employment of a Rural Worker	143
8.8	Determinants of Crop Income and Other Income of Wage Labour Households	144
8.9	Determinants of Crop Income and Other Income of Farm Households	145
8.1A	Description of Variables used in Regression Analysis	148
9.1	Growth of Youth Population and Youth Labour Force	152
9.2	Under-enumeration of Female Youth Population	153
9.3	Labour Force Participation Rate among Youth and Older Population: 2000 to 2010	155
9.4	LFPR among Male and Female Youth and Older Groups	155
9.5	Level of Education of Youth Labour Force (15-29 years): 2000 to 2010	156
9.6	Distribution of Youth Employment by Status in Employment: 2000 to 2010	157
9.7	Distribution of Youth Employment by Broad Sector: 2006 to 2010	157
9.8	Growth of Young Labour Force in Different Sectors of Employment	158
9.9	Unemployment Rate among Youth Labour Force: 2000 to 2013	159
9.10	Unemployment Rate among Educated Youth	160
10.1	Enrolment Rate by Age Group and Income Group	178
10.2	Enrolment Rate among 18-22 Years Aged by Income Group	179
10.3	Distribution of Men and Women Aged 18-22 Years by Level of Education Achieved	179

10.4	Enrolment Rate in Educational Institutions by Age Group and Location	183
10.5	Enrolment Rate in Educational Institutions by Division	184
10.6	Labour Force Participation Rate (LFPR) in Bangladesh: 1991-2010	185
10.1A	Determinants of School Enrolment among 8-12 Years Old Children: Results of Logit Regression	191
10.2A	Determinants of Enrolment among 13-17 Years Old Persons: Results of Logit Regression	191
10.3A	Determinants of 'Whether Studying' for 18-22 Years Aged Persons: Results of Logit Regression	192
10.4A	Determinants of Education Status, SSC or Above among 18-22 Years Aged Persons: Results of Logit Regression	193
10.5A	Determinants of Labour Force Participation (Results of Logistic Regression): Female	193
10.6A	Determinants of Labour Force Participation (Results of Logistic Regression): Male	194
10.7A	Determinants of Wage: Results of Multiple Regression	194
11.1	Poverty Incidence by Division: 1996-2010	199
11.2	Enrolment of Children Aged 6-10 Years by Division and Poverty Status	199
11.3	Infant Mortality Rate by Division	200
11.4	Growth of Consumption: 2000-2010	202
11.5	Household Income, Consumption and Savings Rate: 1991-2010	202
11.6	Results of Savings Function (OLS Regression)	204
11.7	Household Savings Function of Extended Form: Results of OLS Regression	206
11.8	Calorie Inadequacy among Poverty Groups in Rural and Urban Areas	207
11.9	Average Calorie Intake in Urban and Rural Areas	207
11.10	Fish, Meat and Chicken Consumption by Poverty Status	208
12.1	Labour Force Participation Rates of Children (Age 5-14): 1983-84 to 2011	214
12.2	Working Children by Age Group: 1996 to 2006	216

12.3	Formal and Informal Employment among Children: 1996-2003	217
12.4	Distribution of Working Children by Status of Employment: 1996-2003	217
12.5	Working Children's Distribution by Sector of Activity	218
12.6	Parents' Response on Reasons of Children's Employment	222
12.7	Consequence If a Child Stops Work	223
12.8	Share of Children in Self/Family and Paid Employment by Household's Landownership	223
12.9	Households with Children in Economic Activity by Status of Employment of Head of Household by Income Group	224
12.10	Time Gap between Leaving School and Joining Work	226
12.11	School Dropout Children's Experience	226
12.12	Whether Son/Daughter Should Study upto at least Age 15: Parent's Opinion	228
12.13	If Children Do Not Go to School What Should be Done?: Parent's Opinion	228
12.14	Parents' Views on Children's Schooling and Work	229
12.15	What are the Major Reasons for Not Studying: Children's Response	231
13.1	Return Per Hour of Labour Input in Activities Financed by MC	236
13.2	Returns to Labour and Capital: Case Studies of Poultry Farms	238
13.3	Returns to Labour and Capital: Case Studies of Rice Mills and Paddy Processing	239
13.4	Interest Rate of Microcredit	243
13.5	Sources of Funds for the Provision of Microcredit by MFIs: 1999, 2012	245
13.6	Female Share of Borrowers in Major MFIs	246
14.1	Income and Expenditure of Male- and Female-headed Households	255
14.2	Poverty Incidence among Male- and Female-headed Households	255

14.3	Ownership of Land among Male- and Female-headed Households	256
14.4	Literacy Rate and School Enrolment Rate among Male- and Female-headed Households	257
14.5	Employment Rate and Share of Women in Total Employment by Sex: 2000-2013	258
14.6	LFPR by Sex by Location	259
14.7	Age Specific Labour Force Participation Rates by Sex: 2006-2010	259
14.8	Number and Share of Labour Force in Livestock and Poultry Rearing by Sex	262
14.9	Average Annual Growth Rate of Sectoral Employment	262
14.10	Distribution of Employment by Status, Sex and Location, 2010	263
14.11	Type of Employment: Distribution of Employed Labour Force by Sex and Formal vs. Informal	264
14.12	Female and Male Wage by Location	265
14.13	Male-Female Difference in Wage and Salary	265
14.14	Female Participation Rate in Family Employment and Paid Employment	269
14.15	Female Participation in Paid and Self-employment by Education	270
14.16	Women's Control over Decision about Spending Cash Earning by Education and Asset	276
14.17	Male and Female Earner's Role in Decision Making about Spending Own Income	277
14.1A	Determinants of Rural Household's Income: Results of OLS Regression	282
15.1	Total Fertility Rate (TFR) in Bangladesh: 1976-2011	285
15.2	Adoption of Birth Control: 1975-2011	286
15.3	TFR by Education and Asset	286
15.4	Adoption Rate (among 15-46 years aged women) of Birth Control by Education and Asset	289
15.5	Child Health related Outcomes by Asset Group	291

15.6	Desired Number of Children Desired by Ever-married Women Aged 15-49 by Asset	291
15.7	Mean Age at Marriage of Women	293
15.8	Median Age at First Child Birth and Median Age at First Marriage among Women Aged 20-49 by Education and Asset	293
15.9	Percentage of Currently Married Women Aged 14-49 Who Takes a Decision by Herself or Jointly with Husband by Asset Groups	294
15.10	Access to Family Planning Knowledge through Media and Visit by Field Workers: Difference among Asset and Education Groups	296
15.11	Policies for Different Routes to Fertility Regulation	298

Figures

1.1	Fluctuations in GDP Growth of Agriculture and Manufacturing (At Constant Prices)	11
2.1	Share of Sub-sectors in Total Export Earning, 2012	21
7.1	Employment Days and Food Insecurity in Mymensingh	124
10.1	Interrelationship between Education, Labour Market and Household Poverty	176
12.1a	Economic Participation Rate of Children (Age 5-14) by Gender, 1983-84 to 2011	215
12.1b	Number of Children (Age 5-14) in Economic Activity by Gender, 1983-84 to 2011	215
12.2	Factors behind Children's Employment	219
14.1	Linkages among Poverty, Education and Female Employment	268
15.1	Linkages among Poverty, Quality of Children and Fertility	292

Boxes

9.1	Views and Wishes of Unemployed Youth: Results of FGD Sessions among School Dropouts	161
9.2	Case Studies of Unemployed Educated Youth	162

9.3 Recent Case Studies of Young Job Aspirants 165
14.1 Prospects of Self-employment of Rural Women:
Observations Based on FGD among Women 272
14.2 Case Studies on Women's Lack
of Access to Family Employment 273

List of Acronyms

APS	Average Propensity to Save
BBS	Bangladesh Bureau of Statistics
BDHS	Bangladesh Demographic and Health Survey
BFS	Bangladesh Fertility Survey
BRAC	Bangladesh Rural Advancement Committee
CDF	Credit and Development Forum
CHT	Chittagong Hill Tracts
CLS	Child Labour Survey
CMI	Census of Manufacturing Industries
CPR	Contraceptive Prevalence Rate
DTW	Deep Tube-Well
FDI	Foreign Direct Investment
FHH	Female Headed Household
GDP	Gross Domestic Product
GoB	Government of Bangladesh
HIES	Household Income & Expenditure Survey
HSC	Higher Secondary Certificate
HYV	High Yielding Variety
ILO	International Labour Organization
IMR	Infant Mortality Rate
LF	Labour Force
LFPR	Labour Force Participation Rate
LFS	Labour Force Survey
MC	Microcredit
MF	Microfinance
MFI	Microfinance Institution
MHH	Male-Headed Household
MICS	Multiple Indicator Cluster Survey

MoF	Ministry of Finance
MPS	Marginal Propensity to Save
MRA	Microcredit Regulatory Authority
NCLS	National Child Labour Survey
NGO	Non-Governmental Organisation
OLS	Ordinary Least Square
PKSF	Palli Karma-Sahayak Foundation
QIP	Quantity Index of Production
RFH	Residential Female Headed Household
RMG	Readymade Garment
RMH	Residential Male Headed Household
RNF	Rural Non-Farm
SFYP	Sixth Five Year Plan
SFYP/7FYP	Seventh Five Year Plan
SME	Small and Medium Enterprise
SSC	Secondary School Certificate
STW	Shallow Tube-Well
TFR	Total Fertility Rate
TVET	Technical and Vocational Education and Training
UNICEF	United Nations Children's Emergency Fund
YLF	Youth Labour Force
WB	World Bank

Preface

Pessimistic views about the development prospects of Bangladesh during the period following independence are well known. However, these concerns, to some extent, have been proven wrong and the country has achieved considerable success in terms of both economic growth and social development. On the development front, most of the changes have taken place after the mid-1980s, especially during the two and a half decades after 1990. This book provides an understanding of some of the key experiences and issues in the multidimensional process of development of Bangladesh during this period. An elaboration of the objectives of the book requires highlighting what it includes, what it does not, as well as what is outside its scope.

Most books, research monographs, and anthologies on Bangladesh's development involve analysis of a specific aspect such as economic growth or socio-political changes. There is thus a need for analysis of development experience which includes both economic growth and social changes. This objective has motivated the three parts in the book: (i) economic growth: aggregate and sectoral; (ii) unemployment, underemployment and labour market; and (iii) poverty, empowerment, and population dynamics. Within economic growth, the focus is on both aggregate GDP growth and the features of sectoral growth, especially manufacturing and agriculture.

In the realm of social change, only a limited number of subjects could be included due to practical limitations set by the length of the book as well as the author's specialisation. Social changes include unemployment, labour market, child and youth labour, poverty and food security, education, women's empowerment, microfinance, and population dynamics (more specifically fertility trends). Among these topics, unemployment, underemployment and its various dimensions received more detailed attention because of the author's specialisation on the subject and also due to the importance of the topic for both social change and the future growth of the economy. In fact, the existing literature on Bangladesh's development experience has hardly touched this issue. Although a variety of political and sociological issues and governance questions are interlinked with economic growth, these were not covered because a number of studies are available on these aspects.

This book is expected to be suitable for readers who wish to gather a general picture of Bangladesh's overall and sectoral GDP growth, unemployment and the changes in poverty, women's empowerment, population growth, etc. However, the special feature of the book is that within each Chapter it goes in-depth into issues which have not received detailed attention in other books and studies. These less-told-stories can be useful for both academicians and policy makers.

While the book promises to delve into analysis of changes (both in the sphere of economic growth and in the arena of social development), annual time series data are not available for most topics, and, therefore, the analyses involve data at various points of time or even snapshots covering different spatial pictures in two points of time. Even in the face of problems with data availability, the analysis highlights significant progress in different dimensions of development and also focuses on the constraints and challenges which need to be overcome to sustain and accelerate the progress.

While the book draws on some of the author's earlier published works, it also includes newly written chapters. In fact, an attempt has been made to update the analyses through incorporation of recent data. However, the statistics from official sources are available only with a lag. Some of the key statistics are collected through national sample surveys conducted at intervals of four to five years. Therefore, most of the analyses have to depend on such survey rounds of 2005 and 2010. Chapters consisting of works published earlier are based on older data sets. These are still expected to be useful because there is a dearth of new studies on those issues. The analysis can therefore serve as reference points for future research.

The readers of this book are likely to come from various backgrounds and therefore the analyses have been presented in non-technical ways as far as possible. Most chapters use only descriptive tables and the text is usually self-contained and one may read the book without having to refer to the tables. Some econometric analyses have been presented only in a few sections. In other sections, readers have been referred to the original articles which contain more quantitative data and analysis, while the non-technical parts have been included in the book.

In the process of the publication of the book, the author received support, encouragement and concrete suggestions which show that selfless support from her brother and friends is not a fairy tale. In this context, I would like to mention Rizwanul Islam, Zafar Ahmed and Quazi Shahabuddin whose comments have helped improve the arguments and presentations of the book. Support and encouragement from my husband, Md Shafiqur Rahman has been critical for the completion of the book. Publication of the book would not have been possible without the initiative and encouragement of Mohiuddin Ahmed, Founder and Managing Director of the UPL. I am immensely grateful to him and to UPL. In addition, I wish to thank Ms Mahrukh Mohiuddin, Director, Marketing and Business Development of UPL, for her efforts for bringing this out within the shortest possible time. BIDS has given the permission to reprint my works published earlier by BIDS and I am grateful for this. Useful services from Mokbul Hossain and Meftaur Rahman are being acknowledged.

Dhaka, October 2016 **Rushidan I. Rahman**

PART 1
ECONOMIC GROWTH: AGGREGATE AND SECTORAL

CHAPTER 1

GDP Growth and Its Structural Change

In low-income countries like Bangladesh, sustained economic growth is usually accepted as the overriding development goal. At very low levels of per capita GDP, economic growth can help achieve other social development goals including poverty reduction. During the 1970s and 1980s, Bangladesh's growth prospect was generally viewed with skepticism. Stagnation of GDP growth below 4 per cent during the 1980s can be attributed to a variety of factors, including natural disasters, lack of democracy and lack of concerted policy efforts.[1] Against this backdrop, the positive changes in the performance of Bangladesh economy during the 1990s and in the new millennium have generated optimism among all quarters. Nonetheless, it must be recognised that complacence about recent achievements in the economy can be self-defeating. A cautious and realistic assessment of the GDP growth performance and structural change associated with the growth process is required so that policies may be appropriately designed to sustain the positive trends. The objective of the present chapter is to provide such an assessment.

1.1 GDP Growth Scenario: Sustained Progress?

This chapter focuses on GDP growth rates during the last two and a half decades. This can serve as a background for understanding the discussion of subsequent chapters on unemployment, poverty and social development.[2]

---

[1] During the early years after independence, Bangladesh's growth prospect appeared bleak and oft quoted comments by Faaland and Parkinson (1976) and by others revealed such pessimism. Khan (1972), however, adopted a positive view.

[2] An in-depth and comprehensive analysis of macroeconomic scenario and policy reforms influencing economic growth is beyond the scope of the present discussion.

Table 1.1 presents relevant data on GDP growth, which shows clear acceleration of growth during the period 1991-2010. This has led to ambitious targets and projections of economic growth during the Sixth Five Year Plan period (2011-2015). The targets, however, turned out to be unrealistic and achievements of growth have fallen short of targets. This phenomenon received attention when three consecutive years' GDP growth rates were way below the targets. The year 2013-14 witnessed political unrest and violence of an unprecedented extent and non-fulfilment of GDP growth targets were attributed to such political problems. GDP growth remained below the target of Sixth Five Year Plan not only in 2014 but the same was also true for the two previous years. Nonetheless, only 2014's low growth rate and its links with disruption of economic activity have usually been highlighted.

GDP growth rate for the fiscal year 2013-14 has generated concerns about the performance of the economy. The rate of GDP growth, estimated at 6.1 per cent, is lower than the target set by that year's budget and the Sixth Five Year Plan. It is also lower than the growth achieved in 2011.

Is there any valid reason for worrying about this slow GDP growth rate in 2014? Apparently, it is worrying because it is significantly less than the target. However, a decline of GDP growth or non-achievement of target in a single year may not be a serious concern. It may be a temporary downward fluctuation which can be reversed with appropriate policies.

Table 1.1: Bangladesh's GDP Growth Rate: 1981-2014

Year	Annual (Average) Growth Rate (%) Base: 1995-96	Acceleration of Growth Rate (Percentage Point)
1981-1985	3.7	-
1986-1989	3.7	0.0
1991-1996	4.5	0.7
1996-2001	5.3	0.8
2001-2006	5.7	0.4
2006-2011	6.2	0.5
2011-2014	6.1	-0.1

Source: Calculated from MoF, Bangladesh Economic Review (various years).

The question is, whether it is really a minor fluctuation and has occurred only in a single year. In fact, the real cause of concern is that there has been a continuous stagnation of GDP growth rate over the three-year period, 2011 to 2014. The GDP growth rates (*Bangladesh Economic Review*, 2014) in FY2012, FY2013 and FY2014 have been 6.5, 6.0 and 6.1 per cent respectively. Thus the decline has occurred, in larger or smaller increments during these years.

Declining trend of GDP growth during FY2011 to FY2014 can also be observed when one takes a look at three five-year periods and considers the average annual GDP growth rate. During the periods 2001-2006, 2006-2011 and 2011-2014, the average GDP growth rates were 5.7 per cent, 6.2 per cent and 6.1 per cent respectively. Table 1.1 shows that during the period 2006-2011, there was a large acceleration of GDP growth. Even during the period 2001-2006, there was some acceleration of growth.

GDP growth in 2015 shows a reversal of the previous three years' trend. Growth rate stands at 6.5 per cent. In 2016, growth rate rises to 7.1 per cent. Per capita income increases from US$ 684 in 2010 to US$ 1466 in 2016 and Bangladesh is now in the list of lower middle income countries.

When GDP growth stagnates for a number of years as observed, it is a matter of serious concern. Its causes should be identified, even if a reversal of the trend sets in. Some insights into the causes are presented below.

1.2 Factors behind the Downturn: Role of Public and Private Investment

To obtain insights into the factors behind the observed trend of GDP growth, one must take a longer term view of the economy. GDP growth rate in a particular year or over a few years cannot be explained only by the features of the economy during that specific period. Recent explanations about the slower GDP growth in 2013 have emphasised stagnation of investment rate (as a share of GDP). But data show that during the 2010-2013 period, investment as a share of GDP has slightly risen. Public investment as a share of GDP has also shown a significant rise during the same period. Then how does one explain the decline of GDP growth rate in these years?

A closer look at GDP growth rates and investment-GDP ratios during the previous period, i.e., 2006-2010, can throw light on possible long-term reasons. It can be observed that investment-GDP ratio has stagnated during the 2006-2010 period (Table 1.2). This has to some extent contributed to the stagnation of GDP growth in recent years as the investment rate can exert an influence with a time lag. The stagnation is especially true for public investment. Global financial crisis and political instability in the country contributed to the stagnation of investment during this period.

How does this long-term effect of investment take place? This can be explained with reference to specific sectors. For example, GDP growth in agriculture has recently decelerated considerably. This has happened despite good weather. It actually means that more innovation to raise productivity should have been initiated through investment on agricultural R&D. Such investment has high gestation gap. If such investment was made 6-7 years ago, it would bring fruits now. Investment in electricity, gas and other infrastructure are examples where more investment during the 2006-2010 period could have contributed to higher GDP growth during the 2010-14 period and thereafter.

Table 1.2: Private and Public Investment–GDP Ratio: 2001-2013

Year	Private Investment-GDP Ratio (%)	Public Investment-GDP Ratio (%)	Total Investment-GDP Ratio (%)
2001	15.9	7.2	23.1
2002	16.8	6.4	23.1
2003	17.2	6.2	23.4
2004	17.8	6.2	24.0
2005	18.3	6.2	24.5
2006	18.7	6.0	24.7
2007	19.0	5.5	24.5
2008	19.3	4.9	24.2
2009	19.7	4.7	24.4
2010	19.4	5.0	24.4
2011	19.5	5.6	25.2
2012	20.0	6.5	26.5
2013	19.0	7.9	26.8

Source: MoF: Bangladesh Economic Review (various years).

The stagnation of investment rate during 2006-2010 illustrates the discouraging effect resulting from the political instability during that period. This is especially true for public investment, and the ratio of investment to GDP has fallen from six per cent in 2006 to five per cent in 2010. Of course, other factors may have contributed to the stagnation of private investment rate during various segments of the 13-year period. For example, policies adopted for raising savings rate may also have had negative impact on private investment during the period from 2007 to 2011. When one considers private and public investment rates separately, it can be observed that during the entire period of 2001-2009, private investment as a share of GDP increased, although at varying rates. During 2009-2013, private investment rate stagnated as well. Therefore, despite an increase in public investment rate, total investment rate stagnated. Thus an increase in public investment rate alone could not accelerate GDP growth. This is an important message to be taken into account for adopting policies to help improve the performance of the economy in the coming years.

These comments do not mean that only long-term impact can explain the entire problem of slow GDP growth in recent years. Of course, the turn of political events has caused disruptions in the economy and estimates of losses of output have been provided by various organisations. Without entering into further discussion on this, it should rather be emphasised that political turmoil and violence carries the risk of investment disincentive in the longer term as well, thus causing more damage to the economy in the coming years. This has not been captured in the available estimates of potential loss of GDP.

Political instability is, of course, accompanied by other evils, especially corruption and misgovernance. Over the past two decades, Bangladesh has received attention for prevalence of corruption and when it came to international comparison it was in the list of the most corrupt countries. Corruption not only leads to allocative inefficiency but also can act as a disincentive for overall productive investment. It can discourage entrepreneurial effort since income accrual through corruption is a less risky path. Nonetheless, during this period, the country's GDP growth accelerated and this has been labelled as a development puzzle. The puzzle or dilemma can be easily resolved if one looks at the foregone opportunities which could be unearthed in a relatively corruption-free environment, which would possibly lead to better growth performance. Stern (2002), for example, uses other South Asian countries' data and observes that in a corruption-free environment Bangladesh's GDP growth rate would be 1-2 percentage points higher.

1.2.1 How to Reverse the Deceleration of Growth

Bangladesh has no option but to make an all out effort to raise GDP growth, on a sustained basis. To obtain results in the short run, incentives should be provided to greater utilisation of capacity in all sectors. All out efforts should be made to raise private investment rate along with adequate public investment in areas which can bear fruits in the medium-term. Price incentives to agriculture can be an area where policies can bear fruits in the short run. Restoring smooth production environment in readymade garment (RMG) industry can contribute to immediate recovery of the economy.

Increase in investment-GDP ratio can help accelerate GDP growth in the coming years if the instability and violence sparked by confrontational politics come to an end and an investment-friendly environment is created for the economy.

Here it needs to be pointed out that the impact of political turmoil at regular intervals has sometimes been viewed as a cyclical downturn of the economy, which slows down GDP growth in years of change of power or general election. However, given the long-term nature of the impact of declining investment rate, as suggested above, the stagnation of GDP growth in election years will have a dampening impact in the years following the downturn. It is also true that even if one takes into account only the downturns in the election years, the average compound growth rates of GDP over 10/15 years will be lower than the rate achievable without those downturns, other things remaining the same. The nation cannot afford this.

Therefore, a short-term solution and compromise in the political situation is not sufficient for harnessing the growth potentials of the economy. Longer-term expectations about good governance and political harmony can affect the prospects of those investment which have high gestation gap.[3]

1.3 Structural Change of GDP

According to conventional wisdom, an acceleration of GDP growth is expected to be associated with a change in the sectoral composition of GDP. As the economy grows, the emphasis on primary production declines and the industrial and services sectors' shares rise at a faster pace.

---

[3] Khan (2011) has provided a detailed discussion of this issue.

Acceleration of growth in the manufacturing and the tertiary sectors offers prospects of sustained increases in GDP growth rate because of the technological progress associated with such production and less dependence on land as a productive factor which is subject to diminishing returns (Kaldor, 1966, 1967). In contrast, Kuznets (1971) focused on the demand side factors leading to structural change and suggested that income growth usually raises the demand for non-farm products and therefore structural change is likely to raise the pace of GDP growth. Higher productivity also offers the promises of higher wage rate in modern sectors compared to wage in traditional agriculture and can raise demand for non-farm products.

This section examines whether Bangladesh economy has undergone a structural change during the last two decades. The shares of agriculture and non-agriculture sectors in GDP during 1990-2014 show a number of interesting features (Table 1.3). Agriculture's share declined from 38.3 per cent in 1990 to 16.3 per cent in 2014, whereas non-agriculture's share increased from 61.7 per cent in 1990 to 83.7 per cent in 2014. The average annual growth rates of GDP from both agriculture and non-agriculture accelerated during the entire period. But the growth rate of non-agricultural GDP was much higher and therefore its share in the total GDP has risen.

Table 1.3: Share of Agriculture and Non-Agriculture in Bangladesh's GDP: 1990-2014

(Per cent)

Year	Agriculture	Non-Agriculture
1990	38.3	61.7
1995	31.8	68.2
2000	25.2	74.5
2005	22.3	77.7
2010	20.0	80.0
2012	19.4	80.6
2014	16.3	83.7

Source: MoF: Bangladesh Economic Review (various years).

Share of non-agriculture in total GDP is much higher in the middle- and high- income countries. However, this has been made possible by high average GDP per capita, so that even with a lower share of agriculture, a country can meet much of the domestic demand of the primary products.

The conventional wisdom should not dominate the thinking about agriculture's role in the development process of present day Bangladesh. Agriculture can continue to have a large impact on GDP growth of Bangladesh because its share of GDP is large. Bangladesh may have to continue with a high share of agricultural GDP to ensure food security of its growing population. The strategy for structural change in Bangladesh's economy requires faster acceleration of GDP growth in manufacturing through creating an environment for accelerated growth in private investment while agricultural growth should be accelerated through growth of public investment. Prospect of acceleration of GDP growth depends on the simultaneous growth of farm and non-farm sectors and overemphasis on structural change of the economy in the coming years may not be the most desirable option for the country.

In addition to the changes in share of non-agricultural GDP, the changes in the share of industry and service within non-agriculture deserve attention. Bangladesh and other South Asian countries' rising share of service in GDP is being viewed as pre-mature shifts, which may not contribute to sustained GDP growth.[4]

1.4 Complementarities of Sectoral Growth

Agricultural and manufacturing growth in the last two decades shows that Bangladesh has experienced a lack of complementarity of sectoral growth. This becomes clear from data on the annual growth rates of the two sectors (Table 1.4). The annual growth rates moved in the reverse direction in most years (shown by signs in parenthesis). In some years, the growth rates of both agriculture and manufacturing declined. Only in a small number of years (2000, 2003, 2004 and 2006) did both agriculture and manufacturing experience positive changes in growth rates, and in those years growth rate of total GDP accelerated.

This inverse relationship is the result of fluctuations in the growth rates of both agriculture and industry. While the fluctuations in agricultural growth have been associated mostly with natural calamities, the fluctuations of industrial growth have been linked with a variety of factors, including both natural factors and the demand-side forces. The devastating floods of 1998 and 2005 affected both agriculture and industry.

---

[4] A detailed discussion of this issue has been provided by Islam (2015).

Table 1.4: GDP Growth in Agriculture and Manufacturing: 1995-2014

(Per cent per year)

Year	Agriculture	Manufacturing
1995	-1.9(-)	10.5 (+)
1996	2.0 (+)	6.4 (-)
1997	5.6 (+)	5.1 (-)
1998	1.6 (-)	8.5 (+)
1999	3.2 (+)	3.2 (-)
2000	6.9 (+)	4.8 (+)
2001	5.5 (-)	6.7 (+)
2002	-0.6 (-)	5.5 (-)
2003	3.3 (+)	6.8 (+)
2004	4.4 (+)	7.1 (+)
2005	1.8 (-)	8.2 (+)
2006	5.2 (+)	10.8 (+)
2007	4.7 (-)	9.7 (-)
2008	2.9 (-)	7.2 (-)
2009	4.1 (+)	6.7 (-)
2010	5.6 (+)	6.5 (-)
2011	5.0 (-)	9.5 (+)
2012	2.5 (-)	9.4 (-)
2013*	1.5 (-)	10.3 (+)
2014*	2.5 (+)	8.7 (-)

Note: () shows change over previous year. *(at constant 2005-06 prices, rest at 1995-96 prices).

Source: MoF: Bangladesh Economic Review (various years).

Figure 1.1: Fluctuations in GDP Growth of Agriculture and Manufacturing (At Constant Prices)

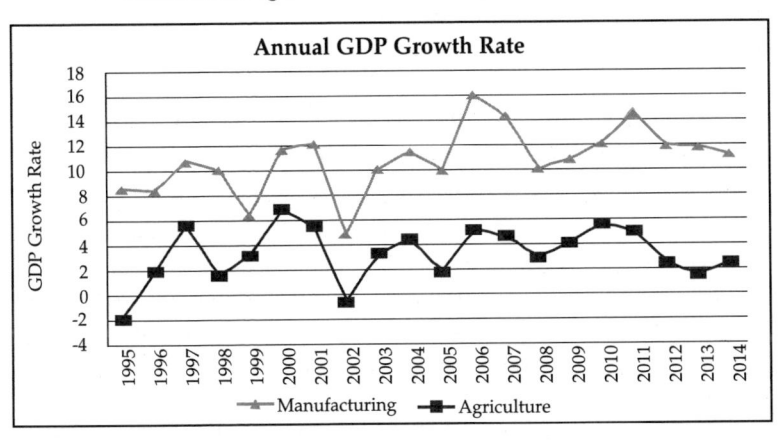

Source: MoF: Bangladesh Economic Review (various years).

The negative association between GDP growth in agriculture and manufacturing also reflects a natural response of the economy where the work force is involved in diversified occupations. When one type of activity faces a setback, people automatically resort to other types and thus the change of sectoral GDP growth is, at least partly, a reflection of the resilience of the large majority of the small producers and low-income groups. In the years of bad agriculture, industrial growth is expected to accelerate as hired labour is more easily available. However, the magnitude of such automatic response is not expected to be so large as to have a sufficient counter cyclical impact.

An important factor that has contributed to the observed phenomenon is the nature of government interventions and conscious policy efforts. For example, during the decline of manufacturing growth rate at the end of the 1990s, the government tried to ease credit facilities and other services for accelerating agricultural growth.

It should be mentioned that a much higher GDP growth rate could be achieved if acceleration of GDP growth in agriculture and industry took place simultaneously. In fact, such speeding up of growth in both sectors is essential if the country's economy has to move to a higher growth path. Lack of complementarities in the growth process cannot be afforded if a sustainable growth of the economy is to be achieved. Policy efforts should not, therefore, slacken in one sector when the other sector is observed to perform well.

It is often emphasised that volatility of GDP growth is low in Bangladesh. The observed pattern of reverse movement of GDP growth rates of major sectors reduces the volatility of GDP growth.

1.5 Growth Performance, Middle Income Status and Lost Potential: International Comparison

While Bangladesh's growth acceleration has been definitely an impressive achievement, whether such growth reflects achievements close to its potential requires closer scrutiny. For such assessment, cross-country comparison can be useful. Such comparison with other neighbouring countries and with low-income countries of other regions can provide insights into change in relative position over various periods.

A comparison with some South Asian and South-East Asian countries can reveal variations with similar regions. In 2013, Bangladesh not only had lower per capita income than Pakistan, India and Sri Lanka, but the difference has been very pronounced (Table 1.5).

A more relevant comparison, which can also throw light on the lost potential for Bangladesh, is a comparison of growth of similar economies over various periods of time. For the purpose of illustration, Mahajan (2005) compared the situation of Bangladesh with Indonesia. In 1971, both countries had similar per capita GDP (Bangladesh was 23 per cent lower). School enrolment rates were quite comparable. Population growth rates were similar (around 2.5 per cent). By the year 2000, Indonesia's per capita GDP had tripled, while Bangladesh's GDP had grown by 80 per cent. This may not reflect lost potential in the strict sense, because there were other differences in initial conditions. In this sense, it may not be very meaningful to say that if Bangladesh had grown as fast as China, per capita income in the year 2000 could have been four times of what was actually achieved. Nonetheless, these high growth rates illustrate that Asian economies have the potential to grow fast.

Table 1.5: GDP Per Capita in Selected Asian Countries: 1980, 2013

	(PPP $)		(GDP per capita) US$	
Country	1980	2013	1980	2013
Bangladesh	334	2,557	220	829
India	432	5,410	271	1,499
Pakistan	620	4,699	296	1,299
Sri Lanka	-	9,736	273	3,280
Vietnam	302	5,293	208	1,911

Source: data.worldbank.org/indicator/NY.GDP.

Comparison of growth of GDP of Bangladesh, India, Pakistan, etc. shows that some of these countries' GDP growth rates have been much higher than Bangladesh during various periods over the last three decades (Khan, 1995, Khan, 2016, Mahajan, 2005). However, the pace of growth has not been uniform. For example, India's impressive performance during the early years of the 21st century was followed by a substantial decline of GDP growth in recent years. The same has been true for Vietnam and Pakistan (Table 1.6).

Table 1.6: Growth Rate of GDP in Selected Asian Countries: 2000-2013

(Per cent per year)

Country	2000-2009	2010	2011	2012	2013
Bangladesh	5.8	6.1	6.7	6.2	6.0
India	7.1	8.6	8.9	6.7	4.5
Pakistan	4.5	1.6	2.8	4.0	-
Sri Lanka	4.9	8.0	8.2	6.4	-
Vietnam	7.6	-1.5	4.2	5.6	-

Source: data.worldbank.org/indicator/NY.GDP.

Since Bangladesh has just attained the status of a lower middle income countries, cautionary remarks about sustaining that status and the possibility of falling in the middle income trap are pertinent. To sustain the new status Bangladesh must make concerted efforts to rise above the present phase of 6.0 to 6.5 per cent GDP growth.

The achievement of lower middle income status has at least partially been due to high remittance inflow. Nonetheless, this component of GNI is vulnerable to risks from international factors outside its own control and therefore cannot be a substitute for domestic growth.

The growth experiences of some of the countries of Asia which crossed the middle income cut-off, reveal that they were unable to avoid the middle income trap. Lack of adequate job creation resulting in growing inequality and stalling of the pace of poverty reduction has taken away the shine out of the achievement of per capita income growth. Moreover, many of these countries experienced slowdown of GDP growth after a phase of acceleration (Table 1.6).

Recent experience of Bangladesh's slow rate of job creation should be noted in this context. During 2010 to 2013, domestic employment generation and overseas jobs were respectively 1.3 and 0.5 million per year. This shows an overdependence on overseas employment.

While the recent concern about jobless growth in some of these countries is being viewed with increasing concern, one cannot ignore the counterfactual that without high growth in some years and even in some segments of the economy, the scenario would have been worse. In fact, the possibility of rising inequality during the initial phase of economic growth has been discussed since the days of Kuznets hypothesis. Nonetheless, careful review of available empirical evidence either shows a mixed result or leans towards positive achievement showing high growth without rising inequality (Deninger and Squire 1996, Dollar and Kraay 2002).

Bangladesh's lost potential of acceleration of economic growth with associated social development can be best illustrated not by looking at better performing neighbouring countries but by projecting on the basis of its own performance during 1992-2005. Such projections show that Bangladesh could have easily attained 7 to 8 per cent rate of growth of GDP by 2013-14. Even if this was accompanied by a non-declining inequality of income, the rate of poverty reduction would be higher with the higher pace of growth.

Slowdown of economic growth in Bangladesh and Pakistan may be aptly attributed to political instability and violence. The need for coming out of such confrontational politics cannot be overemphasised and all recent writings on Bangladesh's growth prospects have highlighted this aspect. However, the downturn of GDP growth in countries like India, Vietnam, etc. illustrates that the initial spurt and easy phase of acceleration of GDP growth can come to a halt due to inherent weaknesses in the growth pattern and policy choices. In this context, various empirical studies have concluded that inadequate infrastructure can be a binding constraint to growth (ADB and World Bank surveys quoted by Islam and Islam, 2015). Nonetheless, these experiences should not discourage Bangladesh from making all out efforts for utilising all feasible routes to maximising the growth prospects in the easy phase.

It is, however, widely recognised that balanced and sustainable growth strategy options are not in abundance, especially for countries with unfavourable initial conditions, including lack of natural resources, high population density, high income inequality and unfavourable international environment. Nonetheless, the lessons from the experience of countries falling in the "middle-income trap" can be taken into account while devising medium-term growth strategies.

CHAPTER 2

Pattern of Manufacturing Sector Growth: Prospects and Challenges

2.1 Growth of Manufacturing Sector: 1980-2014

This chapter provides a brief account of the growth of the manufacturing sector during the last three decades and also discusses a few key constraints to industrial growth. During the years immediately following independence, the manufacturing sector was small and growth was insignificant. In the pre-independence period, industrial growth of this region was neglected. Rather, resources were transferred from this region (the then East Pakistan) to support the industrialisation of the western region (the then West Pakistan). Most industries that had grown in this region were owned by West Pakistanis and they left Bangladesh at the time of independence in 1971. Therefore, it is not surprising that in the years following independence, growth rate of the manufacturing sector was at low ebb and was fluctuating along with policy changes. The objective of this chapter is to get an understanding of the experience of manufacturing sector growth since 1980 and to examine the future prospects of the sector.

Data on manufacturing sector's annual growth during 1980-2014 have been presented to assess how this sector has traversed the growth path during this period. Table 2.1 shows that the path has not been uniform but has gone through phases of change. Table 2.1 and the subsequent discussions on the data from the table have been based on unequal intervals which have been deliberately done to identify the turning points of growth.

During the period 1980-1983, growth rate was low and no sign of upturn was visible, especially in large and medium industry where in three years out of four, growth was negative or very low (Table 2.1). During the period 1984-1989, a turnaround was observed. In most

Table 2.1: Growth of Small and Large & Medium Scale Manufacturing: 1980-2014

Year	Large & Medium	Small	Total	Comments
1980	0.0	4.9	2.1	Slowdown especially in large
1981	7.3	3.0	5.4	& medium enterprises
1982	0.7	2.8	1.6	
1983	-4.9	2.8	-1.6	
1984	4.3	2.8	3.7	Recovery, but fluctuations
1985	3.5	3.0	3.3	
1986	1.0	2.9	1.8	
1987	11.0	2.9	7.4	
1988	0.7	0.5	0.6	
1989	2.7	2.9	2.8	
1990	10.6	2.9	7.3	Accelerated growth & stable
1991	6.0	7.3	6.4	
1992	7.3	7.5	7.4	
1993	9.0	7.7	8.6	
1994	8.3	7.9	8.2	
1995	11.4	8.1	10.5	
1996	5.7	8.3	6.4	
1997	4.0	7.8	5.1	
1998	9.3	6.8	8.5	
1999	4.2	0.8	3.2	Slowdown of growth
2000	4.4	5.8	4.8	
2001	6.7	7.0	6.7	
2002	4.6	7.7	5.5	
2003	6.6	7.2	6.8	Accelerated growth
2004	7.0	7.5	7.1	
2005	8.3	7.9	8.2	
2006	11.4	9.2	10.8	
2007	9.7	9.7	9.7	
2008	7.3	7.1	7.2	Slowdown of growth
2009	6.6	6.9	6.7	
2010	5.5	6.3	5.7	
2011	10.9	5.8	9.5	Accelerated growth, but
2012	10.5	6.5	9.4	slowdown of small scale
2013	10.3	6.8	9.3	industries
2014	9.2	6.6	8.7	

Source: *Bangladesh Economic Review* (various years), Base: 1995-96.

years, growth rates were higher than 3 per cent, although fluctuations were also sharp. During this period small manufacturing achieved a stable growth rate of close to 3 per cent. In the period 1990-1998, there was a impressive high growth of manufacturing sector and this was made possible through stable growth of both large and small manufacturing. This trend could not be sustained and during the 1999-2002 period, a slowdown of growth occurred in both large and small manufacturing. The pattern had gone through two successive changes: an acceleration during the period 2003-2007 and a slowdown during the period 2008-2010. During the period 2011-2014, the situation again reversed and high growth of manufacturing was fuelled by high growth of the medium and large industries.

2.1.1 Pattern of Growth of Small Manufacturing

During the period 2011-2014, growth of large and medium manufacturing has accelerated, while a slower pace of growth of the small scale manufacturing has been observed. Without an acceleration of growth of small manufacturing, it is difficult to maintain the growth of the sector as a whole. During these years (2011 to 2014), annual growth of small manufacturing has ranged between 5.8 and 6.8 per cent. In the previous four years, 2007 to 2010, the range was 6.3 to 9.7 per cent.

Stagnation of small manufacturing sector growth can have adverse impacts not only on GDP growth but also on the income growth of low- and middle-income groups, which may have an adverse effect on income inequality. An earlier study has shown that small industries show larger efficiency and are more labour intensive (Khan and Hossain 1989). More recent studies (Rahman, Mondal and Islam, 2007) show mixed results and have found that medium-size industries are more efficient.

As a result of slow growth of small manufacturing, its share in GDP and in manufacturing GDP has stagnated during the last four years, whereas the share had gone through a continuous, albeit a small increase, during the previous decade. Table 2.1 shows that during the period 1991-2009, the growth of small manufacturing exceeded that of large ones in most years. In fact, growth of manufacturing sector was higher in 2005, 2006 and 2007 when both small, large and medium components experienced accelerated growth.

One can wonder about the reasons behind the recent decline of the growth of the small-scale manufacturing. An obvious factor is that there is inadequate investment flow to small enterprises. The reasons behind slowdown of investment include discouraging effect from deteriorating law and order situation, inadequacy of infrastructure, problems and delays in obtaining new gas/electricity connections, frequent power failure in existing units, etc. The problems are more pronounced in remote areas far from the capital and in small towns.

Lack of credit availability can aggravate the situation. This realisation has led to the adoption of schemes for financing Small and Medium Enterprises (SME). The SME Foundation has taken various steps. SME Refinancing Scheme has also been introduced. The recent decline of growth of small manufacturing GDP castes doubts on the success of these initiatives. Probing into the reasons behind the lack of success of these interventions should be taken up on a priority basis.

2.2 Composition of Medium and Large Manufacturing

At this point, it can be useful to look at the importance of various sub-sectors within medium and large manufacturing. Census of Manufacturing Industries (CMI) provides such data. However, CMI data is usually published with a lag. Therefore, this data has been supplemented by data on QIP (Quantum Index of Production), which is available for recent years.

Table 2.2: Rank of Manufacturing Sub-sectors in terms of Total Value Added/Quantum Index of Production (QIP)

Sub-Sector	(Rank in terms of VA) 2001-2002	(Rank in terms of QIP)* 2005-06	2012
RMG	1	1	1
Pharmaceuticals	2	4	2
Food processing	3	3	4
Cotton textile	4	5	5
Non-metal minerals	5	2	3
Leather goods	6	7	6
Furniture	7	9	8
Printing & publishing	8	6	7
Jute manufacturing	9	8	9
Detergent	10	10	NA

Note: *Value added data is not available for recent years.

Source: BBS (various years), *CMI Report* and *Statistical Yearbook of Bangladesh*.

Table 2.2 shows that readymade garment (RMG) industry dominates the sector. In fact, RMG is at the top of the list in terms of total value added and total employment. Its contribution to manufacturing GDP ranged between 20 and 30 per cent during the last two decades. Therefore, the growth of total manufacturing closely follows the path of growth of RMG sector. Pharmaceuticals and food processing are ranked next. Growth of Pharmaceuticals is a recent phenomenon.

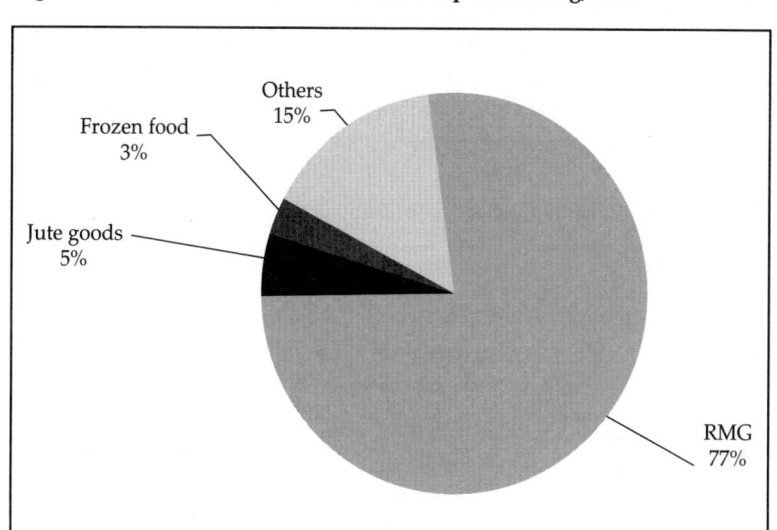

Figure 2.1: Share of Sub-sectors in Total Export Earning, 2012

Sub-sector	Share
RMG	77%
Others	15%
Jute goods	5%
Frozen food	3%

Lack of diversification within manufacturing becomes clearer when one looks at the share of various items in export earnings. RMG accounts for more than 75 per cent and the share has risen during the last one and a half decades (from about 65 per cent). Such lack of diversification can be a matter of concern both in terms of growth prospects of the economy and uncertainty about export earnings.

In this context, it is worth highlighting that none of the developing countries in the region has gone for such narrow specialisation. For example, India's largest export earning comes from engineering industry (21 per cent), followed by gems and ornaments, chemicals and RMG. These three contribute between 8 per cent and 16 per cent. In Vietnam, RMG is a major industry but it accounts for only 17 per cent of export earnings.

2.3 Labour Intensity and Labour Productivity

It is almost definitional that the comparative advantage of a labour abundant and capital scarce country like Bangladesh is in labour intensive sub-sectors. This obvious choice has been reflected in the rapid growth of labour-intensive RMG industry in the recent decades. Nonetheless, the country should not continue to depend on a single sub-sector and must diversify to other sectors where prospect of employment growth is reasonable even if labour intensity is not as favourable as RMG. Sub-sectors must be chosen on the basis of labour productivity and extent of capital intensity. To provide insights into these aspects, capital intensity of the major manufacturing sub-sectors has been examined below. Data on capital intensity (and its reverse, i.e. labour intensity) has been shown in Table 2.3.

Table 2.3: Capital Intensity of Major Sub-sectors of Manufacturing

Labour Intensity	Sector	Capital Asset Per Worker (Tk.)
High	RMG	<50,000
High	Furniture	<50,000
Medium	Food processing	50,000-2,00,000
Medium	Tobacco	50,000-2,00,000
Medium	Chemical	50,000-2,00,000
Medium	Ceramic	50,000-2,00,000
Low	Pharmaceuticals	2,00,000-4,00,000
Low	Textile	2,00,000-4,00,000

Source: Rahman, Mondal and Islam (2007).

CMI data shows that[1] over the past two decades, employment growth in RMG has been the highest. Employment growth in pharmaceuticals has been high even if its capital intensity is high. This has been possible through rapid growth of the industry.

Are these patterns commensurate with positive features of factors productivity? Table 2.4 presents relevant information. The results shown in Table 2.4 provide a non-technical summary of data from production function analysis in Rahman, Mondal and Islam (2007).

---

[1] Rahman, Mondal and Islam (2007) provide these data and the detailed table has not been quoted here.

Table 2.4: Productivity of Labour and Capital in Manufacturing Sub-Sectors

Sub-sectors	Marginal Productivity (MP)			
	Capital	Significance	Labour	Significance
RMG	+	No	+	No
Pharmaceuticals	+	No	+	Yes
Textile	−	No	−	No
Food processing	−	Yes	+	Yes
Tobacco	−	No	+	Yes
Chemical	−	No	+	Yes
Ceramics	+	Yes	−	No
Furniture	+	Yes	−	No
Ginning	−	Yes	−	Yes
Printing & Publishing	+	No	+	Yes
Non-metal-mineral	+	No	+	No
Leather	−	No	+	Yes
Transport equipment	−	No	+	No
Electrical goods	+	Yes	+	No

Source: Rahman, Mondal and Islam (2007).

It can be observed that RMG, pharmaceuticals, publishing, electrical goods, ceramics, leather and furniture have positive marginal productivity of capital. Among these sub-sectors, the first four show positive labour productivity as well. Thus the expansion of these industries is in right track. Textile and ginning are the sub-sectors with doubtful performance.

2.4 A Special Constraint to Industrial Growth: Land Availability for Non-farm Use

The constraint posed by low land–population ratio and its implications for the growth of non-farm sector activities has received inadequate attention in the past. This key feature of Bangladesh can act as a serious bottleneck in its endeavour to economic and social development. The following discussion highlights the nature of problems caused by the shrinking per capita land availability. In fact, it can be argued that the apparent disappearance of surplus labour and demand for higher wages by industrial labourers has indirect links with the tightening of the land constraint (to be elaborated below).

Constraints linked to geographical location of countries have been highlighted in a variety of ways. For example, being land locked or being a small island country poses specific bottlenecks. In a similar manner, too small land area per person can be viewed as a natural resource related constraint faced in the development process. This constraint is quite unique for Bangladesh (apart from the small island countries).

Land constraint, to some extent, has received attention in the context of agricultural production. Since agricultural land is declining (according to some estimates at the rate of one per cent per year), the imperative of producing enough food (especially foodgrain) requires attention to adoption of yield maximising policies. Decline of the size of agricultural land has been caused by many factors. The most important reasons are use of land for non-farm production activities, infrastructure building (roads, bridges, highways, etc.), housing needs of a growing population and social needs (building schools, health centres, entertainment facilities, etc.). Policies for maximising agricultural growth are therefore likely to compete with land availability for industrialisation and this aspect needs careful attention.

2.4.1 Nature of Land Constraint in Service and Industrial Sectors

The way in which land constraint affects the industrialisation process is not always apparent and therefore requires elaboration. To achieve an accelerated growth of industry and services sector GDP, capital investment is essential. A special feature of Bangladesh's industrial growth is that investment on land and premises constitutes a significant part of total resource invested. Land constraint is more acute for the industries with higher labour intensity, e.g., the RMG sub-sector. Rent for buildings forms a large share of current cost of activities operating in rented structure. As a result, there is a tendency to squeeze more workers within a small floor space, causing unhealthy work environment. Nonetheless, this cannot offer a permanent solution to the problem of high cost of building and premises.

One may in this context resort to the theories of "development with surplus labour" and argue that the cost of labour is low in such densely populated countries which may counteract other costs. In fact, the initial success of labour-intensive export industries of Bangladesh has been due to the availability of cheap labour (of course, along with a number of other factors). However, low labour cost cannot help sustain the process of industry and services sectors growth indefinitely. Shortage of land can set an absolute physical constraint to the expansion of industrial enterprises. For example, scaling up of certain production activities may be profitable only if an adjacent building is available. This reduces supervision cost. This is often impossible in crowded cities or the suburbs. In the case of family labour based enterprises which operate in own house, it cannot be scaled up with a rented house which is not adjacent.

Service provision requires certain comfortable area per customer served. If customers are refused service because the "waiting space" is full, then the enterprise cannot survive. An example will make it clear—a fast food outlet (with franchise from an international chain) located in a crowded part of Dhaka is possibly serving the highest (in comparison to other low-income countries) number of customers per square feet per day. Such congested environment may go against food safety standard.

In this context, the constraints faced by urban informal sector enterprises deserve attention. These enterprises are located on roadside spaces, footpaths, outskirts of kitchen markets and other public land. If they have to pay full rental for such land, many of the enterprises are likely to be rendered unprofitable. However, such free spaces have almost been exhausted and further growth of informal sector in large and small cities is not desirable, as it will cause congestion and deterioration of urban services. Toll collection for these spaces emerged as a profitable activity for local unemployed youth because of the scarcity factor.

Moreover, the high cost imposed by land scarcity cannot be always nullified through low labour cost. Cost of hired labour in a big city like Dhaka (or in its suburbs) rises as the cost of living rises. RMG workers' wages have to be linked with the rising cost of living, a large part of such cost being the rent of the living accommodation. Rent per square feet for housing of the low-income earners is often higher than per square feet rent of apartments in good residential areas. Moreover, "safe" shelters for low income employees are getting scarcer as the marginal/low quality land areas are being transferred to real estate agencies ("developers") who use it for construction of houses for higher income groups.

Over the last 3-4 decades, employment generation through public programmes has been an important instrument of poverty alleviation.

Such programmes can create useful physical infrastructure, and generate a long lasting positive impact on economic growth as well. However, the scope of such programmes can be severely constrained by the lack of availability of public land (*khas*) where earth cutting can take place.

2.5 Future Strategies of Industrial Growth in the Face of Land Constraint

The policymakers and the designers of development programmes have to carefully identify strategies to ease the constraints faced by industrial sector.

In the case of land constraint, these policies, if successful, can bear fruit only after a few years, while the decline of land area per person will continue until a zero population growth is achieved. Therefore, specific priorities should be set and the development agenda can include steps for proper use of land. The following are some general suggestions which serve as the basis for specific programmes with detailed time bound targets.

Once the constraint imposed by shortage of land is recognised by the policymakers, programmes can be adopted in phases. A long-term vision of development with adequate emphasis on the constraints related to scarcity of land is an urgent need for sustaining the present development momentum of Bangladesh.

This will imply encouragement of the growth of modern industries in areas outside the existing large cities. Cost of land will be substantially lower in peri-urban areas. Infrastructure facilities should be created by the government to help growth of a few regional growth centres.

Views of entrepreneurs and trade bodies should be invited to correctly identify the facilities they require to make those places attractive for investment. If such initiatives are adopted without examining the demand side, these places may suffer the same fate as the industrial zones created in the past, which did not attract investors.

Creation of facilities for good quality education and health services at costs lower than such services in Dhaka or Chittagong can provide added incentive for regional growth centre based development. This can also form an important step to the reduction of regional inequality. Low cost housing facilities should be created for low-income workers, which may be viewed as a subsidy to the workers as well as their employers. Such schemes may be introduced in new industrial areas.

Growth of hired labour based enterprises in regionally dispersed growth centres can provide an impetus to employment generation, poverty reduction and sustained growth of manufacturing. Entrepreneurs can thrive by drawing upon local labour force, especially the underemployed female labour force. The un/underemployment situation in the labour market of Bangladesh makes it clear that the prevailing magnitude of surplus labour is such that the formal sector may not be able to attract a large supply of labourers from the rural areas. Wages in many formal sectors are close to wages of the informal sectors. In this situation, industrialisation should proceed through a locational dispersion of industrial units moving towards the poorer areas. An expansion of sub-contracting system can utilise the entrepreneurial ability of small enterprises in these interior areas and can provide a useful substitute for a wage labour-based industrialisation. This option can yield the desired outcome only if pursed at a reasonably rapid pace. Otherwise, the rural labourers from poorer regions will continue to migrate to the bigger cities.

An enabling environment for the development of local entrepreneurship can be created through provision of low cost power, transport, communication systems and marketing services. NGOs and private sector financial institutions should be encouraged to provide suitable package of financial services. Protected areas for marketing and storage may be established as a component of peri-urban growth centres. Infrastructure projects for creating linkage between semi-urban growth centres and rural hinterland may lead to direct and indirect employment generation and can help both poverty reduction and economic growth.

Since underemployment rate is much higher among women, a choice open to the labour-intensive industrialisation process is to draw female workers. During the last two decades female labour force participation rate has increased. But still the rate is lower than many Asian countries and there is a prospect of increase of such participation rate if better job opportunities are created in close proximity to their rural homes.

Human capital development strategy must place emphasis on improving the employability of secondary educated school dropouts, who are mostly poor. This is particularly important because the growth centres in the peri-urban areas are expected to draw upon these sources of surplus labour. Vocational and technical training promoted through public investment must link training of these groups with effective employment generation.

Year after year, the relevant organisations of the government are trying to think of steps to attract foreign direct investment (FDI) but with not-so-encouraging results. It is unlikely that success on that front will be bright while our own investors are not coming forward. Investment growth rate is not showing the expected impact of policies on the supply side. Domestic investment growth requires innovative steps to encourage demand.

The recently observed slow growth of real wage in industry[2] implies that the rate of GDP growth in manufacturing sector is not keeping pace with the growth of labour force. A small manufacturing sector confined to large cities cannot influence the wage in the rural and informal sectors. It is difficult to directly implement interventions in the form of minimum wage legislation in rural informal sectors. Rapid growth of a regionally dispersed modern manufacturing sector is, therefore, a top priority not only for sustained GDP growth but also for raising income of the labour force living in backward regions.

---

[2] This aspect has been elaborated in Chapter 6.

CHAPTER 3

Resource Constraints and Agricultural Growth: Availability of Arable Land and Irrigation

The changing role of agriculture in the Bangladesh economy can be better understood in the light of the classical roles of agriculture in a developing/low-income country. These roles have been discussed in various seminal contributions (Meier, 1976, Lewis, 1954). Importance of a discussion of the changing role of agriculture in Bangladesh economy, which started its journey following independence with almost half of its GDP originating from agriculture, cannot be overemphasised. In an economy with such heavy dependence on agriculture, acceleration of overall economic growth in the short and medium term requires sustained agricultural growth. Moreover, agricultural growth can help ensure food security for the large and growing population. The other roles envisaged for agriculture include contributions to export and release of labour for non-farm sectors. The latter, combined with a growth of income of those engaged in farming, leads to growth of demand for products of non-farm activities.

This chapter focuses on the growth of agricultural GDP, especially on the constraint of resources for agricultural growth. In this context, the availability of cultivable land and access to irrigation receives special attention.

3.1 Agricultural GDP: Share and Growth

As expected, the share of GDP derived from agriculture has declined considerably during the last four and a half decades. The decline has been slow during the initial years after independence and faster during the period 1985-2005 (Table 3.1). The share of GDP from crop agriculture has declined at a faster rate than the share of total agriculture in total GDP of the country. The fall in the share of crop agriculture has been at least partly offset by the rise of share of fishery and livestock, especially during the period 2005-2010. During the period 2005-2012, the decline of agriculture's share in GDP has slowed down. Table 3.1 shows that the shares of agriculture in GDP were 44, 38, 25 and 17 per cent in 1980, 1990, 2000 and 2013 respectively.

Table 3.1: Share of Agriculture in GDP: 1974-2014

(Per Cent)

Year	Agriculture	Crop	Non-Crop
1974	48.3	37.4	10.9
1980	43.9	34.6	9.3
1985	41.8	33.2	8.6
1990	38.3	30.3	8.0
1995	31.8	24.3	7.5
2000	25.5	14.5	11.0
2005	22.3	12.5	9.8
2010	20.1	11.2	8.9
2012	19.4	10.9	8.5
2013*	16.8	9.5	7.3
2014*	16.3	9.1	7.2

Note: *The base for these two years is 2005-6, while for earlier years, the base is 1995-96.
Source: BBS, *Statistical Yearbook of Bangladesh* (various years).

However, it should be mentioned that the decline of agriculture's share in GDP has occurred simultaneously with a positive and sometimes accelerated growth of agricultural GDP. Actually, such growth has been accompanied by faster rate of growth of GDP originating from industry and services sectors, thus leading to a declining share of agricultural GDP.

Growth of agricultural GDP (Table 3.2) has gone through fluctuations not only from year to year but also when one considers the averages for five-year periods. Growth of agricultural GDP has been high during three periods: 1981-85, 1996-2000 and 2005-2010. In the five-year periods immediately following these high growth years, agricultural growth has slowed down. The fluctuation, to some extent, has been due to exhaustion of benefits of short term policy initiatives in each of these periods. The need for assessment of resource constraint and the urgency of adoption of longer term policies for sustained growth becomes evident from these fluctuations.

Table 3.2: Rate of Growth of GDP from Agriculture: 1970-2014

Period	(% Per Year)
1970-80	1.3
1981-85	2.7
1986-90	2.4
1991-95	1.5
1996-2000	4.9
2001-2005	2.5
2005-2010	4.2
2010-2013*	2.3
2013-2014*	2.5

Note: *The base for these two years is 2005-6, while for earlier years, the base is 1995-96.
Source: Calculated from *Bangladesh Economic Review*, MoF.

3.2 Availability of Arable Land[1]

Land constraint deserves close scrutiny in a densely populated country like Bangladesh. In fact, the country has the highest population density when the small-island countries of Asia are excluded. Moreover, agriculture continues to be the major source of employment and livelihood in its rural areas where 70 per cent of population live. Availability of agricultural land can, therefore, pose a key constraint to growth of output and employment.

Cultivation of new agricultural land can be one of the easiest sources of agricultural growth, and the prospect of such expansion can be assessed on the basis of available data from the recent rounds of Agricultural Census. Three rounds of such census data (conducted in 1984, 1996 and 2008) are available from Bangladesh Bureau of Statistics. Relevant data from the three rounds have been shown in Table 3.3.

---

[1] This section draws from Rahman (2012).

Table 3.3: Use of Land in Rural Areas of Bangladesh and Changes during 1984-2008

Year	Agricultural Use ('000 Acres)	% Change Over Previous Census	Homestead Land ('000 Acres)	% Change Over Previous Census
1984	22,678		966	
1996	19,957		1,318	
2008	21,945		1,995	
	Difference (000 acres)		*Difference (000 acres)*	
1984 to 1996	- 2721	-12.0	+ 352	36.4
1996 to 2008	+ 1988	+10.0	+677	51.4
1984 to 2008	- 733	- 3.2	1,029	106.5

Source: BBS (various years), *Report on Bangladesh Census of Agriculture*.

When the 1996 Agricultural Census data was released, alarms were raised about the decline of arable land in 1996 compared to 1984. During the 12-year period from 1984 to 1996, the total agricultural land lost was 12 per cent of the area in the base year, thus generating the figure of average loss of 1 per cent of arable land every year. Projections based on this data imply that within the next 50 years, arable land would be cut into half of the area in the year 1984.

The release of the 2008 agricultural census data provided a scope for reassessment to check whether the decline continued at the same rate, and whether the projections made on the basis of 1984 and 1996 census data can be treated as realistic. The following findings emerge on the basis of data on rural land use from the three rounds of census (Table 3.3).

a. During 1984-1996, area of agricultural land decreased by 27,21,000 acres; the decline per year was 226.8 acres and the total decline during the 12-year period was 12 per cent.

b. A comparison of 1984 and 2008 data shows that cultivable land shrank by 733,000 acres, which amounted to 3.2 per cent in 24 years.

c. Comparing 1996 and 2008 data one finds a reverse trend. An increase in the total arable land took place, which was 10 per cent of the area in 1996.

d. During 1984-1996 and 1996-2008, area under homestead increased by 352,000 and 677,000 acres. This is somewhat expected in view of population growth.

Points (c) and (d) noted above appear somewhat contradictory because an increase in homestead area is likely to be achieved through diversion of cultivable land. One obviously wonders why the reverse happened. Two possible explanations are: first, there may be accretion of arable land through siltation and emergence of new chars and second, homestead areas may expand through use of fallow land and land under other use. However, the supply of such "other land" is not plenty and therefore there may be some skepticism about data problem, especially in the case of 1996 round of the census.

Data on "Dhaka Division" can be used to illustrate the possibility of anomalies in the agricultural census data. During the period 1996-2008, area of agricultural land increased in this Division. It is, however, well known that during this period there were huge inflow of people into Dhaka city and the surrounding areas. Growth of non-farm and industrial enterprises contributed to the influx of in-migrants. Such developments require diversion of agricultural land to other uses. It is difficult to reconcile this fact with the data showing increase of agricultural land in this Division, thus casting doubt on the quality of the 1996 round data.

Even if there is difference in the direction of change of available cultivable land in the latest two rounds of data, if 1984 and 2008 are considered, there is a net decline of agricultural land and thus there is no scope for complacence. Average annual decrease per year is 0.13 per cent over the entire 24-year period. A recent study (Quasem, 2011) shows a decline of 0.56 per cent per year during 2001-2010.

It may be worthwhile to highlight the fourth finding listed above. It shows a significant increase in the area under homestead use in the rural areas. Therefore, the need for planned use of rural land and setting guidelines for use of arable land for non-farm use cannot be overemphasised. Technologies for low cost and land saving homestead must be developed and made available to rural households. Restrictions on sale of arable land for use by non-farmers and imposition of taxes on non-residential construction activities on rural land should be seriously considered.

The effect of aggravating land constraint on the farmers can also be observed from the distribution of households by farm size and extent of landlessness. The share of small and marginal farms significantly increased during this period. The share was 70 per cent in 1984 and 84 per cent in 2008. The implications of the change in distribution of landownership merit serious investigation. Studies show that small farmers have higher production per unit of land. Such higher productivity results mainly from use of higher number of days of labour input per acre by the small farms. This, in turn, is due to the fact that small farms use family labour with low opportunity cost, whereas large farms use hired labour with higher opportunity cost as reflected in the market wage.

When farming is the only option for rural households' employment and earning, the rising share of small farms may imply higher growth of production as well as greater equity in income distribution. It is in such a context that Sen (1962) and others have discussed this issue and have drawn the conclusion that small farms are more efficient.

In Bangladesh today, options other than farming are also available. The small farms are gradually changing into marginal farmers. Data from agricultural census show that the number of farms under one acre is growing rapidly. About one million farms are being added to this size group each year. Whatever may be the per acre production from such a farm, it cannot ensure livelihood of a 4-5 member household. Earning members resort to multiple occupations to supplement farm income of such households. Such farms also lease in land under sharecropping or other tenurial arrangements. However, with the decline of medium and large farms, land for leasing has become scarcer.

Marginal farmers who rent in (out?) land on lease or on sharecropping face certain constraints. In the cases of fixed advance rent, the farmers' cash supply is depleted reducing their ability to invest in inputs. In the case of sharecropping, a disincentive is likely to operate due to the need to share the output. Policy measures to ease these constraints can enhance the productivity of these farms. Moreover, such dependence on tiny plots must ultimately be reduced through expansion of rural non-farm activities. Subsequent chapters present quantitative analysis of relationship of farm size with adoption of modern inputs and land productivity.[2]

---

[2] Chapter 5 examines the relationship on the basis of 1996 and 2010 data.

3.3 Irrigation

Land constraint may, to some extent, be eased through more intensive use of land which can be possible through application of modern irrigation. Therefore, a discussion of the expansion of irrigation can throw light on the prospects of agricultural growth in this country.

Data presented in Table 3.4 show growth of irrigation as a whole and for groundwater and surface water irrigation separately. Growth of irrigated areas has been high during the period 1991-2001. After that phase, growth of irrigated areas has slowed down. The decline is quite pronounced for groundwater irrigation. This has occurred due to lowering of groundwater level, which implies that in many areas groundwater irrigation has been rendered unprofitable.

Table 3.4: Use of Irrigation on Agricultural Land: 1986-2011

Year	Irrigated Area (00 Ha)		
	Total*	Using Groundwater	Using Surface Water
1986	21156	9516	11640
1991	29917 (41.41%)	17617 (85.13%)	12300 (5.67%)
1996	35112 (17.36%)	23290 (32.20%)	11822 (-3.88)
2001	45165 (28.63%)	32852 (41.05%)	12213 (3.3%)
2006	54096 (19.77%)	38213 (16.31%)	15884 (30.5%)
2011	64350 (18.95%)	42240 (10.54%)	22110 (39.20%)

Note: *() Per cent changes during the last five years.
Source: *Bangladesh Economic Review* (various years).

The positive development which has accompanied the decline of groundwater irrigation is the growth of surface water irrigation. Before 2001, such irrigation constituted 27 per cent of the total irrigated area and the area covered did not expand during the period 1986-2001. Between 2001 and 2011, however, there was a rapid growth of surface water irrigation and its share in the total irrigation reached 34 per cent.

The slowdown of growth of groundwater irrigation using either deep tubewell (DTW) or shallow tubewell (STW) does not reflect only the technical aspect of access to water level. The constraint results from a combination of various technical problems and demand-side choices. It may be useful to delve briefly into both sides of the problem.

While most analyses of failure of public sector initiatives of DTW irrigation emphasise the technical problems of machines, fielding at the wrong site (due to slope or soil type), lack of repair facilities, etc., a deeper investigation shows that the organisational aspects and demand-side problems also played a critical role. Rahman (1998) highlighted some of these problems which are also relevant for other modes of groundwater irrigation. An important demand-side factor in this context is the high cost of irrigation which reduces profitability. Since irrigation is used mostly for rice crops, a fall of relative price of rice vis-à-vis other non-irrigated crops also accounts for the decline of return from irrigation. Informal discussions with farmers reveal that they describe the constraints related to irrigation in simplistic terms, like "not having access to sufficient irrigation water," and do not go deeper into the forces affecting profitability. Insufficient access to irrigation water includes actual technical access as well as timely availability, which can be influenced by the regularity of power supply and farmers' willingness to pay enough for fuel for getting the desired quantity of water.

However, from the experience of groundwater irrigation it is clear that access to water cannot be neglected and the technical aspects of water availability, in the short, medium and long term, deserve attention. Excessive use of surface water can also affect the availability of surface water for various uses in the coming years. Therefore, more judicious planning and use of water resources are essential.

3.4 Cropping Intensity and Modern Variety Seeds

During the last two and a half decades, production growth in the crop sub-sector has been associated with rising cropping intensity. Farmers resorted to higher cropping intensity (i.e., double and triple cropping) since there is hardly any scope of bringing in additional land for cultivation. Data presented in Table 3.5 show that cropping intensity has increased slowly during 1972-1986. The pace accelerated during the next decade (1986 to 1996) and increased from 154.5 to 173.2 per cent. This may be due to the reduction of agricultural land, as shown in Section 3.2. During the period 1996-2006, however, cropping intensity stagnated, which indicates that the scope for more intensive cultivation of the land has been more or less exhausted. But cropping intensity has again shown a jump during the period 2006-2011.

Table 3.5: Cropping Intensity: 1972-2012

Year	Cropping Intensity (%)
1972	138.3
1976	141.6
1980	153.2
1986	154.5
1990	168.4
1996	173.2
2000	175.4
2006	175.9
2008	178.7
2010	183.4
2011	190.5
2012	190.0

Source: BBS, *Statistical Yearbook of Bangladesh* (various years).

The rising intensity of cropping during the period 1976-1996 has, to a large extent, been associated with the use of high yielding variety (HYV) paddy. More than 60 per cent of Bangladesh's cropped land is under paddy. Therefore, the prospect of growing an additional crop of paddy can enhance food production as well as total agricultural production. This has been made possible through the development of new seeds. These varieties were initially developed abroad. During the 1980s and 1990s, Bangladeshi scientists have developed several high yielding paddy varieties suitable for local conditions. These varieties are mostly grown with mechanised irrigation during the dry season. Thus the additional crop raises cropping intensity. Table 3.6 shows that during the period 1980-2005, the share of paddy land with HYV increased very fast, from 19.7 per cent in 1980 to 69.8 per cent in 2005. The rise was slower during the period 2005-2008, with a subsequent decline. Scientists are trying to develop new varieties for areas with adverse ecological features, e.g., drought and salinity prone and waterlogged areas. Such varietal improvements can contribute to further rise of cropping intensity.

Coming back to the question of rise of cropping intensity, how does one explain the recent (2008-2013) jump in cropping intensity? This has happened despite the slowdown of irrigation expansion, particularly groundwater irrigation. An important factor in this context is the growth of vegetable production. In fact, vegetable cultivation often involves short maturity period and several crops can be raised within 3-4 months, which is reflected in high cropping intensity.

Table 3.6: Coverage of High Yielding Variety (HYV) Paddy: 1980-2013

Year	HYV As Per Cent of Total Land under Paddy
1980	19.7
1985	27.2
1990	40.7
1995	50.1
2000	61.9
2005	69.8
2008	72.4
2010	65.7
2013	64.6

Source: BBS, *Statistical Yearbook of Bangladesh* (various years).

However, use of land for quick maturing non-cereal crops will go against the objective of higher growth of food production. Of course, crop diversification is also an important objective of agricultural development. Thus, with the shrinking of agricultural land and the declining availability of groundwater, the country will, in the near future, face a critical choice: between higher growth of irrigation intensive cereal crops and other crops requiring less land and less water.

3.5 Policy Recommendations

On the basis of the above discussion on constraints faced by Bangladesh's agriculture, especially in terms of availability of arable land and irrigation water, the following policy suggestions can be made.

a. Planned rural housing should receive priority and guidelines for rural land use should be formulated so that the area of land used for productive activities can be maximised.

b. Land administration and systematic maintenance of land records possibly with computerisation can play a critical role in this context.

c. In the design of safety net "Employment Scheme," detailed plans should be drawn for rural infrastructure building which require use of public (*khas*) land.

To help planned use of irrigation, continuous monitoring of the technical aspects of water availability should be done and the information should be disseminated to all stakeholders. Agricultural growth has to focus on development of new variety of seeds of paddy and other crops which require less water. Crop diversification and growth of non-crop agriculture may provide some answer to this constraint.

Measures should also be adopted to raise the efficiency of use of irrigation water. Government's support for on-farm water management and for improving technical services for operation, repair and maintenance of irrigation equipment is needed.

Most commonly discussed policies for encouraging the expansion of irrigated area include the provision of subsidy on diesel and electricity for operating irrigation equipment. Without going to the details of the subsidy issue, it should be emphasised that small and tenant farmers need special attention and provision of subsidy must take into consideration special constraints faced by these groups due to lack of resources for financing irrigation. In addition to providing incentives through input price subsidy, the timely availability of the inputs and price support for outputs are also important. Policies in these areas are relevant for big and small farmers alike. In this context, policies for ensuring timely availability of other modern inputs like seeds and fertilisers can be helpful.

CHAPTER 4

Factors Affecting Adoption of Modern Agricultural Technology: Evidence from Early Phase[1]

4.1 Introduction

Early studies on the adoption and cultivation of high yielding varieties (HYV) of foodgrains have emphasised role of the factors related to the agrarian structure operating on the demand side of technology adoption. Some of the structural factors may also have implications for the supply-side problems and affect adoption practices. But few of the early studies on technology adoption have dealt with the problem of supply and availability of inputs directly. This problem is especially relevant in the early phase of adoption of a new technology and for a country like Bangladesh, where the supply mechanisms are usually not very efficient.

The present analysis, therefore, examines how the availability of the inputs influences the adoption of HYV paddy and other related modern inputs. It focuses on the question of spread of knowledge and access to irrigation. For modern inputs, cash expenses have to be incurred. So the question of availability of cash and the supply of credit becomes important. The other side of the question is the supply and cost of labour use on the new crops. This chapter sheds light on this issue as well.

The analysis, based on early years of HYV paddy cultivation in Bangladesh, can offer important insights even for the present day because supply channels in this country are still not as efficient as desirable. Moreover, the analytical findings on factors affecting adoption in the early phase can be compared with findings presented in later chapters (Chapter 5 and Chapter 8) which are based on data from more recent years.

---

[1] This chapter is an edited version of Rahman (1983).

4.1.1 Notes on Data Used

This section uses data from an irrigated village to verify the hypotheses. Data were collected through a household level survey carried out in the early months of 1980. All households in the village were covered by the survey. The village covered is Dhanbari in Savar thana of Dhaka district with 178 households. Among these, 110 households were engaged in farming. All other villages around Dhanbari were more or less backward villages with traditional cropping pattern, whereas HYV boro was extensively grown in Dhanbari with the help of DTW irrigation. So the village Dhanbari serves as an illustration in the following discussion of factors influencing the adoption of HYV.[2]

4.2 Role of Knowledge

In general, the adoption of an innovation is preceded by users' knowledge about it, which consists of awareness of its existence, the scope of its profitable use and the actual practices. Such knowledge is almost definitionally a prerequisite to the adoption of HYV crops as well. What needs investigation in this respect is whether the spread of knowledge is almost automatic in a locality so that once some farmers start growing HYV, others become automatically aware and there is no inter-farm difference in adoption of HYV technology. If not, knowledge may pose an obstacle to the expansion of HYV for a group of farmers in general in a locality or for some backward farmers in particular. Such lack of knowledge may be due to two factors: (a) lack of access to the mechanisms which are responsible for the dissemination of such knowledge, and (b) lack of basic education and literacy to learn the new management practices. But one may doubt the role of education in relation to adoption of HYV in the villages. This is because mere literacy may not be of much help in learning the cost-benefit calculations for the new crops or the management practices. If one considers secondary level education as the requirement for such efficiency, few villagers will qualify and still many of them are efficient adopters. On the other hand, it is noteworthy that many of the farmers, without being able to read and write, can still do the basic arithmetic of cost and return calculations verbally. Out of necessity they learn this from the elders. So, one does not expect the formal schooling to

---

[2] The survey also covered households from a neighbouring village (Parannagar) to obtain data on wage, income, employment, etc. But the village did not have access to modern irrigation. Data from this survey have also been used in Chapter 7.

FACTORS AFFECTING ADOPTION OF MODERN AGRICULTURAL TECHNOLOGY 43

have much influence on technology adoption. Even then, lack of general knowledge may prove to be an obstacle to the expansion of the new input use.

The present study has collected information on the source of information for becoming aware of the HYV crops and for learning the related cultivation practices. Farmers were also asked about the factors which really work as obstacles to the expansion of HYV.

As to why HYV is not grown, the frequency distribution of households stating different reasons are presented in Table 4.1.

Table 4.1: Distribution of Households by Causes of Not Growing High Yielding Variety (HYV)

Causes*	% of Households
	Dhanbari
Lack of irrigation	7.9
Land is not suitable	6.7
High cost of production and lack of cash	1.0

Note: *In this village only a small percentage of households do not grow HYV.
Source: Household Survey 1980.

None of the households has mentioned "lack of knowledge" as a cause, though it was suggested to them as a possible answer.

Another question seemed pertinent for the high-adoption village, Dhanbari. This was about why they did not start HYV earlier than the year reported. This question revealed that lack of irrigation was the most important reason. But in this respect, lack of knowledge was the second most frequent answer (Table 4.2). So knowledge is an important factor for an innovation like HYV to make headway; but once some farmers start it, knowledge may not be a problem for other non-adopters.

Table 4.2: Causes of Not Growing HYV Earlier than the Year Reported

Causes	% of all Households
Lack of irrigation	21.9
Lack of knowledge	4.5
Lack of other inputs	1.7
Others	1.0

Source: Household Survey 1980.

To judge whether this knowledge is associated with formal education, the process of dissemination of such knowledge, and more specifically whether it comes from any reading material, has been examined. Table 4.3 shows that the most important channel of spread of knowledge is through other villagers. Second in importance is listening to radio programmes. A few villagers have learnt HYV cultivation from extension agents. So it seems that a practical demonstration to a few cultivators could be enough to start a process of spontaneous diffusion.

Table 4.3: Source of Knowledge of HYV Cultivation

Source	Per Cent of Farmers Reporting this Source for	
	Becoming Aware	Learning Cultivation Practices
Other villagers	47.3	64.5
Extension agents	5.5	14.5
Radio	29.1	3.6
At market places	4.5	-
Newspapers/books	1.0	-

Source: Household Survey 1980.

Given the above information on the source of knowledge, it can be concluded that formal education should not matter much in this context. Knowledge as such, no matter what its source, could very well be a constraint. To examine this question, farmers were asked about the reasons for (a) not growing HYV in aus and aman seasons, and (b) not using adequate doses of fertiliser. The reason for particularly asking about the aus and aman seasons was that knowledge is more likely to be a constraint here, since cultivation practices for HYV aus and aman are not widely understood. The results are shown in Tables 4.4 and 4.5. It seems that lack of knowledge is a relatively unimportant constraint for the growing of non-boro HYV, but it is more important in the case of fertiliser.

Table 4.4: Reasons of Not Growing HYV in Aus and Aman Season

Reasons	% of Households
Land is not suitable	18.0
Greater risk	9.6
Lack of irrigation facility	7.3
Lack of knowledge	5.6
Non-availability of other inputs	1.0

Source: Household Survey 1980.

Table 4.5: Reasons of Not using Adequate Fertiliser

Reasons	% of Households
Lack of cash	18.0
Lack of Knowledge	9.6
Higher market price than government rate	8.4
Lack of supply of fertiliser	-

Source: Household Survey 1980.

Thus it can be concluded that lack of knowledge is a fairly important constraint to the spread of input use although formal education may not be important in this context.

However, a note of elucidation is in order here. When the farmer knows that he is not using adequate fertiliser, his reply of lack of knowledge may sound inconsistent and would require further elaboration. Their observation in this respect is that these days they need to use more fertiliser to achieve the same increase of yield or even to maintain the same yield. The first is quite reasonable but a higher dose of fertiliser to maintain the same yield may simply mean that loss of yield due to deterioration of the quality of land or loss of land fertility due to higher cropping intensity is being compensated by fertiliser use. Whatever be the case, this situation along with the requirement of proper mix of various types of fertiliser to achieve good yield of HYV crops creates confusion among the farmers as to what amount and mix of fertiliser they should use (of course "lack of knowledge" may be a simplistic expression of such confusion).

4.3 Role of Irrigation

Without taking a proper account of the irrigation system that is available in a locality, it is not possible to explain the role of other factors on HYV adoption. It will be useful to take a look at how some other studies bypass this issue and the inadequacy of analysis resulting from this.

For example, studies have shown (Ahmed, 1981) that farm size is directly related to the rate of HYV adoption.[3] The reasons stated are that large farmers can better withstand the risk associated with HYV crops and they have better access to resources. On the other hand, the

---

[3] Rate of HYV adoption means percentage of adopters in a group, whereas the extent of adoption of HYV means the proportion of land devoted to HYV crops.

relationship between farm size and "extent" of adoption of HYV is less clear. Some authors (Ahmed, 1981, Muqtada, 1975) found it to be negative, whereas others (Asaduzzaman, 1979) obtained a positive relation. Ahmed found a negative relation because once the small farmers decide to adopt, they adopt on a greater portion of their land to justify what he calls the fixed cost of adoption (cost of collecting information, getting access to the inputs, etc.). But once the importance of irrigation is understood, the type of relationship observed can be explained more easily than to attribute it to such subjective "fixed cost" consideration.

Some simple arguments can elaborate how the scope of irrigation influences adopter ratio and "extent" of adoption. The choice of growing HYV boro is open only to these farmers whose land has access to irrigation. On a land which has access to irrigation, it is likely to be profitable to grow HYV rather than local boro. Coming to the question of risk, it is not proper to put all HYV in the same category of riskiness. HYV grown on irrigated land in the dry season is less risky than rain-fed HYV's. Ahmed (1981) shows that among the four crops, aman local, aman HYV, boro local and boro HYV, the boro-HYV has the lowest coefficient of variation of output. So when a land has access to irrigation, it is likely that the farmer will grow HYV boro. In some areas where the risk of flood damage is high, HYV boro replaces risk prone local aus or local aman.

Given the system of fragmented holdings, large farms usually consist of much larger number of fragments and thus have more chances of having some pieces of land in the irrigable zone once DTW or STWs have been fielded. So, irrigated farms and adopters of HYV will be in larger percentage among the large farmers.

The small farmers have their land in fewer segments. So once one piece is irrigated and is covered by HYV, it shows a larger percentage of farm area under HYV. So, simply because of the fact that the small holding cannot be economically subdivided, the small farms may devote larger percentage of area to HYV and thus the extent of adoption may show an inverse relation with farm size, as obtained by Ahmed (1981). Asaduzzaman's (1979) results, which are contradictory to this, can also be explained by extensions of the above argument. Asaduzzaman's adoption study concerns rain-fed aman HYV. In this case, it may be possible to further subdivide a plot and grow different varieties. So, the small farm can take this advantage and devote a small portion of land to the risky HYV aman. In the case of HYV boro, it is convenient to irrigate one whole piece of land when it has access to irrigation, since a farmer is eager to have such access (given the lower output variability of irrigated boro HYV and its higher yield).

So a major variable explaining the adoption of HYV or its absence is the existence of irrigation facility. Apart from its direct impact for boro varieties, it may have indirect impact on rain-fed aman or aus HYV's. When one considers the impact of family's consumption pressure on crop choice, one should consider all the crops feasible on a piece of land during all crop seasons in a year. Some land is specific to certain types of crop. On some land with access to irrigation, HYV boro may be the only profitable choice. So the dictates of consumption pressure will be residually determined after taking into account those obvious choices, and it should not be analysed only with reference to a single crop if it is a multi-cropped area.

Table 4.6: Pattern of Adoption of HYV by Different Size of Farms

Cultivated Land (in acres)	% of Owners Adopting HYV	% of Area Devoted to HYV by the Adopters
.01-1.0	27.0	85.0
1.0-2.0	89.0	45.0
2.0-3.0	94.0	28.0
3.0 & above	96.0	28.0
All groups	70.0	33.0

Source: Household Survey 1980.

Table 4.6 shows the pattern of HYV adoption by different farm size groups. As expected, the table shows that percentage of cultivators adopting HYV increases gradually with farm size, but the proportion of area they devote to HYV declines. At the beginning of this section, it was explained that the smaller farms have lower probability of having land under irrigation but once they have one fragment of the holding irrigated, it covers a large part of his land.

Data from a direct question on why the small farmers cannot adopt HYV and the large farmers cannot expand their HYV acreage is presented below. For the HYV growers, the reasons for not covering more land with HYV are given in Table 4.7.

Table 4.7: Reasons of Not Growing HYV on More Land by Different Farm Size

(Per Cent of Farmers)

Reasons*	Farm Size (Operated, in Acres)				
	.01-1.00	1.01-2.00	2.01-3.00	3.1 & Above	All Groups
No access to irrigation on remaining land	17.5	46.4	76.5	64.0	44.5
No more land/No more suitable land	12.5	32.1	17.6	12.0	18.2
Lack of cash	-	7.1	5.9	8.0	4.5
Others	-	-	11.8	8.0	3.6

Note: *Multiple reasons have been reported.
Source: Household Survey 1980.

For all holdings, access to irrigation is the most important reason, whereas, for smaller groups, the absolute limits of land or suitable land also set an important constraint for expanding HYV acreage. In the boro season, the consideration of risk does not seem to pose any constraint to the adoption or expansion of HYV. No one considered this as a reason even if it was suggested to them as a factor to consider. Apart from land suitability or access to irrigation, causes like lack of cash enter into consideration for expansion of HYV acreage, whereas, for preliminary adoption, only land suitability and access to irrigation seem to be limiting factors, as revealed by Table 4.8. Thus it can be concluded that adoption of HYV in the boro season and the pattern of adoption by various sizes of farms can be explained mostly by the availability of irrigation.

Table 4.8: Reasons of Not Adopting HYV by Farm Size

(Per Cent of Farmers)

Reasons	Farm size (in acre)			
	.01-1.00	1.01-2.00	2.01-3.00	3.1 & Above
Land is not suitable	25.0	3.6	-	-
No access to irrigation	25.0	7.2	-	7.2
Lack of cash	2.50	-	-	-
Lack of knowledge	-	-	-	-
Risk factor	-	-	-	-

Source: Household Survey 1980.

No one considers risk as a reason behind non-adoption. The adoption of HYV in aman or aus season are likely to be influenced by risk and other factors no doubt, but it is also related to the adoption of HYV in the boro season and thus indirectly depends on availability of irrigation in the case of multi-cropped land.

4.4 Cash Availability and Credit Facilities

Does the above discussion imply that once all land is irrigated, it will be covered with boro HYV? Possibly it does not. Once the possibility of growing HYV is expanded with the provision of irrigation, other constraints will be felt. Lack of cash for investment is likely to be an important obstacle to the expansion of HYV acreage in the use of optimum doses of related inputs like fertiliser. There is a greater possibility that cash constraints create bottlenecks for HYV crops than for traditional crops. The obvious reason is that these crops need larger quantities of purchased inputs, including both physical inputs and labour.

Given the large increase in cash cost, it may not be possible for the farmers to adopt HYV and more so, to expand the acreage of HYV. For the small farmers, the initial capital may be in short supply. While the large farmers have better access to credit facilities, they have to incur a larger amount of cash cost per acre than the smaller farms because they rely more on hired labour. So even if the physical facilities are available, lack of investible cash may retard the process of diffusion of the HYV technology. While the large farmers may reinvest the surplus generated from agriculture, the first round expenses need to be financed. This constraint is more likely to operate after some time, when HYV covers larger share of cultivated area. Data from the survey village can be used to examine whether the farmers have begun to feel the constraint.

Direct enquiry reveals that few farmers (2 cases only) consider lack of cash as a barrier against adoption of HYV. Responses to a follow up question on the problem of expansion of HYV acreage show that lack of cash is the third most important (Table 4.8) reason. Thus even in a village where irrigation and HYV still covers a small part of the village area, the constraint is making itself felt.

To understand the cash availability problem, the credit situation is also relevant. In fact, the government has been taking measures to increase the credit supply to enable farmers to use modern inputs.

But the problem usually affecting in this sphere is the inequality in the access to credit by different groups of farmers. Large farmers with the ability to provide collateral get loans from institutional sources, while small or tenant farmers may have to resort to non-institutional sources. Still if the absolute amount of credit remains inadequate, the large farmers will also be unable to overcome the bottleneck of the constraint of cash requirement. Apart from the problem of absolute shortage of loanable funds, cost of credit and its timely availability are also important for its proper utilisation.

The situation of credit availability and its related aspects in village Dhanbari has been presented in Table 4.9. The table gives the picture of borrowing by different farm sizes. As expected, the large farms borrowed larger amounts. But whether this satisfied their credit need fully is not obvious. So they were asked a question as to who sought more credit and was unable to get it. Table 4.10 shows pertinent data. Both small and large farms wanted to borrow more, though the sources they preferred differed. A higher share of large farmers wanted to obtain more loans.

Table 4.9: Amount Borrowed by Households with Different Farm Size

Size of Farm (in acres)	Average* Amount from		
	Bank	Private Interest Free Sources	Private with Interest
00	0	460	845
.01-1.0	600	1,883	1,621
1.0-2.0	629	0	5700
2.0-3.0	880	0	5350
3.0 & above	743	2,600	3,514
All group	742	1,259	3,274

Note: *Average for only those who actually borrow, in taka value in 1980.
Source: Household Survey 1980.

Another interesting feature of the credit situation may be mentioned here. Timelines of credit supply is crucial if it is to be used for agricultural inputs. In the year of the survey, the government decided to supply credit in kind in the form of fertiliser. But it was reported that the fertiliser, which was supposed to be given for use in boro season, actually reached the farmer in the next aman season. Its usefulness was much less in the aman season. Similarly, it also takes time to get cash credit from institutional sources. Though the cash may be used for another HYV boro crop next year, it is usually spent on other things. So to provide useful credit facilities for HYV inputs, the timeliness aspect of such credit needs to be emphasised.

Table 4.10: Willingness of Households of Different Farm Sizes to Borrow More Money

Farm Size (in acres)	% of Households Trying to Borrow More Funds
00	5.9
.01-1.0	20.0
1.0-2.0	39.3
2.0-3.0	41.2
3.0 & above	52.0

Source: Household Survey 1980.

Though it is expected that a shortage of credit will constrain the use of inputs, mere provision of credit may not necessarily lead to the use of that credit on improved inputs. In the absence of direct supervision, greater profitability of activities like relending and trading will attract credit for use in those activities even if on paper it is given for agricultural activities.

4.5 Labour Availability

In the previous section it was mentioned that HYV crops require larger investment on purchased inputs including labour. We turn now to the question of physical availability of labour, in view of the changed pattern of labour use.

The constraint with respect to labour has two aspects: (a) the total labour may be in short supply, and (b) family labour may be inadequate and hired hands have to be used.

Cultivation of HYV crops increases labour use in two ways. First, total labour for an HYV crop is higher than its local counterpart. Second, growing HYV crop in the winter season raises cropping intensity and increases labour use over the year. Concern with the latter may not be serious because labour use spread over the year will not create problems where a large part of the workers are underemployed. Rather, the labour use for a single season and its implications should receive attention.

Data from the present survey and a study by Muqtada (1983) show that the amount of labour used in each HYV crop is greater than the respective local variety. Does it mean that there will be shortage of labour? In fact, from the ex post data it cannot be resolved whether there was labour shortage. On the other hand, one can judge the possibility of labour shortage through various indirect questions.

The possibility of shortage emerges not so much from the larger labour requirement in total. In fact, a large part of the agricultural labour force remains underemployed in the case of traditional technology. But the underemployed labour force cannot provide the entire supply of labour for the new crops because the requirement is concentrated in some short periods. The difference specifically comes in the peak weeding period and harvesting period. The HYV crops use mere fertiliser and weeds grow fast. So the labour needed for weeding is much higher. The constraint is further aggravated by the fact that within an area, this task is done simultaneously on all the fields. Labour requirement for harvesting of the larger yield is also higher. When a field is ready, it needs to be harvested as quickly as possible.

The analysis of whether a constraint is felt would involve the direct enquiry of what is the maximum number of hands required simultaneously and how many are available. While requirement itself may have been adjusted by adjusting the acreage of various crops, the availability question is also complicated by the inter-village and inter-regional migration of labour and resulting flexibility of supply. So the labour supply constraint has to be examined in terms of the reactions which are likely to be the impact of such a constraint. For example (a) whether the farmers, especially the large farmers, fear a shortage in labour availability in the peak seasons, (b) whether a large part of the labour used is supplied by migrant labourers, and (c) whether in the fear of labour shortage, farmers choose to reduce the acreage of labour-intensive crops.

With respect to (b) above, it may be mentioned that the progressive village in the present survey was dependent on outside labour to a much larger extent than the other village. Other studies also show that large groups of labourers migrate from non-irrigated areas to HYV growing areas, which helps both the labourers and the growers (Chowdhury, 1980). But this has implications for the future expansion of HYV acreage simultaneously in all regions, which may create a real shortage of labour.

Ahmed's (1981) study gives some evidence on reactions of types (a) and (c) above. In a direct enquiry, he has found that, in a village in Comilla, large farmers faced a shortage of labour in the peak season. He has related this to the observation that large farmers devoted lower percentage of their land to labour-intensive crops like HYV boro. Similar findings have been given by Asaduzzaman (1979), which shows that the extent of adoption of HYV is negatively related to relative labour scarcity (defined as land area per family labourer). If this trend is even partly due to the fear of labour shortage, one should consider this seriously while discussing the problems of expansion of new technology.

The other aspect of the labour constraint is related to the composition of labour in terms of family and hired component. In addition to shortage of total labour for a village, some households may face a problem from a shortage of either component. For the large and richer households, the likely problem is the shortage of family labour to supervise the hired workers who are employed in large numbers in the peak season. For the small farmers, the family labour may be in surplus in some seasons; but the labour requirement for HYV's being very concentrated in some weeks, the small farmers also have to hire a small portion of total man days required.

On the whole, it can be said that even in a labour abundant country like Bangladesh, there is a possibility of labour shortage becoming a constraint to the expansion of HYV acreage. Such possibility is mainly due to the marked seasonality of labour use, which creates seasonal scarcity of labour or at least a fear of such shortage.

In areas where mechanised means of irrigation is not available, but HYV is grown in winter with the help of manual irrigation, labour will be a more critical question. Labour requirement for manual irrigation is quite large for each acre and the productivity of such labour would not be so high. So it is worthwhile only for small farmers who are underemployed. Then the larger farms are likely to devote a lower share of their land to HYV, thus explaining the inverse relationship between farm size and extent of adoption of HYV observed in these villages. However, manual irrigation is likely to decline in future.

4.6 Summary of Findings and Conclusion

The above analysis shows that the availability of inputs may pose obstacles to the adoption of HYV and expansion of its acreage. Irrigation is the most important among such supply-side constraints. Lack of knowledge does not seem to be an obstacle. Supply-side factors like irrigation are important not only for adoption practices but also for explaining the pattern of adoption among different farm sizes. When access to irrigation is limited, percentage of HYV adopters varies directly with farm size, while the extent of adoption varies inversely.

The new technology involves greater use of material inputs and increases the requirement of cash for current investment. Availability of cash may be an obstacle to the expansion of HYV acreage, if not for its adoption. Supply of timely and supervised credit can ease the situation.

Labour availability also deserves consideration as a supply-side constraint. Labour is underemployed if we consider the whole year or entire crop season. Still labour constraint may be felt in periods of peak demand. There are symptoms which suggest the existence of such a constraint. This also helps explain inverse relationship that is observed between farm size and extent of adoption. Inter-village and inter-regional migration of labour from low productive areas to HYV growing parts shows the existence of labour shortage in some areas. However, this can be a possible solution to the problem as long as HYV technology is not uniformly spread in all regions.

It should be mentioned that by emphasising the supply-side constraints, we do not want to de-emphasise the demand-side factors in explaining adoption practices and pattern. Ultimately, the demand-side factors will determine the extent of adoption when the supply-side bottlenecks are entirely removed.

CHAPTER 5

Agricultural Productivity: Role of Farm Size, Tenancy and District Level Variations

5.1 Introduction

The objective of the present chapter is to analyse the district level variations of agricultural productivity and the determinants of the use of modern inputs that enhance productivity. The chapter examines the complementarities between crop and non-crop production and between cereal and non-cereal production. Analysis of such data is useful for the identification of the advanced and backward areas. This can have important implications for policies of regionally balanced agricultural growth. Most of the past research on agricultural growth and productivity have been based on either aggregate data or household data (except studies by Boyce 1986 and Hossain 1986) and therefore a study on district level difference can play an important role in the context of determinants of modern inputs use and productivity.

Bangladesh has been described as a plain alluvial land with a small area of hilly regions in the northeast and southeast corner. The description conveys a picture of lack of physiographical and ecological diversity. Such an implicit assumption may have been responsible for inadequate attention to the analysis of the regional aspects of agricultural growth. Almost all research on agriculture (except some analysis of regional price variation) has been conducted at the aggregate level. Therefore, it will be useful to begin with an elaboration of two important rationales for the district level analysis presented here.

First, the assumption of uniformity of physiographical and ecological characteristics is actually not as correct as generally portrayed. The general description of Bangladesh as a flat and fertile alluvial land conceals the differences in soil and rainfall characteristics which influence the choice of crops and the interregional variations in the productivity of the same crop. Recent soil surveys and other detailed analysis of ecological characteristics have identified important regional variations in these characteristics.

The second rationale lies in the concern about a regionally balanced growth which emerges as an important issue, especially after three decades of development experience. At the early stages of agricultural modernisation, an aggregate analysis of the constraints to agricultural growth is adequate for guiding the policies; since all the regions are backward during the early phases, development initiatives may be spread as evenly as possible. After three decades of experience of agricultural development in Bangladesh, the relative performance of different regions (districts) should be analysed. Given the differences in the agro-ecological characteristics and in the socio-economic features of different areas, it is pertinent that a disaggregated analysis of agricultural productivity and its determinants is taken up.

District level analysis by Hossain (1986) and Boyce (1986), taken up during the mid-1980s (when the 1983/84 Census of Agriculture by BBS had been published), focused only on the impact of irrigation on the growth of crop production. These two studies provide important reference points and the results of the present study have been compared with the findings of these studies.

This chapter has been organised as follows.

The relative performance of the districts in terms of agricultural productivity level and the productivity of crop, non-crop, cereal and non-cereal crops have been discussed in Section 5.3. Growth rates of value added in agriculture and its components (crop and non-crop) have been examined in Section 5.4.

Determinants of the extent of adoption of HYV technology and the use of other modern inputs, namely irrigation and fertiliser, have been examined in Section 5.5. Section 5.6 focuses on whether irrigation continues to be the leading input. Section 5.7 examines the determinants of the use of farm machinery. Section 5.8 discusses the relationship between farm size and productivity on the basis of more recent data. The last Section provides some concluding observations.

5.2 Notes on Data

Absence of district level analysis of agricultural production has been, to some extent, due to the lack of availability of pertinent data. For the period 1985-1996, relevant data have been available in disaggregated form for the 20 (often termed as greater) districts. This data set provides disaggregation for crop and non-crop sectors and the number of observations with comparable data is sufficient to obtain a picture of the time path of ranking of districts and the growth rate of value added (Sections 5.3 and 5.4). This data set has been discontinued after 1999 and therefore the analysis cannot be extended to recent years.

The analyses of input use and intensity of cultivation (Sections 5.5, 5.6 and 5.7) are based on data from the Census of Agriculture 1996 which has been published in 1999 (BBS, 1999). This source provides data on input use and the relevant explanatory variables for explaining the input intensities. Data on all of these variables are not available in the other source (*Statistical Yearbook of Bangladesh*). The *Census of Agriculture 1996* provides disaggregation for 64 new districts (compared to the 20 greater district level disaggregation in the other source) and therefore offers greater degrees of freedom for the regression analysis. Section 5.8 uses recent data from the HIES 2010 to examine the relationship between farm size and productivity.

It should be mentioned that the analysis at district level is not sufficient to capture the impact of variation of soil types and other physical factors on productivity because ecological zones do not perfectly match with district boundaries. However, data on socio-economic variables are not available for the ecological zones. Therefore, the chapter limits itself to district level analysis.

5.3 Differences in Agricultural Productivity across Districts

This section addresses the following issues:[1]

a. Identification of the advanced and the backward districts in terms of agricultural productivity;
b. Variation in the relative position of districts over time;
c. Relative importance of various types of agricultural products in different districts.

Table 5.1 provides data on agricultural value added per hectare[2] and the rank of the districts in terms of this indicator.

---

[1] Sections 5.3 to 5.7 draws from Rahman (2002).

[2] Agriculture includes both crop and non-crop (forestry, fishery and livestock). Value added per hectare is calculated on the basis of total land area of the district, which is more logical than using arable land as the denominator because we have included forestry, fishery, etc. in agriculture.

Table 5.1: Gross Value Added in Agriculture and Rank of Districts

District	Gross Value Added in 1996 Per Ha (Taka, 1984/85 Prices)	Rank 1995/96	Rank 1990/91	Rank 1985/86
Chittagong	15,174	10	14	8
Chittagong Hill Tracts	7,952	20	20	20
Comilla	20,316	1	2	3
Noakhali	12,240	15	16	13
Sylhet	12,104	16	17	19
Dhaka	15,442	9	8	6
Faridpur	13,340	12	13	9
Jamalpur	16,904	5	7	7
Mymensingh	15,548	8	10	5
Tangail	17,430	4	4	4
Barisal	11,853	17	9	16
Jessore	18,646	3	3	11
Khulna	9,340	19	19	18
Kushtia	16,395	7	6	10
Patuakhali	11,802	18	18	17
Bogra	19,366	2	1	1
Dinajpur	13,654	11	12	15
Pabna	13,278	13	15	12
Rajshahi	12,889	14	11	14
Rangpur	16,414	6	5	2

Source: Calculated from BBS (Statistical Yearbook of Bangladesh, various years).

The three districts with the lowest productivity are Chittagong Hill Tracts, Khulna and Patuakhali, with per hectare value added of Tk. 7,952, Tk. 9,340 and Tk. 11,802 respectively. The three districts at the top are Comilla, Bogra and Jessore. The districts with the lowest productivity are the ones with adverse ecological characteristics. Chittagong Hill Tracts is located in the hilly region while Khulna and Patuakhali are affected by salinity problem. The next three districts with low ranks are Barisal, Sylhet and Noakhali. These are located in the plain land but two of them are partly affected by salinity problem. The very low "haor" areas of Sylhet pose special ecological constraint to crop productivity.

One should also examine whether the range of variation of productivity is sufficiently large to call for an analysis of inter-district variation. It can be observed from Table 5.1 that the range of variation is not small, the largest value added per hectare is more than twice that of the smallest one (Tk. 7,952 and Tk. 20,316 respectively).

The ranks of each district in the years 1985/86, 1990/91 and 1995/96 have also been shown in Table 5.1. From Table 5.1 the following points emerge: It is observed that the relative position of a few districts at the top and the bottom had hardly changed during these years. Only at two points the position of two topmost districts interchanged and in 1995/96 they were again in the same rank as in the beginning. Similarly, the districts in the bottom also continued with almost the same ranks over this period. There have been changes in the relative position of some of the districts in the middle positions.

5.4 Growth of Agriculture: Performance of Districts

The annual rate of growth of value added in agriculture per hectare of area of a district has been estimated through a semi-logarithmic function fitted to the data. The estimated average annual rates of growth have been presented in Table 5.2.

Table 5.2: Growth Rates of Value Added in Agriculture (Crop Plus Non-Crop) Crop, Non-Crop, Cereal Crop and Non-Cereal Crop

District	Agriculture	Crop	Non-Crop	Rank of Growth Rate of Crop	Rank of Growth Rate of Non-Crop
Chittagong	2.29***	0.94	4.32***	15	17
Chittagong H. Tracts	2.86***	1.39*	3.27***	9	18
Comilla	1.65**	0.65	6.34***	16	12
Noakhali	0.30	-0.82	4.61***	18	15
Sylhet	3.80***	3.32***	6.30***	1	13
Dhaka	3.13***	1.51	7.60***	7	2
Faridpur	0.16	-0.98	5.79***	19	14
Jamalpur	2.52***	1.64*	7.53***	6	3
Mymensingh	1.97***	1.04	7.23***	12	8
Tangail	2.46**	1.47	6.74***	8	11
Barisal	-1.98*	-2.57**	-0.85	20	20
Jessore	3.23***	2.65***	7.44***	3	4
Khulna	3.09***	1.95*	4.54***	5	4
Kushtia	1.85***	0.99	7.42***	13	5
Patuakhali	0.50	0.95	-0.35	14	19
Bogra	3.19***	2.52**	7.29***	4	7
Dinajpur	2.11**	1.18	7.11***	11	9
Pabna	2.34***	1.36	6.92***	10	10
Rajshahi	3.69**	2.99*	7.62***	2	1
Rangpur	1.66***	0.64	7.38***	17	6
Bangladesh	2.08***	1.19*	4.88***	-	-

Note: ***, ** and * indicate significance at 1 per cent, 5 per cent and 10 per cent level respectively.
Source: Estimated from data provided by BBS (Statistical Yearbook of Bangladesh, various years).

The range of the rate of growth of agriculture among the districts is quite large: the lowest is -1.98 and the highest is 3.80 per cent per year. The next question one should ask is whether the districts with a high level of production in the initial year have slowed down or is it the reverse, that is, the low productive areas have continued with low growth rate. This has been examined through a rank correlation analysis.

There are certain areas where the initial productivity levels as well as the rates of growth are low. The districts in this category are Noakhali, Faridpur, Barisal and Patuakhali. In contrast, Mymensingh and Rangpur started with a higher base and have slowed down during the period 1986-1995. Sylhet, Jessore, CHT and Khulna were the initially low ranking (in terms of value added per hectare) but later became high growing areas, with ranks 1, 3, 6 and 7 in terms of growth rate. Bogra started with a high rank of value added per hectare and maintained its rank through a high rate of growth during this period (in terms of growth rate, its rank is 4). Thus, one cannot say that the initially stagnating areas have picked up. Among the areas with better initial rank, some have continued with a high rate of growth, while most of them have experienced stagnation.

5.5 Determinants of the Use of Modern Inputs: Role of Farm Size and Tenancy

This section focuses mainly on the determinants of productivity in the crop sector. The analysis of productivity in the crop sector highlights the impact of population density as a growth augmenting factor, and in that context examines (at the end of this section) the association between population density and overall agricultural productivity.

The analysis of productivity of crop sector has been based on a number of indicators. Increased productivity in crop sector has been achieved through a rise in cropping intensity and through the expansion of the percentage of area under modern inputs. The set of modern inputs include irrigation, fertiliser and high yielding varieties of crops, especially paddy. Adoption of HYV paddy in different seasons may be determined by different sets of factors and therefore these are considered as separate indicators (though an analysis of all HYV has also been included). In this chapter, the extent of adoption of irrigation has been used as an indicator of productivity growth (and thus as a dependent variable in the multiple regression). With an increase in the number of shallow tubewells (STWs), which require much smaller fixed capital compared to deep tubewells (DTWs), and may be owned by single individuals, irrigation becomes an endogenous variable. In contrast, in the earlier studies, when DTW and large-scale gravity flow methods were predominant, irrigation had been used as an independent variable. Physical features of the land and location of a DTW or a gravity flow project were the dominant exogenous determinants of irrigation (Rahman, 1998).

The independent variables used in the equations include physical features and a number of economic and social factors which are expected to explain the district level variation of productivity. Among the physical features, district level data is available only on rainfall and land elevation. Two variables have been included to take the latter factor into account. These are per cent of high land and per cent of low land. Total amount of rainfall over a year has been included as an explanatory variable.

Among the social features, the following variables have been included:

  i. Per cent of households with land under tenancy in each district;[3]
  ii. Per cent of households in a district, with small holding;
  iii. Per cent of households with no cultivated land (and own land less than 0.04 acre);
  iv. Population density.

The disincentive impact of share tenancy has been widely discussed in the past studies, though the empirical results have not been conclusive on the lower level of modern inputs used by tenants (compared to owner farmers). Therefore, a variable (listed as item i) has been incorporated to test this hypothesis. The distributional impact of agricultural growth induced by the modern rice technology and access of small farmers to such technology has been a matter of considerable debate since the introduction of the irrigated HYV paddy. From the early days of introduction of modern technology, it has been pointed out that due to risk averseness of small farmers and a number of institutional biases working against them, the use of the modern inputs may be less among the small farmers compared to the large farmers. Griffin (1974) and Frankel (1971) are some of the early studies expressing this concern. India's experiences during the 1970s have been examined by a large number of studies and they demonstrate that the adoption rate of

---

[3] During the 1990s sharecropping was the predominant mode of tenancy.

modern technology is higher among large farms compared to smaller ones and among owner cultivators compared to tenants (Rudra, 1970, Mukharjee, 1970, Rao, 1975). In the context of Bangladesh, empirical findings on these issues have been mixed (Rahman, 1983, Hossain 1988, Hossain et. al., 1994). Therefore, it is pertinent that the role of farm size is examined with more recent data sets. To assess the current situation in this respect, an indicator of farm size (per cent of households with small farms with less than 2.50 acres of land) has been included as an explanatory of adoption of HYV and irrigation.

Per cent of households with no cultivated land has been included to test the hypothesis of the presence of a constraint of wage labour supply. Most hired labour for agriculture is supplied by this group. The possibility of such a constraint arises because HYVs require larger amount of labour input.

To analyse the impact of population density on the efforts to increase agricultural production, two explanatory variables have been included: the area of a district and total population. Population pressure or smaller average size of holding per household/person is expected to be positively associated with land productivity. This may be considered as a reflection of the Chayanovian hypothesis, which predicts a more intensive use of land and family labour by households with larger family consumption demands for own produce. In the present case, the Chayanovian hypothesis may, however, take a slightly modified form. Higher land productivity in a situation of higher population density may be viewed as an attempt to maximise family income as well as to maximise the return from existing resources because alternative opportunities of employment and investment are rather limited in the rural areas. It may be noted that in recent years, marketable surplus of rice crops has substantially increased. The positive relationship between population pressure and production may, therefore, not be motivated by families' subsistence only but by the need for enhancing family income as well and thus may not be in a contradiction to the observed trends of increase in the marketable surplus. The positive impact of population on modern input use is also likely to be due to the larger labour requirement of these inputs.

The results of the equations on the extent of adoption of HYV have been presented in Table 5.1A. The results of the regressions with cropping intensity, fertiliser and irrigation intensity as the dependent variables have been presented in Table 5.2A.

The discussion begins with a focus on the impact of the physical characteristics. Land elevation variables have the expected sign and are statistically significant in most equations. For example, HYV aman cannot be grown in deeply flooded low land. The percentage of cultivated area under this category has a significant negative coefficient. This variable has a positive coefficient in the equation for HYV boro. Low land can retain moisture in winter and thus is suitable for growing HYV boro. The per cent of high land does not always have an impact in the expected direction. The reason may be that high land in different districts has greater variations in quality, access to surface water, etc. The quantity of rainfall has an insignificant coefficient in all equations except equation 1 (Table 5.1A). This is because HYV paddy is usually grown with irrigation.

The coefficient of the percentage of small farms is negative in all the equations except equation 1 (for per cent of net cropped area under HYV aus). The coefficient is significant at less than 5 per cent probability in the case of equations with dependent variables, "per cent area under HYV aman," "per cent area under all HYV," and "per cent area irrigated." It has already been mentioned why such a relationship may prevail. Hossain (1989) obtained a positive relationship between HYV adoption in aman season and farm size and the result is in conformity with the present findings. In his study, the coefficients of farm size in the equations for HYV boro were insignificant, as in the present case.

The variable representing tenancy is positively related to the cropping intensity and the coefficient is statistically significant. In other equations, its coefficient is insignificant.

As expected, the districts with higher population (after controlling for area of the district) are associated with higher intensity of cropping, extent of HYV adoption and irrigation. In most equations, the coefficients are statistically significant.

Per cent of landless households, who are expected to be the supplier of wage labour, does not have significant coefficients in some of the equations (equations 1 and 5). Thus, the availability of labour is not working as a constraint to the increased intensity of HYV cultivation during boro and aus season when the total area cropped is smaller and thus total labour demand is smaller than in aman season. But this constraint becomes significant in the case of HYV aman, the season in which total cropped area is the largest. Therefore, one cannot really ignore the possibility that this constraint may become more pressing for HYV cultivation in other seasons as well if the area cropped expands in future. Values of adjusted R square are in the range of 0.19 to 0.54, which are considered plausible for regressions with district level data (values of F are significant in all the equations).

Table 5.3 shows data on density of population and the ranks in terms of population density and agricultural (crop plus non-crop) value added per hectare. It is observed that the ranks based on land productivity have a positive correlation with the ranks based on population per hectare. Table 5.3 also presents data on per capita value added in agriculture. It is observed that the ranks of districts in terms of this indicator are more or less in the reverse direction of the ranks based on value added per hectare. The districts with lowest value added per hectare have risen to the top of the list in terms of value added per person because population density is low in these districts.[4]

Table 5.3: Rank of Districts in terms of Value Added Per Capita and Population Density

District	Population Density (Persons Per Hectare)	Value Added, Taka Per Capita, 1995-96	Rank Based on Population Density	Rank Based on Per Capita Value Added	Rank Based on Value Added/ha
Chittagong	19.40	2,575	1	4	10
Chittagong Hill Tracts	9.16	13,843	19	1	20
Comilla	18.63	1,592	2	19	2
Noakhali	15.39	1,600	5	18	16
Sylhet	9.65	2,207	18	7	18
Dhaka	18.55	1,638	3	17	8
Faridpur	11.38	1,693	13	16	11
Jamalpur	13.53	1,896	8	14	6
Mymensingh	12.30	1,954	10	12	9
Tangail	12.56	1,950	9	13	7
Barisal	11.90	1,863	12	15	13
Jessore	10.32	2,553	14	5	3
Khulna	10.28	2,733	15	3	19
Kushtia	12.22	2,124	11	9	5
Patuakhali	6.28	2,899	20	2	17
Bogra	14.14	2,152	6	8	1
Dinajpur	10.02	2,278	17	6	15
Pabna	15.73	1,557	4	20	14
Rajshahi	10.27	1,952	16	11	12
Rangpur	13.78	1,996	7	10	4

Source: Calculated from BBS (Statistical Yearbook of Bangladesh, various years).

[4] Thus, the productivity of agriculture does not provide an indication of the level of per capita agricultural income and the incidence of poverty in a district.

5.6 Is Irrigation the "Leading Input"?

A rapid increase in agricultural growth during the late 1970s and 1980s has been possible through the expansion of irrigation. Promotion of groundwater irrigation through subsidy on the imported equipment and gravity channel irrigation under government's direct management has been based on the notion of irrigation as the leading input (Hossain, 1986, Boyce, 1986). Irrigation has been considered as the leading input because it came first in the chain of technology adoption. Provision of irrigation facility opened up the possibility of adoption of HYV paddy and the increased application of chemical fertiliser.

Boyce (1986) estimated regression equations between extent of input use (HYV adoption, extent of fertiliser adoption) and irrigation. Irrigation's role as the leading input has been confirmed through the highly significant regression coefficients and high value of adjusted R square. Hossain (1986) criticised Boyce for using outdated data. Hossain's study (1986) used the 1983/84 Agriculture Census data and his findings provide strong support to Boyce's conclusion with significant regression coefficients for the same variables.

In recent years, the mode of irrigation has undergone a change and the expansion of irrigation has experienced a deceleration. Upto the late 1980s, there has been an acceleration of the number of DTWs as well as the area irrigated by DTWs. With the increased pace of economic reform policies during the late 1980s and 1990s, subsidies on DTWs were first reduced and then completely withdrawn. As a result, the DTWs became unprofitable. Installation of new DTWs was not viable. Standardisation restrictions on the import of STWs were lifted. As a result, there was drastic fall in the prices of STWs. The zoning restrictions on sinking STWs (around DTWs) were discontinued. Due to these favourable changes, the number of STWs used for irrigation and the area irrigated by STWs increased rapidly.

With the expansion of STW irrigation, the role of irrigation as the leading input is expected to change. STW irrigation does not involve a large fixed investment and/or an institutional mechanism to set up the operation. STWs can be fielded quickly and it may be easily shifted and used in a new site. Therefore, this form of irrigation may not necessarily be considered as a precondition for the use of other inputs. The small capital requirement and quick installation procedure mean that this input may be procured simultaneously with other inputs.

Therefore, irrigation may no longer be considered as an exogenous variable.

Whether irrigation still continues to be the leading input may be influenced by the farmers' attitude as well. How far the sinking of a STW and its operation is an easy option also depends on the access to market and related physical infrastructure and on the availability of the services of the mechanics, repair facilities, etc. Moreover, the gravity flow irrigation and the DTW's already in operation continue to occupy a significant percentage of irrigated acreage. Therefore, it is likely that "irrigation as the leading input" phenomenon may continue though its significance may have declined.

To test whether irrigation is the leading input, the earlier studies relied on a regression analysis with irrigation as the explanatory variable. Rahman (2002) estimates similar equations with the district-wise data set and the regression results have been compared (Tables 5.4A to 5.6A) with the regression results from the earlier papers.[5] This will reveal whether the role of irrigation as a determinant of the use of other modern inputs has been weakened or not.

Equations have been estimated for the dependent variables: various types of HYV as per cent of net cultivated area, total HYV cultivation as per cent of net cultivated area, per cent of area fertilised and cropping intensity. Two sets of equations have been estimated: one with irrigation as the only independent variable and in another, irrigation and rainfall have been included. This has been done to obtain comparable results with Boyce's and Hossain's study.

The coefficients of irrigation are significant in both sets of equations. Therefore, it may be concluded that the importance of irrigation as the contributor to the adoption of modern inputs has not declined. This factor alone still accounts for a significant per cent of the variations in HYV adoption (especially in aman and boro crops) and fertilised area (adjusted R-square values are in the range of 0.54 to 0.66). Thus, irrigation can be considered as the leading input, which implies that policies related to expansion of irrigation have an important role for agricultural growth. Nonetheless, it may be noted that the level of significance, the values of the coefficients and the values of adjusted R-square are lower in some of the new equations.

---

[5] Both data sets are from the "Census of Agriculture" and are disaggregated for districts. However, the data set for the later year (1995/96) has been presented for 64 districts, while the earlier set was for 20 districts.

5.7 Determinants of the Use of Farm Machinery

The other important component of modern technology in agriculture consists of the farm machinery used for land preparation. In Bangladesh, use of farm machinery has been rather limited until recently. During the last decade, the use of tractors and power tillers for land preparation has made rapid progress. An analysis of the factors that contributed to the mechanisation process is therefore pertinent.

In most areas of Bangladesh, use of mechanised tillage practices is possible only in the dry seasons. Therefore, the popularity of machinery had to wait till a substantial expansion of irrigated winter paddy has been achieved.

With the expansion of farm machinery, the following questions about its determinants should be examined:

i. Whether this has been due to inadequacy of draught power;
ii. Whether the shortage of labour contributes to the increase in the number of tractors and power tillers; and
iii. Whether the preponderance of small and landless farmers impedes the expansion of mechanised tillage practices.

Analysis of these questions has been undertaken through multiple regression equations. The dependent variable has been specified as the number of machinery in a district. The explanatory variables include area, population, number of draft animals, landless holdings (per cent) and small farm holdings (per cent).

After controlling for area of a district, the coefficient of "population" shows the impact of two counteracting forces. First, a larger population would require an increase in food production and encourage mechanisation, which will help to increase productivity and cropping intensity. Second, larger population implies a larger potential supply of labourers and thus will have a negative impact on mechanisation.

The shortage of supply of draft animals may act as a constraint to swift land preparation for winter crops or summer crops and thereby encourage mechanised land preparation.

The other two variables, share of landless and small farm holdings, can test whether the structure of landownership in favour of small holdings discourages the use of machinery. This may be due to two forces: first, small farmers may not be endowed with capital required for investment on machine and second, the more numerous the small farms are, the smaller will be the average size of holding. Tractors may not be suitable for tilling small fragments of land.

The results of the estimated equations have been presented in Table 5.3A. One equation has been estimated with "number of tractors plus the number of power tillers" as the dependent variable and the results of this equation have been discussed below. The other equation uses "the number of tractors" to see whether the results significantly differ when the two items are not added.

The results show that "population" has a significant negative coefficient. Thus, the availability of workers is found to be a critical constraint, which counteracts the positive impact of subsistence pressure encouraging mechanisation to achieve higher production.

It may be useful to elaborate on this issue. Bangladesh has been traditionally known as a surplus labour economy and therefore one may wonder why and how the labour constraint may emerge as a factor leading to mechanised tillage practices. To understand this, one must distinguish between an absolute shortage of labourer and the shortage of labour for land preparation. The ploughing activity is one of the most time bound activities in the crop cycle. Ploughing with bullock labour is also the most physical labour-intensive operation. Therefore, the labourers engaged in this activity usually work for only 5-6 hours a day (this is also because the animals need rest as well). Therefore, when all the fields in a village have to be completed within a short span of time, there is inadequacy of labour.

Results presented in Table 5.3A show that the coefficients of the variables representing the extent of small holdings and landless holdings are positive and significant. These variables raise the number of machinery in a district and thus the small size of holdings does not pose a constraint to the mechanisation process.

The coefficient of draft animal was hypothesised to be negative: a constraint of the availability will necessitate machine use. The result is contrary to expectation. The obvious implication is that mechanisation is not taking place as a result of the draught power constraint and, as already mentioned, labour power is the critical constraint in this respect. It is not difficult to perceive a situation where the number of machinery and the number of livestock increase simultaneously and thus contribute to the increase in cropping intensity.[6] This has a positive implication

---

[6] In fact, another study on the determinants of mechanisation obtained a regression of the per cent of machine cultivated area on draught animal per acre and cropping intensity. Possibly due to the inclusion of cropping intensity as an explanatory variable, the paper obviously obtained a negative coefficient of draught animal (Ahmed, 2001).

for the growth of the livestock sector which may grow simultaneously with the progress of mechanisation.

5.8 Importance and Efficiency of Very Small Farms: Evidence from the HIES 2010

An earlier chapter (Chapter 3) has shown that arable land per rural household of Bangladesh has been declining during the last two decades. It is not, therefore, surprising that a large majority of farms are of small size. Another related feature that has so far remained unnoticed is that the number of tiny holdings of less than one acre was growing during 1998-2008.

Holdings below half acre (or one acre) are often referred to as marginal farms. The term instantly flashes their low importance within the farm sector. This group attracts attention as candidates for safety net allocations or poverty reduction strategy. In the process, important aspects of the role of this group of tiny farms (in this chapter referred to as "very small farms") in the rural and agricultural growth have been lost sight of. In the following discussion two issues are addressed in turn.

- Share of very small farms and the factors contributing to the rise in the number of such farms;
- Whether this group demonstrates productive efficiency.

According to *Agricultural Census of 2008*, less than one acre sized farms constitute about 52 per cent of all farms, while only 15 per cent farms own above 2.50 acres. However, the very small farms own only 17 per cent of all agricultural land, while the medium and large owners own 49 per cent. The very small farm size group, which accounts for more than half of the total farms, should not be relegated to an unimportant position by viewing them as "marginal" farms. Moreover, the share of very small farms is increasing with an addition of about one lakh farm households sliding down to less than half acre group annually.

One obvious question is that as long as the owners of the small farms intend to continue as farmers, why they do not purchase more land and become owners of a more viable or economical size of farm? On the contrary, they may also give up farming, sell the farm land and invest in alternatives. Land market situation provides answers to these questions. Land price is so high that low-income people cannot buy a significant parcel of land. Moreover, land price is escalating and such price expectation explains why they cling to the possession of the land.

The reason behind the rise of price of land is that arable land frontier has already been reached and there is no scope of bringing in new land for cultivation. In fact, not only arable land has been exhausted, a process of decline of total arable land has already set in due to the non-farm uses of land. Decline of total farm land makes it clear that the situation is irreversible with no chance that the farms with very small size will have better chance of getting access to land in future.

A farm area of less than an acre can be hardly sufficient for the subsistence of a family. Although there is no readily available figure of standard size of farm that can ensure subsistence of an average family, past studies have used 2.5 acres as the norm. Using the recommended rice consumption per person, expenditure share of low-income groups on non-food, the current rice production per acre and assuming an average family size of four persons, one can obtain an estimate of the area of farm needed for ensuring subsistence. This estimate stands as two acres, slightly less than earlier estimates, which is quite natural as productivity per acre has increased over the last two decades.

The other concern in this context is whether the very small farms can be as efficient as their larger counterparts. A number of forces may work together to hinder their efficiency. They have low savings and therefore cannot invest on modern inputs. They cannot use farm machinery because the investment will not be fully utilised on the tiny plot.

On the contrary, there may be reverse forces at work as well. Small and very small farmers may even be more efficient. To eke out subsistence from their small piece of land, they use all means to raise productivity. In fact, studies on Indian agriculture have demonstrated that smaller farmers have higher productivity. Previous studies in Bangladesh show mixed results. Some studies found medium farmers more efficient than small and larger ones.

Data for 1984 and 2008 have been quoted in Table 5.4. Data show that the share of small farms (including marginal) adopting HYV or irrigation is very close to the adoption rate of medium-size farms and is only slightly less than the large farms.

Table 5.4: Adoption Rate of High Yielding Variety (HYV)/Irrigation by Farm Size

Farm Size	Per Cent of Households who Grow HYV, 1984	Per Cent of Households who Irrigate their Land, 2008
Small	75.0	72.0
Medium	74.0	74.0
Large	77.0	79.0

Source: BBS: *Census of Agriculture, 1984, 2008.*

The question of efficiency of farms of smallest size did not receive separate attention in those studies.

Analysis of HIES data on households' farm production shows that production per acre of land of small farms is higher than large[7] and medium farms and for the smallest farm size it is even higher (shown in Table 5.5).

Table 5.5: Paddy Production and Family Labour Days Per Acre by Farm Size

Farm Size (Acres)	Production of Paddy (Kg Per Acre)	Days of Family Labour Per Acre of Land
< .99	1,746	465
1.00-2.49	1,647	183
2.50-4.99	1,587	112
5.00+	1,337	61

Source: HIES 2010.

The factors contributing to their high land productivity can have useful policy implications and therefore these are being highlighted. These farmers have the required motivation. Therefore, they aim to obtain subsistence from the tiny holding. They use larger dose of family labour to achieve this. This "self-exploitation" of self-employed farmers has been borne out by analysis of HIES (2010) data. Table 5.5 shows that the smallest holdings use much larger number of days of family labour per acre of land. Data also show that total labour use (including family labour and hired labour) per acre is also smaller among large and medium farmers.

---

[7] Regression of production of paddy on area of cultivated land provides statistically significant positive relationship.

One will obviously look for strategies and policies for raising the productivity of large farmers and for increasing the labour use in those farms. One of the ways to raise productivity is that they resort to mechanisation of some of the operations of cultivation. This may further reduce their labour input per acre. At present, women and young persons of large and medium farms contribute only a small share of family labour to field crop production. The constraints here are mainly social factors. Therefore, overcoming these barriers requires a change in social attitude. Farming should be made an attractive occupation for young men and women and this requires such transformation that cultivation will be viewed as farm enterprises. Awareness raising and application of modern devices can contribute to such change.

Evidence of higher productivity of very small farmers gives a clear message that they are by no means marginal farmers. They deserve policy attention to improve their access to credit and farm inputs. At the same time, these data highlight the fact that production per acre can be increased through application of more labour inputs in the medium and large farms.

The findings also have implications for land redistribution. Whenever possible, *khas* land should be distributed to very small farmers. This will not only reduce inequality but will also raise productivity.

5.9 Concluding Observations

Inter-district variation of per hectare value added in agriculture has been found to be quite large. Bogra, Comilla and Jessore have been at the top of the list of productivity, while Chittagong Hill Tracts, Khulna and Patuakhali have been the three districts with lowest agricultural value added per hectare. Low value added from agriculture is not, however, reflected in low value added per person because the districts with low land productivity are characterised by high land-population ratio.

Most of the districts have experienced high rate of growth of non-crop agriculture, whereas only five districts (out of 20) have achieved significant growth of crop production. Two districts have shown negative growth rate in both crop and non-crop production. Most of the districts experiencing low growth rate of crop production have also performed poorly in terms of growth of non-crop agriculture.

It has been observed that the growth rates of value added in agriculture and in crop production are high in some of the districts which have low ranks based on the "level" of value added per hectare. The exceptions are the districts of Faridpur, Barisal and Noakhali. Particular attention should be given to enhance productivity in these districts since these are characterised by low level of productivity as well as low growth rate.

It should be recognised that all districts are not equally suitable for cereal production. Fruits and vegetables are important products in some of the districts. To facilitate the growth of production of these crops, special infrastructural development and policies are required to enable the farmers to market these products. Special storage and transport facilities must be created through public sector investment as well as through directed support for private sector initiatives. The districts which produce non-cereal crops are often far from the metropolitan cities. Therefore, the need for improved transport facilities for encouraging the growth of production of these items in remote districts should not be overlooked.

The analysis of the determinants of farm machinery shows that the density of livestock and machinery may grow simultaneously. The availability of labour for land preparation is a critical constraint which encouraged mechanisation. Whether such changes are welcome features in the context of agricultural productivity and the gains made by various strata of rural population are yet to be ascertained.

Among the factors affecting technology adoption in agriculture, the role of farm size deserves attention. Some of the earlier studies found a positive association between farm size and extent of adoption of HYV inputs. In contrast, the present study observes negative impacts of the variable "per cent of small farms," especially on the percentage of area irrigated and on HYV in aman season (the coefficient is significant) when HYV cultivation is associated with greater risk. For further expansion of area under HYV aman, the constraints that limit the small farmers' access to irrigation and to HYV expansion must be removed.

Percentage of households in the "landless" category has a positive impact on the extent of adoption of high yielding varieties and other modern inputs. Landlessness being a proxy indicator of the availability of hired labourers, this result implies that a shortage of hired labour is emerging as an important constraint to the expansion of modern inputs in crop production.

Population density has a strong positive impact on modern input use. It implies that pressure of demand can lead to acceleration of growth. So there is scope for accelerating agricultural growth through enhancing demand through better inter-district linkage and infrastructure development.

Analysis of HIES (2010) data shows an inverse relationship between farm size and productivity. Productivity of land is the highest among the "very small farmers." Their productivity may be further enhanced through appropriate policies for easing their access to inputs.

Appendices

Table 5.1A: Determinants of the Area under HYV in Different Seasons: Results of Ordinary Least Square (OLS) Regression

Independent Variables	Equation 1	Equation 2	Equation 3	Equation 4
	Log of Area under HYV Aus as % of Net Cropped Area	Log of Area under HYV Aman as % of Net Cropped Area	Log of Area under HYV Boro as % of Net Cropped Area	Log of Area under HYV Paddy as % of Net Cropped Area
Rainfall (mm)	.00036**	.00013	-.00019	.00012
Population (million)	.00000016	.00000021**	.0000003**	.00000017**
% of Small Farm Holdings (.04-2.49 acres)	.0144	-.0284**	-.0202	-.0229**
Low Land as % of Total Operated Area	-.0044	-.0358***	.0232*	-.005
% of Landless Holdings (upto 0.04 acre)	.0000014	.0000031***	.0000028*	0000021***
Tenant and Owner cum-tenant Holdings as % of Total Holdings	-.0431*	.016	.0211	-.0019
High Land as % of Total Operated Area	.0291***	.0138*	.0226*	.0134**
Total Area of the Districts (Acre)	-.00000051	-.0000014***	-.0000019**	-.0000011***
Constant	-.0639	3.15**	1.92	3.67***
N	64	64	64	64
F	3.65***	7.97***	2.88***	3.55***
Adjusted R-square	.25	.47	.19	.24

Note: ***, ** and * indicate significance at 1 per cent, 5 per cent and 10 per cent level respectively.
Source: Estimated from BBS, Census of Agriculture, 1999.

Table 5.2A: Determinants of Irrigation, Fertiliser Use and Cropping Intensity: Results of OLS Regression

Independent Variables	Equation 5	Equation 6	Equation 7
	Log of Cropping Intensity (%)	Log of Area under Irrigation as % of Net Cropped Area	Log of Area Fertilised as % of Net Cropped Area
Rainfall	-.000042	-.000076	.0000017
Population	.000000047**	.0000002**	.00000012***
% of Small Farm Holdings (.04-2.49 acres)	-.000059	-.0292**	-.0085*
Low Land as % of Total Operated Area	-.0026*	.0083	-.0047*
% of Landless Holdings (upto 0.04 acre)	.0000003	.0000031***	.0000014***
Tenant and Owner-cum-tenant Holdings as % of Total Holdings	.0099**	-.0046	.0098
High Land as % of Total Operated Area	-.0019	.0196***	-.0025
Total Area of the Districts (Acre)	-.00000032***	-.000002***	-.0000011***
Constant	4.93***	4.4***	4.59***
N	64	64	64
F	4.14***	5.16***	10.34***
Adjusted R-square	.29	.35	.54

Note: ***, ** and * indicate significance at 1 per cent, 5 per cent and 10 per cent level respectively.
Source: Estimated from BBS, Census of Agriculture, 1999.

Table 5.3A: Determinants of the Number of Farm Machinery: OLS Regression Results

Explanatory Variables	Equation 1 Number of Tractors Plus Number of Power Tillers Coefficient	t-value	Equation 2 Number of Tractors Coefficient	t-value
Cultivated Area ('000 ha)	.0003	.96	.0006	1.68*
Population ('000)	-.000015	-2.29**	-.00001	-.12
Number of draft animals (Cattle and Buffalo) ('000)	.0003	7.47***	.0002	4.27***
Per cent Landless	.086	5.98***	.083	4.52***
Per cent Small Farm Holdings	0.59	4.73***	.071	4.43***
N	64		64	
F	34.77**		22.44***	
Adjusted R-square	.73		.63	

Note: ***, ** and * indicate significance at 1 per cent, 5 per cent and 10 per cent level respectively.
Source: Estimated from data provided in BBS, Census of Agriculture, 1999.

Table 5.4A: Regression of Per Cent of Area under HYV, Fertiliser Use and Cropping Intensity on Per Cent of Area Irrigated

Independent Variables	Equation 1 Area under HYV Aus as % of Net Cropped Area	Equation 2 Area under HYV Aman as % of Net Cropped Area	Equation 3 Area under HYV Boro as % of Net Cropped Area	Equation 4 Area under HYV Paddy as % of Gross Cropped Area	Equation 5 Cropping Intensity (%)	Equation 6 Area Fertilised (%)
Area under Irrigation as % of Net Cropped Area	.0313	.4344***	.544***	.5253***	.4354***	.6202***
Constant	3.80***	3.92	.0612	9.44***	139.8***	47.45***
N	64	64	64	64	64	64
F	2.28*	34.99***	123.8***	76.37***	12.37***	84.85***
Adjusted R Square	.02	.35	.66	.54	.15	.57

Note: ***, ** and * indicate significance at 1 per cent, 5 per cent and 10 per cent level respectively.
Source: Estimated from data provided in BBS (1999).

Table 5.5A: Regression of Per Cent of Area under HYV, Fertiliser Use and Cropping Intensity on Per Cent of Area Irrigated and Rainfall

Independent Variables	Equation 1	Equation 2	Equation 3	Equation 4	Equation 5	Equation 6
	Area under HYV Aus as % of Net Cropped Area	Area under HYV Aman as % of Net Cropped Area	Area under HYV Boro as % of Net Cropped Area	Area under HYV Paddy as % of Net Cropped Area	Cropping Intensity (%)	Area Fertilised (%)
Area under Irrigation as % of Net Cropped Area	.0478**	.4593***	.5548***	.5762***	.3428***	.5897***
Rainfall	.0019**	.0028	.0012	.0057***	-.0104**	-.0034
Constant	-.7656	-2.98	-2.93	-4.64	165.45	55.88***
N	64	64	64	64	64	64
F	4.56***	18.08888	61.60***	46.06***	9.56***	44.10***
Adjusted R Square	.10	.35	.66	.59	.21	.58

Note: *** and ** indicate significance at 1 per cent and 5 per cent level respectively.
Source: Estimated from data provided in BBS (1999).

Table 5.6A: Regression Results from Other Studies on the Impact of Irrigation on Inputs Use

Explanatory Variables	Source: Hossain (1986)			Boyce (1986)		
	Equation 1	Equation 2	Equation 3	Equation 4	Equation 5	Equation 6
% of Cultivated Area Irrigated (BBS Estimates)	0.49	6.15 (8.12*)	0.61 (3.57*)	0.49 (3.64)*	1.83 (6.42)*	2.99 (8.90)*
Medium High Land as Per cent of Cultivated Area	-0.09 (-0.47)	0.40 (0.68)	-	-	-	-
Annual Rainfall	0.16 (3.16)*	-0.26 -1.71	-	-	-	-
Constant	-22.71 (-1.69)	48.74 (1.21)	1.36 (n.a)	3.17 (n.a)	7.45 (n.a)	17.98 (n.a)
F-statistics	5.40*	24.1*	n.a	n.a	n.a	n.a
R-bar Square	0.41	0.78	0.42	0.45	0.72	0.83

Note: *indicates significance at 10 per cent level.

Dependent Variables in:

Equation 1: land cropped with aus and aman HYV as per cent of cultivated area in a district (data from 1983/84 census).
Equation 2: Kg. of fertiliser used per hectare of land (data from 1983/84 agricultural census).
Equation 3: Percentage of aman acreage sown to HYVs.
Equation 4: Percentage of aus acreage sown to HYVs.
Equation 5: Per cent of gross cropped area fertilised (1976/77 agricultural census data).
Equation 6: Per cent of gross cropped area fertilised (1976/77 agricultural census data).

PART 2
EMPLOYMENT, UNDEREMPLOYMENT AND LABOUR MARKET

CHAPTER 6

Unemployment, Underemployment and Structural Change in the Labour Market

6.1 Introduction

Previous chapters have highlighted that during the last two decades Bangladesh has experienced an acceleration of economic growth. Economic growth in a resource poor country hinges on the proper utilisation of its labour force. Higher pace of GDP growth is expected to generate an accelerated pace of employment growth, whereas the nature and extent of employment generation is likely to depend on the nature of growth.

Bangladesh and a number of other South Asian countries with high population densities and low land population ratios have been characterised as "surplus labour economies." Dual sector theories of development formulated on the basis of such characterisation visualised that industrialisation would proceed through the absorption of the "unlimited supply of labour" from the traditional sectors where they subsisted through the sharing of family income (Lewis, 1954).

The assumption of "unlimited supply of labour", or in other words, the existence of un- and underemployment implies that the policies for acceleration of GDP growth and industrialisation should focus mainly on the removal of other relevant constraints. The success of such policies will, to some extent, depend on the correctness of the assumption of availability of surplus labour.

When a growing industrial sector is unable to absorb the underemployed labour force, such labour tries to find gainful employment in other sectors. Therefore, there is a need for periodic reassessment of the extent of surplus labour in the economy. The objective of the present chapter is to provide such an assessment.

The labour market processes in the densely populated developing countries reflect the changing labour demand in the economy as well as the livelihood strategies of the poor workers who resort to various types of informal employment. An understanding of these processes can shed light on the scope of future labour-intensive growth of the modern sectors and therefore these issues deserve attention.

Unemployment and underemployment may accentuate poverty of households dependent on labour income. Bangladesh has achieved significant success in poverty reduction. How far this can be sustained will depend on further reduction of unemployment and underemployment. This chapter therefore primarily focuses on the analysis of the presence of surplus labour in the form of unemployment or underemployment (Section 6.2).

Employment growth can lead to tightening of the labour market and thereby result in a rise of real wage in both the modern sector and the traditional/agricultural sector. This can have a positive effect on income of wage labourers and therefore recent thinking has emphasised employment growth as an important route to inclusive growth (Islam and Islam, 2015). However, it may also result in a slowdown of labour supply to the modern sector. Therefore, the changes of real wage need close scrutiny. The pattern of changes of real wage in agriculture and other sectors is discussed in Section 6.4.

An upward trend of real wage cannot provide sufficient evidence to conclude that the "surplus labour" from traditional sector has been exhausted and a structural change in the labour market has taken place. So the present chapter includes a direct assessment of the changes of structure and type of employment (Section 6.3). Section 6.5 discusses two special aspects of the structure of Bangladesh's labour market: employment in readymade garment sector and overseas employment. The concluding section summarises the positive features as well as the negative features of the labour market.

6.2 Unemployment and Underemployment

6.2.1 Unemployment

In usual economic analysis unemployment rate is used as an indicator of the health of the economy. Nonetheless, the concept of "open involuntary unemployment" has been developed in the context of industrial economies and therefore its applicability to low-income traditional economies of South Asia has been doubted. This has led to the formulation of alternative concepts of partial unemployment (termed as underemployment). Before moving on to that discussion, data on the unemployment rate in Bangladesh and the problems with such data also need attention.

The unemployment rate among the labour force in Bangladesh (as presented in official statistics) appears to be incredibly low, lower than the current rates in many high income industrial economies (Table 6.1). According to Labour Force Surveys (LFS) conducted by the Bangladesh Bureau of Statistics during the period 2000-2013, unemployment rate in Bangladesh remained unchanged at a very low figure of 4.3 per cent (only slightly higher in 2010). Census data (1981, 1991) also revealed similar low unemployment rates. A discussion of the definition and data generation process contributing to such a low rate of unemployment can help make a proper interpretation of the data.

Bangladesh's apparent low unemployment rates have been largely due to the problems of the definition used by labour force surveys of the country which adheres to the international definition which is actually more appropriate for developed labour markets of industrial economies. Definitional problems arise from two sources. First, the survey question for identifying the unemployed is such that few people fit into that category. It consists of two parts: "whether one was without work for last one week (a reference period) and whether one was willing to work or was looking for work." Being "without work" can be afforded only by persons from rich households and especially by the educated labour force (educated unemployment has been discussed in Chapter 8).

Table 6.1: Unemployment Rates in Bangladesh: 1995-2013

Unemployment Rate (%)	1995-1996	1999-2000	2006	2010	2013
Total	3.5	4.3	4.3	4.5	4.3
Male	2.8	3.4	3.4	4.1	3.0
Female	7.1	7.4	7.0	5.8	7.2

Source: BBS; LFS (various years).

The second factor is that the definition used by LFS allows that during the reference week, only one hour spent on income earning activities is enough for being counted as "employed" and therefore the chances of being unemployed are low. This liberal definition is also responsible for giving a high labour force participation rate as well as a high ratio of "employed" in total population. The scope of employment for only a few hours a week is very high in Bangladesh's labour market where self/family employment is predominant. It means that people who want to engage in work can easily spend a few hours a week in taking care of the family's livestock, kitchen garden or other family enterprise. In urban areas, entry into low productive informal sector may provide such scope for employment.

Another source of under-enumeration of unemployment is the form of the questions used in the interview. The question "whether one was looking for job or trying to start self-employment" lacks practical applicability. In the informal labour market where there are no formal routes of job search, most people without work are not involved in actual the search process. Employers in the rural areas approach them when there is a need. Petty self-employment may not require any prolonged period of "trying to start," as mentioned in the survey instrument. Moreover, women who wish to work may not go for job search because of social inhibition and may not report that they are willing to work. Thus the social reality makes the concept of open unemployment inapplicable to the large majority of the labour force.

The term "informal labour market" mentioned above and its links with unemployment need clarification. Informal employment consists of employment with one or more of the following characteristics: it is without written contract, employment may be terminated without notice, it can be paid on an irregular basis or may consist of unpaid family work, etc. A common misconception is that "informal/unpaid work" is not actually "employment" and these workers may be counted as "unemployed." It must be recognised that such informal work is an essential component of employment[1] and often forms a larger subset of employment compared to formal jobs (these data are presented in a later section). There may be need for rethinking whether a minimum cut off in terms of weekly hours of work should be introduced for counting an informal worker as employed.

6.2.2 Underemployment: Definition, Concepts and Estimates

Given the problems of application of the concept of open unemployment discussed above, an alternative concept of "underemployment rate"

---

[1] This point may be obvious to the labour economists, but misconception has been seen to prevail among development practitioners or even survey organisations.

has emerged. It can provide a better measure of surplus labour when only a part of the time of workers is unutilised.

Before presenting data from LFS, it may be worthwhile to clarify a few conceptual issues. Time criterion is the most commonly used concept of underemployment in Bangladesh. While "time criterion" of estimation of underemployment is based on a comparison of actual hours worked and hypothetical norms, various other methods of estimation of surplus labour/underemployment have been used in the past studies in Bangladesh and India. The concept of "disguised unemployment" in the sense of work sharing by family workers, which takes place due to inadequate employment opportunity, has also been used in this context.[2]

Some studies have obtained estimates of surplus labour force/days from total supply of labour and total demand in existing economic activities (Muqtada, 1974, Mehra, 1966). Others have taken into account the peak labour requirement due to seasonal nature of labour demand (Rudra, 1982). These methods have been used in view of the lack of availability of data on actual hours worked by the employed persons.

With the rapid decline of the joint/extended family systems, "disguised unemployment," which applies more appropriately to family workers, is giving way to open underemployment. "Time criterion" and "willingness criterion" are being used for its empirical estimation and these can be applied to both family workers and hired labourers who are in disguised or open underemployment situation.

Bangladesh's Labour Force Survey and a number of other studies based on micro surveys have used "time criterion" (on the basis of various cut off lines as standard hours) to measure the underemployment rate. Application of time criterion requires data on hours of employment during a reference period. LFS of Bangladesh has set the cut off line for full employment at 35 hours per week and those who work less than this norm are counted as underemployed.

---

[2] Initially, disguised unemployment was used by Robinson (1937) as a slightly different concept "... to describe the adoption of inferior occupation." Without tracing the full history of conceptual evolution (Krishnamurty 2008) it may be mentioned that later it was identified with work sharing in family farms. In this sense, disguised unemployment consists of family workers whose work is not essential for the family farm, and who are still not openly unemployed. The present chapter uses time criterion based estimates of underemployment which is applicable to both work sharing family workers and paid workers with inadequate hours of work.

Comparable data on the basis of time criterion are available for 1996 to 2013. Underemployment rates disaggregated by sex and location (rural-urban) are shown in Table 6.2.

Underemployment rate increased from 16.6 per cent in 1996 to 24.5 per cent in 2006 and decreased slightly in 2010 when it stood at 20.3 per cent. A further decline of underemployment occurred during the period 2010-2013, especially among the female labour force. In 2013, male and female underemployment rates were 13.1 and 29.5 per cent respectively.

Nonetheless, the figures especially for male workers, which are in the range of 7 to 14 per cent, cannot be considered as very high.[3] Moreover, one should take into account the fact that all of the underemployment may not be of involuntary category. LFS (2010) questionnaire does not include a question on whether underemployment is involuntary, or, in other words, whether a person is willing to work more and whether the willingness is due to inadequate income or other reasons.[4]

Table 6.2: Underemployment Rates in Bangladesh: 1996-2013

Underemployment Rate (%)	1995-96	1999-2000	2006	2010	2013*
Total	17.6	16.6	24.5	20.3	17.8
Male	13.0	7.4	10.9	14.4	13.1
Female	45.5	52.8	68.3	34.2	29.5

Note: *Estimated from unit records of LFS 2013.
Source: BBS, LFS (various years).

Underemployment rates are higher in the rural areas compared to the urban areas of Bangladesh (Table 6.3), which is not unexpected. In the rural areas, most of the underemployed workers can derive a livelihood through resorting to various low productive activities, work sharing with other family members and drawing upon the family's consumption basket. In contrast, workers opt for moving to urban areas only when there is a prospect of a job because one cannot survive without a job.

---

[3] Osmani et al. (2015) give much higher underemployment rates. The rates for male and female labour force were 43 and 57 per cent in 2010, much higher than all existing findings.

[4] India has chosen "willingness criterion" to identify and estimate the rate of underemployment. In various rounds of Indian NSS, this criterion has been used without any reference to hours of employment. Krishna (1973) has formulated three criterion of underemployment: time criterion, willingness criterion and income criterion.

Table 6.3: Rural and Urban Underemployment Rate in Bangladesh

Underemployment Rate (%)	1999-2000	2006	2010	2013
National	16.6	24.5	20.3	17.8
Rural	17.8	27.8	22.7	20.5
Urban	12.2	13.9	12.4	10.8

Source: LFS (various years).

Moreover, a large part of rural underemployment takes the form of "seasonal underemployment" and is due to seasonal variation of labour use in economic activities. This aspect is so important that it should receive separate attention and Chapter 7 presents a detailed analysis of seasonal un/underemployment and its implications.

Data presented in Table 6.2 show that the underemployment rates among women were much higher than men. Underemployment rates among women were 34 and 29 per cent respectively in 2010 and 2013. The high average underemployment rate was due to the very high underemployment among female workers. The rise of underemployment rate in the period 1996-2006 was also linked to this phenomenon. During this period, there has been a rise of the weight of female labour force and this rise combined with higher underemployment among women pushed up the average underemployment rate.

Although the male underemployment rate is around 13 per cent, this does not really mean that surplus labour is 13 per cent of available male labour supply. Surplus labour available from the underemployed workers is usually only a fraction of their total hours. Moreover, all workers may not be willing to work more, as has been mentioned above. It may be particularly true for higher income earners who have entered the negative income effect regime.[5] Female labour force's willingness to accept more employment may also be low due to their burden of domestic chore, which is a major reason behind their current underemployment.

A comparison of data of the recent decade and the 1970s and 1980s shows an improvement in terms of the extent of underemployment. Although comparable LFS data is not available for the earlier decades, a number of sample survey-based studies provide similar data. These

---

[5] It implies that a rise of wage can push up the income to such an extent that the income earned by working additional hours does not compensate the disutility of work. So a rise of wage reduces his hours of work.

studies arrived at underemployment rates in the range of 16 to 40 per cent during the 1980s and 1970s (Muqtada, 1975, Alamgir, 1978, Hossain, 1989, Rahman, 1981). These rates refer to underemployment rates mainly among the male labour force, because the share of female workers was very small in those samples.

Low unemployment rates observed above imply that the growth rate of labour force and the growth rate of employment have been very close. Data (Table 6.4) confirms that this has been the case. The growths of labour force and employment have moved in the same direction. This association may have resulted from the fact that in most cases the labour force entrants generate employment for themselves if other types of employment cannot be obtained. In addition, the reverse is also true, i.e., those who cannot find employment either exit from the labour force or do not report themselves as unemployed, as mentioned above. These observations imply that more probing needs to be undertaken into the nature of employment. These aspects receive attention in the following section. The rate of growth of labour force and employment, especially for the women, has been high during 2000 to 2010 (Table 6.4) when female labour force participation rate (LFPR) increased significantly.[6] This has been partly due to better enumeration of female labour force because of increasing awareness about the need to recognise women's family employment.

At this point, it may be mentioned that according to the projections made for the Sixth Five Year Plan (SFYP), 1.8 million would be added to the labour force each year during the Plan period (2011-2015) and a total of 1.8 million employment would be generated domestically (SFYP, Part 1, p. 79). In addition, 0.4 million would avail overseas employment. Therefore, 1.8 million employment opportunities created in the domestic labour market would absorb not only the growing labour force but also reduce the existing underemployment. However, domestic employment growth has been only 1.3 million per year during the period 2010-2013, (MoF, 2015, Budget Speech FY2016), which is much smaller than the projections of SFYP. The shortfall in generating additional employment has been due to lower GDP growth achieved during these years compared to the targets set by the Plan. In addition, the growth of less labour-intensive sectors has contributed

---

[6] Even after such increase, female labour force participation rate in Bangladesh is much lower than in India and a number of other Asian countries.

to the sluggish employment growth.[7] SFYP has emphasised a strategy of structural change of the economy in favour of industry for achieving its GDP growth targets. As a result, employment growth in agriculture has been smaller during this period compared to the 2006-2010 period. This calls for a more balanced policy initiative for future GDP growth and employment generation.

Table 6.4: Growth Rates of Labour Force: 2000-2013

(Average Annual Growth Rate, %)

Period	Sex	Labour Force Growth	Employment Growth	LFPR*
2000-2003	All	4.6	4.4	57.3
	Male	3.9	3.4	87.4
	Female	7.1	7.7	26.1
2003-2006	All	2.2	2.2	58.5
	Male	1.2	1.5	86.8
	Female	5.5	4.6	29.2
2006-2010	All	3.4	3.3	59.3
	Male	1.4	1.2	82.5
	Female	8.4	9.1	36.0
2010-2013	All	2.4	2.4	57.1
	Male	2,6	2.9	81.6
	Female	1.9	1.3	33.5

Note: *LFPR values are for the years 2003, 2006, 2010 and 2013.
Source: LFS (various years).

6.3 Quality of Employment: Type (Formal/Informal), Status and Sector

Acceleration of the pace of economic growth is expected to result in a rise in the share of employment in modern sectors. Such structural change can be used as an indicator of the quality of employment. In the process of structural change, the secondary sectors are usually expected to lead and tertiary sectors are likely to follow, and such employments are usually considered as superior to agricultural employment. To assess whether such positive changes have been taking place, the present section discusses the composition of employment in terms of sector and status (paid and self-employment).

---

[7] Islam (2015) discusses the link between GDP growth and employment generation and provides useful insights into employment generation capacities of various sectors.

Table 6.5 presents data on broad sectoral distribution of the labour force. The share of agriculture increased from 48.9 per cent of the labour force in 1996 to 51.7 per cent in 2003. After 2003, it went through a decline and stood at 45.1 per cent in 2013. During the seventeen-year period (1996 to 2013), the share of agriculture in total employment fell by only 3.8 percentage points. The decline was rather small, especially in view of the decline of agriculture's share in the GDP during this period. The share of GDP had gone down from 32 per cent to about 19 per cent. The slow change of sectoral composition of employment needs an explanation.

The difference in the changes of male and female employment in various sectors deserves attention in this context. Male and female labour force show different direction of changes in sector composition of employment (Table 6.5).

The share of agricultural employment among female labour force increased although the share of male labour force in agriculture went through a continuous decline during the period 2000-2010. The net result was that agriculture's share of total labour force went through only a small decline during this period. This aspect of female employment has been discussed in Chapter 14.

Table 6.5: Distribution of Male and Female Labour Force by Broad Economic Sector: 1995-2013

(Per Cent)

Period	Male			Female			Male and Female		
	Agriculture	Non-Agriculture	Total	Agriculture	Non-Agriculture	Total	Agriculture	Non-Agriculture	Total
1995-1996	52.3	47.7	100.0	27.8	72.2	100.0	48.9	51.1	100.0
1999-2000	51.8	48.2	100.0	46.9	53.1	100.0	50.8	49.2	100.0
2002-2003	49.8	51.2	100.0	58.7	42.3	100.0	51.7	48.3	100.0
2006	41.8	58.2	100.0	68.3	31.7	100.0	48.1	51.9	100.0
2010	40.2	59.8	100.0	64.8	35.2	100.0	47.6	53.1	100.0
2013	41.6	58.4	100.0	53.7	46.3	100.0	45.1	54.9	100.0

Source: LFS (various years).

The pattern reversed in the latest round of LFS (2013) data. The share of female labour force in agriculture fell drastically, whereas the reverse was true for the male labour force. Nonetheless, the share of female labour force in agriculture was still higher than it was in

2000. Thus, the male labour market has experienced a progress in terms of change in sectoral structure while the situation in the female labour market has been fluctuating.

One must, therefore, examine the reasons behind the change of sectoral composition of female employment. The large increase of female employment in agriculture actually consists of women's work in family-based animal husbandry (Salmon 2002).[8]

Detailed sector classification (Table 6.6) of labour force shows that the percentage of the labour force employed in the manufacturing sector has risen continuously during the period 2000-2010, from 9.5 per cent to 12.5 per cent. The share increased by 1.5 percentage points during the period 2006-2010. Share of trade, hotel and restaurant, and transport and communication also increased during the period 2000-2006 but the pattern reversed during the period 2006-2010. In addition to the share, the absolute figures of employment are presented in Table 6.7. Employment in manufacturing increased by 1.5 million over the period 2000-2006 and by another 1.5 million during the period 2006-2010. Construction and community/personal services absorbed a significant number of additional workers during this period.

Table 6.6: Distribution of Employed Persons by Industry and Sex: 2000-2013

(Per Cent)

Major Industry	1999-2000			2006			2010			2013		
	Total	Male	Female	Total	Male	Female	Total	Male	Female	Total	Male	Female
Agri. forestry and fisheries	50.8	51.8	46.2	48.1	41.8	68.3	47.6	40.18	64.8	45.1	41.7	53.5
Mining & quarrying	0.5	0.3	1.0	0.1	0.1	0.1	0.2	0.25	0.1	0.4	0.5	0.1
Manufacturing	9.5	7.5	17.7	11.0	10.9	11.5	12.5	12.75	11.8	16.4	13.9	22.5
Electricity, gas and water	0.3	0.3	0.2	0.2	0.2	0.0	0.2	0.24	0.0	0.3	0.3	0.2
Construction	2.8	3.2	1.3	3.2	3.9	0.9	4.8	6.31	1.4	3.7	4.8	1.0
Trade, hotel & restaurant	15.8	18.2	6.3	16.5	20.4	4.1	14.0	17.24	6.3	14.5	18.2	5.3
Transport, storage and communication	6.3	7.8	0.6	8.4	10.8	0.6	7.4	9.87	1.5	6.4	8.8	0.7
Finance and business services	1.0	1.2	0.6	1.6	1.7	1.1	0.7	0.83	0.3	1.1	1.4	0.6
Community and personal services and others	12.9	9.6	26.2	10.9	11.0	13.6	12.7	12.33	13.7	12.0	10.3	16.2
All	100.0	100.0	100.0	100.0	100.0	100.0	100.0	100.0	100.0	100.0	100.0	100.0

Source: LFS (various years).

---

[8] Salmon (2002) pointed out that there are problems in the sector/occupational classification of LFS data and inconsistency between sector and occupational category. Better enumeration may partly explain the rise of female employment in agriculture.

From the disaggregated data of the LFS 2010 (3 digit sector classification, tables not shown here), it is observed that female employment has increased in food manufacturing in rural areas and in RMG in urban areas. Both are at least partly due to correction of past error in sector classification and better enumeration of women's employment in manufacturing, rather than actual change.

Still LFS data provides an underestimation of women's employment in RMG sector, which shows that the number of women employed was one million in 2010. Data from Bangladesh Garment Manufacturers and Exporters Association (BGMEA) sources, however, show it to be above 2 million.

Table 6.7: Number of Employed Persons by Industry: 1996-2013

(In Million)

Major Industry	1996	2000	2006	2010	2013
Agri. forestry and fisheries	17.0	19.8	22.8	25.7	26.2
Mining & quarrying	-	0.2	0.1	0.1	0.2
Manufacturing	3.5	3.7	5.2	6.7	9.5
Electricity, gas and water	0.1	0.1	0.1	0.1	0.2
Construction	1.0	1.1	1.5	2.6	2.1
Trade, hotel & restaurant	6.0	6.1	7.8	8.4	8.4
Transport, storage and communication	2.2	2.5	4.0	4.0	3.7
Finance and business services	0.2	0.4	0.8	1.0	0.5
Community and personal services and others	5.1	5.1	5.2	5.5	7.0

Source: LFS (various years).

6.3.1 Status of Employment

Family based employment is the predominant type of activity in a subsistence agriculture based production system, as in Bangladesh. The growth of industry and service sectors is expected to lead to commercial production and thereby lead to increases in the share of hired employment. LFS provides data on distribution of employment among five major statuses of employment: regular employee, self-employment, unpaid family employment, casual/day labourer and employer (with a residual category of others). Among these categories, self-employment and unpaid family work have often been referred to as vulnerable employment. In fact, in Bangladesh casual/daily employment can be even more vulnerable. There is no security of employment in the latter category. Self-employment is better in this respect. None of the three has any retirement benefit.[9]

Table 6.8 presents the relevant distribution. Data show that self-employment absorbed the largest share of labour force. The share was 41 per cent in 2013, which was around 45 per cent in the earlier years. In 2010, irregular/casual daily employment contributed 32.5 per cent of all employment and was much higher than the share in 2006.

Table 6.8: Distribution of Employed Persons by Status of Employment: 1995-2013

(Per Cent)

Status of Employment	1995-1996	1999-2000	2005-06	2010	2013
Self-employed	45.4	46.7	42.0	40.8	40.6
Employer	0.4	0.3	0.3	0.2	0.9
Employee	16.8	16.7	13.9	14.6	23.2
Unpaid family helper	12.0	12.0	21.7	22.5	18.2
Day labourer/irregular	25.3	24.3	20.1	32.5	15.5
Others	-	-	2.0	0.8	1.6
All	100.0	100.0	100.0	100.0	100.0

Source: BBS: LFS (various years).

Share of regular employee fell from 16.8 per cent in 1996 to 13.9 per cent in 2006 and then increased to 14.6 per cent in 2010. Within the hired employment category, "day labourer" is an inferior type compared to "employees." Share of day labourers was 32.5 per cent in 2010 compared to 20.1 per cent in 2006. However, there has been an improvement in this context and during the period 2010-2013, the share of day labourers drastically declined, while share of regular employees increased substantially. In 2013, these shares were 15.5 and 23.2 per cent respectively.

Self-employment and unpaid family employment play important roles in absorbing the fast growing labour force (Table 6.8). Share of

---

[9] The objectives of "decent employment," proposed by ILO (ILO, 1999, Ghai, 2006) and accepted and pursued by Bangladesh, include "security" of work as an important component. The other components of decent work include "sufficiency" of employment, which is equivalent to absence of un/underemployment. This aspect has already received attention in this chapter. Progress with government's endeavours of "decent employment" deserves detailed discussion and has not been attempted here.

unpaid family employment increased substantially between 1996 and 2010 (from 12 per cent to 22.5 per cent). In 2013, the share stood at 18.2 per cent. Self-employment plus unpaid family employment contributed 57.4, 63.3 and 58.8 per cent of total employment in 1996, 2010 and 2013 respectively.

Table 6.9 presents pertinent data on share of male and female employment in various categories. Data show that 25.1 and 47.5 per cent of Bangladesh's employed men and women were in the self-employed category respectively in 2010. About 56.3 per cent of the employed female labour force was in unpaid family work. Among the male labour force, 7.1 per cent was in this status. About 8.9 per cent of the female labour force and 17 per cent of the male labour force were in regular paid employment, while 7.1 per cent women and 29 per cent men were employed as day labourers/irregular paid employees.

Table 6.9: Distribution of Status of Employment by Sex: 1999-2013

(Per Cent)

Status of Employment	1999-2000 Female	1999-2000 Male	2006 Female	2006 Male	2010 Female	2010 Male	2013 Female	2013 Male
Self-employed	26.6	51.4	15.9	50.0	25.1	47.5	12.3	52.2
Employer	0.0	0.3	0.1	0.3	0.2	0.2	0.1	1.2
Employee	20.3	15.8	11.7	14.5	8.9	17.0	32.8	41.2*
Unpaid family helper	34.1	6.4	60.1	9.7	56.3	7.1	50.1	5.1
Day labourer	19.0	26.1	7.9	24.0	7.1	28.9	-	-
Others	-	-	4.3	1.5	2.4	-	4.7	0.3
All	100.0	100.0	100.0	100.0	100.0	100.0	100.0	100.0

Note: *Combines employee & day labourer.
Source: BBS: LFS (various years).

Among female workers, the share of regular employees and day labourers went through a large decline during the period 2000-2010.[10] The decline in the share of hired employment as a whole (regular plus irregular/casual) was larger among female workers compared to male workers. Share of self-employment also showed a small negative change. This has been made up by a large increase in the share of unpaid

---

[10] The picture of status of employment of Bangladeshi women stands in contrast with the situation of other South Asian Countries. Share of paid workers in total female employment is much higher in India.

family helpers. The rise in the number (Table 6.10) and share of "unpaid family workers" among women has been, to some extent, a reflection of increasingly better enumeration, as mentioned earlier.

Table 6.10: Number of Male and Female Labour Force by Status of Employment: 2006-2010

Status of Employment	2006 ('000) Female	2006 ('000) Male	2010 ('000) Female	2010 ('000) Male	% Change during 2006-2010 Female	% Change during 2006-2010 Male
Self-employed	1789	18056	2544	9789	42.2	-45.8
Employer	13	117	30	89	130.8*	-23.9
Employee	1318	5249	1439	6440	9.2	22.7
Unpaid family helper	6780	3488	9116	2677	34.4	-23.2
Day labourer	893	8667	1145	10979	28.2	26.7

Note: *Due to small base.
Source: BBS: LFS (various years).

One may also attribute this to women's deliberate choice because family employment is more flexible in terms of hours of work as well as location of work compared to paid work. However, this is more likely due to the fact that there is hardly any choice for women as paid employment opportunities for them are scanty.

Overall, it may be concluded that an improvement in the quality of employment in the desired direction of higher share of workforce in paid employment has not become a reality, especially for women. Growth of family employment alone may lead to overcrowding in the family farm/enterprise and drive down marginal productivity. It may not, therefore, be desirable to depend only on self/family employment for absorbing the growing labour force.

6.3.2 Formal vs Informal Employment

Data on the extent of informality and its changes are presented in Table 6.11. Considering the 10 year period of 2000 to 2010, the share of employment in the formal sector fell from 24.7 per cent to 12.5 per cent. Informality is one of the important indicators of backwardness of the present day labour market in Bangladesh. In 2013, the share of formal employment increased to 21.6 per cent, which was close to the 2006 figure, but was less than the share of formal employment in the year 2000.

Table 6.11: Size and Share of Labour Force in Formal and Informal Sector: 2000-2013

Years	Share of Employment (%)		Size of Employment (Million)	
	Formal	Informal	Formal	Informal
2013	21.6	79.4	12.0	46.1
2010	12.5	87.5	6.8	47.3
2006	21.5	78.5	10.2	37.2
2003	20.8	79.2	9.2	35.1
2000	24.7	75.3	9.6	29.3

Source: LFS (various years).

The sudden decline in the share of formal employment and a decline in the absolute number of persons (Table 6.11) engaged in formal sector in 2010 leads to doubts about the quality of this specific data. A commonly recognised fact is that there has been increase in employment in RMG and other formal services. So the decline in the absolute number of formal sector employment is difficult to explain.

In fact, data on informality should, however, be used cautiously. Neither the employees nor the field enumerators would have sufficient information as to whether the unit where they are employed is formally registered. Even the registered formal enterprises may sometimes provide employment on an informal basis as it is more convenient for the employer. Moreover, some workers may consider themselves as regular formal employees, even if they do not have any written contract or job offer which would include a clear statement of the terms of employment.

6.4 Real Wage

Changes of real wage and the difference between real wage in traditional and modern sector can be important indicators of quality of employment. According to the predictions of dual sector theories, the presence of surplus labour in the traditional sector is likely to result in a stagnant real wage in both modern and traditional sectors as long as the surplus is not completely exhausted. Presence of significant underemployment in Bangladesh's labour market makes it pertinent that the changes of real wage receive attention. The magnitude of underemployment has gone through a decline in recent years and whether this has been associated with a rise of real wage needs to be examined.

Table 6.12: Growth of Nominal Wage Index and Inflation Rate

(Per Cent)

Year	Growth of Nominal Wage Index (GNW) in			Inflation Rate
	Agriculture	Manufacturing	Construction	
1998	3.66	10.83	7.68	8.66
1999	4.28	5.30	8.69	7.06
2000	4.46	7.10	5.67	2.79
2001	5.11	4.85	3.06	1.94
2002	5.65	7.17	3.74	2.79
2003	8.00	15.35	7.36	4.38
2004	5.69 (76)*	7.55	1.69 (110)	5.83
2005	5.30	6.64	3.33	6.49
2006	7.61	6.92	4.75	7.17
2007	7.86	7.99	8.52	7.22
2008	11.66 (136)	12.10	13.20 (129)	9.93
2009	21.28	17.91	21.47	6.66
2010	12.37	6.40	8.70	7.31
2011	10.87	3.96	7.55	8.80
2012	15.17 (260)	6.54	32.10 (267)	10.62

Note: *(Nominal wages in Tk. are in parentheses).
Source: MoF: Bangladesh Economic Review (various years).

The most commonly used source of wage data is *Bangladesh Economic Review* (MoF, various years).[11] The MoF data provide "growth of nominal wage index" (GNW) and inflation rate (IR) and the two together (Table 6.12) can provide an idea about the trend of real wage in each sector.[12] Main features emerging from Table 6.12 are:

- During the period 1999-2002, growth of nominal wage index in manufacturing was much higher than inflation rate and thus

---

[11] There are problems with this data and especially with manufacturing wage (which does not cover the main sub-sectors including RMG) and it should be used cautiously. A study by Islam (2015) uses this data along with CPI and concludes that real wage index in industry has stagnated during 2007-2012 and it is less than the real wage index of agriculture. The study concludes that this is because of presence of surplus labour in agriculture. However, the real wage in agriculture is then expected to stagnate as well, which actually has gone through a rapid growth.

[12] Ideally one should compare the growth of nominal wage index with changes of CPI for workers in each sector. However, BBS discontinued the industrial workers CPI series and so the "inflation rate" has been used here. Rahman (2009) uses rice price as a deflator and "rice wage" shows similar pattern, as obtained in this section.

real wage in manufacturing increased. In contrast, real wage in construction sector stagnated and in agriculture it increased at a slow pace.
- During the period 2005-2006, inflation rate was higher than the growth of nominal wage in manufacturing and construction and thus there was a decline of real wage.
- Real wage in agriculture and construction increased during the period 2008-2012. Manufacturing sector's real wage index stagnated or even declined during the period 2010-2012 when inflation rate was higher than GNW in this sector.

One would obviously wonder about the links among real wage growth and sectoral GDP growth, and government's policy interventions. Government interventions in the form of minimum wage legislation and trade unionism can result in a rise of real wage despite the presence of surplus labour.

The rise of real wage in the informal labour market in agriculture and construction cannot really be attributed to these interventions since there has been hardly any government initiative to extend coverage of minimum wage to these sectors. Trade unions are also non-existent in the informal sectors. Government's minimum wage boards cover only some of the formal sectors, mostly within manufacturing.

At this point, it may be useful to look at the ratio of urban and rural wage. The ratios of nominal wages in urban and rural areas are 1.11 and 1.17 in 2010 and 2006 respectively.[13] It indicates that urban real wage is not substantially higher than the rural wage. However, the daily wage conceals the fact that even the same real wage gives higher earning in urban areas since they obtain employment for higher number of days and underemployment rate in urban areas is lower. This is supported by data on poverty incidences estimated from the HIES 2010, which shows that 35.2 and 25.0 per cent of agricultural and non-agricultural casual/daily workers respectively are in extreme poverty (Rahman, 2015).

The observed growth of real wage in agriculture and construction has occurred mainly due to the pressure of peak season demand when surplus labour is hardly available although underemployment is prevalent in the slack season.

---

[13] In 2010, rural and urban nominal wages were 200 and 179 taka respectively; in 2006, the values were 106 and 90 taka respectively (LFS, various years).

Rise of real wage in agriculture is likely to contribute to demand for higher wages in urban sectors including RMG. The increases of minimum wage in RMG during 2005 to 2014, to some extent, reflect the narrowing of gaps between wage increase in agriculture and manufacturing (this is not reflected in the official data presented in Table 12.5). Thus the modern sectors can no longer be certain about the availability of elastic supply of unskilled workers.

Moreover, the supply of unskilled labour in farm activities has been declining because school educated persons are not enthusiastic about employment in these occupations. Thus a segmentation of labour market is at work.

Such preference implies that labour supply to the manufacturing sector is likely to be more elastic than what is suggested by the rising trend of agricultural real wage discussed above. In addition, secondary educated women who are outside the labour force and female workers with high underemployment rate are likely to be the potential suppliers of labour to the manufacturing sector. This may contribute to a dampening effect on real wage. Even if these workers expect higher wages than the prevailing rates, growth of sub-sectors with higher productivity may be able to employ them profitably, thus contributing to both economic growth and better living standards of workers.

The growth of real wage in agriculture and construction shows more or less similar cycles as the growth of GDP in these sectors. For example, during the period 2001-2007, GDP growth in agriculture slowed down, resulting in stagnation of real wage in this sector and also in other informal sectors. After 2007, agricultural growth picked up and this was associated with a rise of real wage.

Apart from the wage index, Table 6.12 provides values of nominal wage of male labour in agriculture and construction in some years. Data show that these were quite close and in some years even higher in agriculture, e.g., 136 and 129 taka per day in 2008 and 260 and 267 taka in 2012 in agriculture and construction respectively.

6.5 Employment in Readymade Garment and Overseas Labour Market

The changes in the structure of employment in terms of broad sectors cannot capture the full picture of transformation of the labour market. Two features must be highlighted to understand the dynamism among

the labour force in Bangladesh and the importance of government policies in this context. These are:
a. growth of employment in readymade garment, and
b. growth of overseas employment.

6.5.1 Employment in Readymade Garment

Dramatic growth of employment in the "wearing apparel" sector, commonly known as readymade garment (RMG), has taken place since the early 1990s. While the experience of export led industrialisation in fast growing countries of Asia provided imitable examples of employment growth in this labour-intensive export industry, the prevailing multi-fibre agreement's (MFA) provisions created a right environment for undertaking initiatives by the not-so-experienced new entrepreneurs of Bangladesh. At that time, the industrial base was confined to a small number of traditional sub-sectors like jute textile, paper, fertiliser, etc.

Employment in RMG increased from .33 million in 1990 to 1.2 million in 1995 (Table 6.13). Growth of RMG employment slowed down during the subsequent years, especially during the period 1995-2005. However, it accelerated again during the period 2005-2010. In 2012, the number of workers was more than double the figure of 2000. Along with growth of employment, RMG's share in Bangladesh's export earnings also increased and stabilised around 75 per cent during the last twelve years.

Table 6.13: Employment in RMG Sector

Year	Employment (In Million)	% Change during the Last Five Years	RMG's Share in National Export (%)
1995	1.2	-	65.6
2000	1.6	33.3	75.7
2005	2.1	31.3	74.2
2010	3.6	71.4	77.1
2012	4.0	11.1 (in two years)	78.6
2016	4.0	0.0 (in four years)	82.0

Source: BBS (various years), *Statistical Yearbook of Bangladesh*, & BGMEA website.

Many analysts have attributed the initial spurt of growth of the sector to the facilities offered by MFA. Although MFA has provided the impetus during the early phase, the role of new entrepreneurs' enthusiasm to capture the benefits of export oriented growth must be recognised. In addition, a number of government policies also played a supportive role, which needs mention.

The most important policy in this context has been "back to back letter of credit" introduced in 1986-87, which meant that RMG entrepreneurs were not required to invest money to open L/C or to pay the suppliers of imported inputs (fabrics, etc.) from their own resources or bank credit obtained for this purpose. The other important policy was "Special Bonded Warehouse" scheme, which provided an efficient system to exempt exporters from import duties. During the period 2000-2005, a number of other policies were adopted to help entrepreneurs cope with the MFA withdrawal.

However, the industry must resolve more challenges as it moves ahead. The most important challenges the industry will have to overcome in the coming years are related to compliance with labour standards, including working hours, overtime payment, safety in places of work, timeliness of the payment of wages and bonuses, and freedom of association and collective bargaining. Studies show that the level of compliance has improved in recent years (McKinsey, 2011) although there are some unresolved issues (Lopez-Acevado and Robertson, 2012). In fact, the safety standards, which are recently receiving attention from international buyers and from ILO, require much improvement in the building structures where production takes place. A number of serious accidents during the last few years have been followed by planned measures to improve safety standards. Monitoring mechanisms in this respect have been geared up.

Other challenges faced by RMG (as well as other industries) include inadequate infrastructure, port services, supply of skilled labour and political stability, which influence the relative costs and competitiveness, especially, vis-à-vis countries like Vietnam, Pakistan, etc. These challenges can be addressed with appropriate policies and the industry should be able to continue its growth or even move to a higher growth path in the coming decade and contribute to employment growth along with rise of real wage.

Employment of women in the RMG industry has been significant from the early years of its growth and initially their share was 60-70 per cent of total RMG employment.

Employment growth in this sector is likely to lead to growth of demand for female labour. However, during 2012 to 2016, total employment in RMG has stagnated at 4.0 million. Nonetheless, the value of export of RMG products has grown at more than 9 per cent per annum during this period. Thus the growth of export has not generated an expected employment growth. Without properly planned policies, such "jobless growth" may continue resulting in higher unemployment rate and declining female labour force participation rate.

6.5.2 Growth of Overseas Employment

Overseas employment is an essential and growing factor in the context of Bangladesh's labour market. Employment in international market not only helps absorb a significant share of Bangladesh's growing labour force, it also contributes to the economy through inflow of remittance. Overseas employment increased from 0.22 million in 2000 to 0.6 million in 2012. The new century also saw a fast growth of remittance from US$ 1,950 million in 2000 to US$ 12,843 million in 2012.

Growth of overseas employment and remittance flows has been aided by policies and active initiatives of the government, of course, along with private sector initiatives. Government policies included steps for reducing the expenditure of taking up overseas employment and for ensuring welfare of the expatriate workers. Policies have gradually evolved for ensuring safe expatriation as well as for improving safety and security at the destination. In addition, during the last few years, initiatives have been taken for search of new labour markets. Policies and measures adopted for easing remittance inflow through formal channels have resulted not only in growth of remittance but also encouraged growth of overseas job seekers.

Progress has also been made in terms of growing female migration for overseas employment. During the 1990s, various restrictions on female overseas employment were enforced by the government. These were gradually removed since 2001 and female migrant workers' share in total migrants increased from 0.2 per cent in 2000 to 4.7 per cent in 2006 (Table 6.14). The change has been spectacular during the period 2012-2013. Women's share jumped to 14 per cent and their employment increased while male overseas employment saw a decline (of course after a rapid rise during the period 2009-2012). The government has adopted various measures to ensure growth of female migration and their safe and sustainable employment at the destination. Such measures include special briefing for female migrants, training and awareness raising about safe channels of migration, and capacity development of Bangladesh Missions abroad for monitoring female migrants' situation.

Table 6.14: Overseas Employment: 2000-2013

Year	Total	Male	Female	Female as % of Total
2000	222,686	222,232	454	0.2
2003	254,190	252,837	2,353	0.9
2006	381,516	363,471	18,045	4.7
2009	475,278	453,064	22,214	4.7
2012	600,000	562,696	37,304	6.2
2013	400,000	344,000	56,000	14.0

Source: MoF (various years).

To reap the full benefits of overseas employment, areas of weakness in the present scenario require attention. Improvements in the sphere of overseas employment require emphasis on shifting the composition of foreign jobseekers towards higher share of skilled workers and exploring a diversification of destinations. Both government and private initiatives should be steered to these directions. In addition, the overseas job seekers frequently fall prey to fraudulent practices of middlemen and agents. They face breach of contract and exploitation at the workplace. Insecurity, harassment and accidents are not uncommon. Improvements in all these spheres require government policy initiatives.

6.6 Concluding Observations

Assessment of the labour market of Bangladesh shows some significant improvements in terms of employment growth and performance of the labour market. Simultaneously, shortcomings are also noteworthy, especially in the quality of employment. It may be useful to summarise the major positive and negative features of the employment scenario.

- Unemployment rate has been incredibly low during all three decades, 1980 to 2010, which has been mainly due to the inappropriateness of the concept of "open unemployment" in the context of Bangladesh's labour market. The overall low unemployment rate conceals the fact that "educated unemployment" rate,

especially among the youth labour force, is high and this has been discussed in detail in Chapter 8.
- Underemployment rate is low, especially among male workers and has been in the range of 7 to 14 per cent at various points in time during the period 1996-2013. This is much smaller than the underemployment rates during the period 1974-1990, when 20 to 40 per cent underemployment were rather common. Female underemployment rate is higher, although it has gone through a decline during the period 1996-2013 (from 45 to 29 per cent).
- The decline of underemployment rate, despite high rate of growth of the labour force, reflects a growth of labour demand, which has resulted in a growth of real wage. Real wage has risen in both agriculture and in non-farm sectors, although the changes have not been uniform during the last two decades. Employment growth has been lower during the period 2010-2013 compared to the previous five year period. Additional domestic employment generation per year from 2010 to 2013 was only 1.3 million. This was much smaller than the projections of the Sixth Five Year Plan. During this period, 0.5 million workers have been absorbed annually through overseas employment. This shows a high dependence on foreign employment with associated uncertainty and other repercussions.
- Success in employment growth during the period 1996-2010 cannot conceal the fact that there have been weaknesses in terms of the changes in type and sector of employment. Structural change in terms of rise of the share of modern non-farm sectors has been small. In 1996, 48.9 per cent of the labour force was employed in agriculture, which came down to 45.1 per cent in 2013. The decline was higher for men, while for women the change was in the reverse direction—the share of farm sector employment actually increased from 27.8 to 53.7 per cent. Commensurate with such sector composition, most of the employment has taken the form of self-employment or unpaid family work, which are categorised as vulnerable employment. The latter category accounted for 56.3 per cent of female employment in 2010.
- Another aspect of the performance of the labour market where improvements are required is the predominance of informality

of employment. Eighty per cent of all employment is of informal type. It implies that labour hiring of even the formal sector takes the form of informal employment. Such informal employment falls short of features of "decent employment" (including job security, leave provision, right to organise and to bargain with employers, etc.). While it is difficult to adopt and implement direct policies for growth of formal employment, indirect policies for growth of labour-intensive modern sectors and for raising productivity of informal employment can have positive influence on wage and quality of employment.
- Despite the observed shortcomings in the quality of employment, progress towards higher employment growth, especially among women, can help both economic growth and social change in the future. While an elastic supply of male labour to the modern sector no longer provides an easy route to industrialisation, female labour supply may help meet the growing labour demand. This supply may come not only from the underemployed women, but also through entry of the "discouraged workers" into the labour market and a rise of labour force participation among young unmarried women through offers of a rising real wage and better terms of employment.
- Policy suggestions for improvement of the performance of the labour market and for accelerating employment growth have been presented at the end of Chapter 9. These suggestions are based on the findings of analysis of all relevant chapters.

CHAPTER 7

Seasonal Underemployment and Its Implications

7.1 Introduction

Seasonality of labour use is inherent in agriculture, as production in this sector depends on climatological and biological factors. Many of the non-agricultural activities in the rural areas are also dependent on weather. As a result, employment pattern of rural labour force shows pronounced seasonal fluctuation.

Such seasonality of productive activity has important implications for the problem of unemployment and consequent poverty and household food insecurity. The question of labour allocation may also be related to the seasonal pattern of labour demand. Consequently, the nature and implications of seasonality need to be fully analysed for the purpose of adoption of proper policies to enhance the welfare of the rural labourers and to ensure proper allocation of resources, especially labour. This chapter highlights the seasonality of employment and its mirror image, seasonal underemployment in rural areas.[1]

The initial sections (Sections 7.2 to 7.5) provide analyses of seasonal employment on the basis of a survey conducted in 1980. Section 7.2 provides a description of the nature of seasonal labour use in agriculture, while Section 7.3 examines the extent of seasonal underemployment of labour force. The other side of the picture is the influence of seasonality on decisions of allocation of labour in agriculture. A related question is how the forms of labour hiring in the labour market respond to such seasonality, which is discussed in Section 7.4. Decision of labour allocation in non-agricultural activities has to take the seasonal pattern of labour use in agriculture into account and this receives attention in Section 7.5. Section 7.6 provides a snapshot from another recent set of data. The final section summarises the discussion.

---

[1] In this chapter, seasonal underemployment and seasonal unemployment have been used synonymously.

7.1.1 Notes on Data

To illustrate the arguments, micro level data from some villages in Bangladesh have been used. The first set of data is from the sample villages of Dhanbari and Parannagar in Savar Thana of Dhaka district. Data relate to the Bengali calendar year corresponding to April 1979 to March 1980. The survey covered all households in the sample villages; the number of households is 107 in Parannagar and 178 in Dhanbari. For each household, information was collected on relevant socio-economic variables and on the pattern of employment for all people actively engaged in income-earning activities. Some qualitative information on the cultivation practices and timing of different crops activities was also collected to supplement the quantitative data.[2]

One may wonder whether seasonal pattern of employment existed only during the early years of agricultural growth. With the advent of new HYV technology in agriculture, the extent and pattern of seasonality are likely to change. Therefore, Section 7.6 presents more recent data on monthly employment and monthly variation of wage. This section is based on data from some villages in Mymensingh (greater district). The survey conducted in 2008 covers 657 households in six villages. This data set focuses on household food insecurity and the link between seasonal unemployment and seasonal food insecurity faced by households.

7.2 Nature of Seasonality of Labour Use in Agriculture

Labour use in agriculture, especially in crop production, is highly seasonal because of the very nature of crop growing practices. The amount of work and attention required at different stages of plant growth are different. Labour days required in each month or each operation for any crop is an indicator of the nature and extent of such variation. Monthly data on labour use in crop production for all farms of the two sample villages show that the extent of variation is quite large (Table 7.1). In the slack months, labour use is 12 per cent of the peak month in Dhanbari and 16 per cent in Parannagar. The coefficient of variation is also high.

---

[2] Such detailed data collected on the basis of memory may suffer from the problem of memory lapse. But cross-checking within the questionnaire and with village-level information ensured workable reliability. Also, our experience is that memory-based data have greater reliability if information is collected as disaggregated components, which is done. Data from this survey have also been used in Chapter 4. Section 7.2 to 7.5 draws from Rahman (1981).

Table 7.1: Monthly Pattern of Labour Use in Crop Production in two Villages in Savar

Months	Village Dhanbari Total Labour Used in Each Month	Village Dhanbari Labour Used in Each Month as % of Labour Used in Peak Month	Village Parannagar Total Labour Used in Each Month	Village Parannagar Labour Used in Each Month as % of Labour Used in Peak Month
Baishakh*	4,736	100.0	2,082	92.2
Jaishtha*	3,308	96.9	2,285	100.0
Ashar	2,390	50.5	1,810	80.2
Shraban	3,372	71.2	1,939	85.9
Bhadra	2,899	61.2	1,052	46.6
Ashwin	564	11.9	468	20.7
Kartik	598	12.6	352	15.6
Agrahayan	1,196	25.3	707	31.3
Poush	2,321	49.0	1,117	49.5
Magh	2,260	47.7	739	32.8
Falgun	2,172	45.9	964	42.7
Chaitra	2,978	62.9	1,140	50.5
Total	28,798	-	14,660	-
Coefficient of variation	48.05%	-	51.05%	-

Note: * The index has been put at 100 for the month providing the maximum amount of employment. *Baishakh* extends from mid-April to mid-May, *Jaishtha* corresponds to mid-May to mid-June, etc.

Source: Village Survey 1980.

Table 7.2: Pattern of Labour Use in Different Crop Seasons

Seasons	Dhanbari Total Acreage under Crops	Dhanbari Labour Use in 100 Mandays	Dhanbari % of all Labour Use	Parannagar Total Acreage under Crops	Parannagar Labour Use in 100 Mandays	Parannagar % of all Labour Use
Boro	206.5	137.8	46.3	114.5	49.2	34.1
Aus	131.3	115.5	33.9	110.6	86.1	59.7
Aman	78.3	44.0	14.3	29.4	9.0	6.3

Source: Village Survey 1980.

The season-wise distribution of labour use is shown in Table 7.2. As can be seen from the table, total acreage and labour requirement is the lowest in aman season. This pattern, however, is not consistent with the national picture where in the aman season, the amount of labour used as well as the acreage under crop is the highest amongst all seasons (Table 7.3). It is, however, interesting to note that the deepest intra-season slack occurs in the months of Bhadra and Ashwin which are within this aman season. This is true not only for these two villages but for many other areas of Bangladesh, as revealed by other studies (Clay, 1978, Muqtada, 1975).

Table 7.3: Seasonal Labour Use in Bangladesh Agriculture

Season	Acreage under Crop (100 Thousand)	Total Labour Use (in Million Mandays)	% of all Labour Use
Boro	56.2	487.9	19.5
Aus	93.7	786.0	31.4
Aman	142.6	1233.3	49.2

Source: Calculated from BBS, Statistical Yearbook of Bangladesh (1983).

However, the data cannot fully reveal the qualitative dimension of the problem. Monthly data may not adequately reflect the intensity of the peaks and slacks, because labour use may not be evenly spread out within a month. A description of the type of operations involved for a crop may help clarify this point by revealing the true nature of seasonality in crop production.

In crop cultivation, the periods of rush are those when certain operations have to be performed within a limited period of time. Table 7.1 shows that at the beginning of the Bengali year (mid-April), there is a marked peak in labour use. This is because *Baishakh* and *Jaishtha* are the months of land preparation for aus and jute. Moreover, in certain areas the boro crop is also harvested in end *Baishakh* after which the land has to be prepared for aus. The combination of these operations accounts for the rush of activities in this period. Moreover, the work of land preparation for aus is very much dependent on weather. The land being dry and hard, it can be ploughed only after the first few showers of rain. When the rain starts, all the fields in an area have to be ploughed as soon as possible. Hired labour finds itself in great demand at that time. But supply may be constrained because labourers who possess tiny plots of land give priority to preparation of their own plot. As a result, in this period, for a few days at least, there may be a severe scarcity of labour.

This may again happen in the period of peak weeding and peak harvesting. In Shraban, for instance, we find another peak of activities. In early Shraban the rush is due to the requirement of weeding of aus and jute, and the transplantation of the seedlings of aman. Transplantation, once started on a field, has to be completed as soon as possible so as to leave all the plants in the same stage of growth, which is essential for the next steps like application of fertiliser, water, etc. On the other land, when weeds start to grow in aus and jute land after the rains, most fields need simultaneous weeding. Also, the nature of this task is such that if it is not done fast, weeds start to multiply and require more labour. As a result, there is again a scarcity of labour in this period often resulting in attempts on the part of labour-hirers to bid away labour from each other, at least for a few days. The same may happen when a large acreage of aman needs immediate harvesting, when delays may result in a significant loss of yield.

This description helps to show how labour shortage may be felt for a brief period although there may be a surplus when one considers a longer period such as a month or even a fortnight. Such shortage is due to the particular practices with respect to cultivation operation, and their dependence on an uncertain monsoon weather.

7.3 Seasonal Underemployment and Food Inadequacy

The seasonal pattern of labour use in agriculture obviously gives a seasonally fluctuating level of employment for workers of the village. Data presented in Table 7.1 cannot show the exact magnitude of such fluctuation, because workers may be engaged in more than one occupation. They may also go out to other villages and seek work. Moreover, people from other villages may have come to this village and contributed labour. Still the data in Table 7.1 can be used to assess the problem hypothetically.

Given the labour use pattern in Table 7.1, it can be assessed whether the labour force of the village would remain fully employed if they supplied all the labour required by the agricultural sector of the village. If labour use in both crop and non-crop agricultural activities is added up, the monthly pattern of labour use turns out to be significantly seasonal, as shown by columns 3 and 5 of Table 7.4. The number of workers who are engaged in agriculture as their main occupation is 184 and 88 in Dhanbari and Parannagar respectively. On the basis of these numbers, a hypothetical potential supply has been calculated. A "hypothetical surplus" for each month can be estimated from this hypothetical supply and total labour demand (or use) in the agricultural sector of these two sample villages. If the potential is compared with the actual supply of labour of those whose major occupation is agriculture, the "potential surplus" among these workers can be obtained.

The results are presented in Table 7.4. The percentage of potential surplus assumes a very high positive value in some months and a high negative value in others. This indicates that a village cannot be self-contained with respect to labour use, because in that case the workers will not be able to cope with the work in the peak period. On the other hand, in the slack season they will be almost idle and this implies that they must resort to occupational diversification and inter-village migration to seek work. The results indicate that it may not be easy to withdraw surplus labour from agriculture, though a large amount of seasonal surplus exists.

Table 7.4: Comparison of Hypothetical and Potential Surplus Labour in Agriculture in two Villages in Savar

Months	Dhanbari				Parannagar			
	Mandays of Labour in Agriculture	% Hypothetical Surplus Labour $(S_i-L_i) \times 100 / S_i$	Mandays of Agricultural Days by Workers (A_i)	% Potential Surplus $(A_i-S_i) \times 100 / S_i$	Mandays of Labour in Agriculture	% Hypothetical Surplus Labour $(S_i-L_i) \times 100 / S_i$	Mandays of Agricultural Days by Workers (A_i)	% Potential Surplus $(A_i-S_i) \times 100 / S_i$
Baishakh	6,313	-56.0	3,657	9.7	2,775	-43.3	2,496	-28.9
Jaishtha	4,410	-9.0	4,145	-2.4	3,047	-54.4	2,580	-33.3
Ashar	3,187	21.3	2,889	28.6	2,414	-24.1	1,738	10.2
Shraban	4,495	-11.1	3,131	20.2	2,585	-23.5	1,800	7.0
Bhadra	3,865	4.5	2,901	28.4	1,402	27.6	1,259	35.0
Ashwin	752	81.4	2,099	48.2	624	67.8	1,041	46.2
Kartik	797	80.3	2,743	32.2	469	75.8	1,490	23.0
Agrahayan	1,595	60.6	3,309	18.3	942	51.3	1,698	12.3
Poush	3,094	23.5	3,059	14.4	1,489	23.1	1,314	32.1
Magh	3,017,	25.5	2,429	40.0	986	49.1	1,191	38.5
Falgun	2,896	28.5	2,660	34.3	1,285	33.6	1,515	21.7
Chaitra	3,970	1.9	2,927	37.6	1,520	21.5	1,991	23.0

Note: S_i = workers whose major occupation is agriculture x 22 days and S = 184 x 22 days in Dhanbari and 88 x 22 days in Parannagar.

Source: Village Survey 1980.

How far such surplus is balanced by supplementary activities and inter-village migration is revealed by an account of total employment of a worker in all types of activities where one is engaged. In rural areas, non-agricultural activities are also seasonal, either by their very nature or because they are consciously taken up to counteract agricultural seasonality. The resultant picture has been presented in Table 7.5.

Table 7.5: Monthly Underemployment Rate among Workers in two Villages in Savar

Months	Dhanbari			Parannagar		
	Total Days of Employment (E_i)	Employment Per Member of Labour Force	Rate of under-Employment *(S_i/E_i) x100	Total Days of Employment (E_i)	Employment Per Member of Labour Force	Rate of under-Employment *(S_i/E_i) x100
Baishakh	6,403	19.6	10.7	4,165	20.0	8.9
Jaishtha	6,620	20.3	7.7	4,060	19.5	11.2
Ashar	5,263	16.1	26.6	3,441	16.5	24.8
Shraban	5,661	17.3	21.0	3,492	16.7	23.6
Bhadra	5,181	15.8	27.7	2,928	14.0	36.0
Ashwin	5,039	15.4	29.7	2,942	14.1	35.7
Kartik	5,831	17.8	18.7	3,441	16.5	24.8
Agrahayan	6,348	19.5	11.4	3,589	17.2	21.5
Poush	6,458	19.8	19.9	3,464	16.6	24.3
Magh	6,186	18.9	13.7	3,423	16.4	25.2
Falgun	6,604	20.2	7.9	3,685	17.7	19.4
Chaitra	6,430	19.7	10.3	3,694	17.7	19.2
Total (all months)	72,024	220.9	16.3	42,324	203.4	22.9

Note: S_i = 326 x 22 mandays for Dhanbari and 208 x 22 for Parannagar.
Source: Village Survey 1980.

The extent of variation in monthly underemployment[3] (Table 7.5) is much less pronounced than what has been found in the potential sense (Table 7.4), considering agriculture alone. The coefficient of variation of this actual monthly surplus is only about 8 per cent in both the villages.

For a fuller utilisation of this underemployed labour time, it is useful to identify the extent of underutilisation that is due to seasonality alone and the part that is due to non-seasonal reasons. The underemployment rate in the month with the highest employment can be taken as the measure of underemployment due to non-seasonal reasons

---

[3] In this chapter, the terms "monthly unemployment" and "monthly underemployment" have been used synonymously.

(u_p). For other months, the difference in the percentage of actual underemployment (u_i) and u_p can provide the estimate of seasonal underemployment. Table 7.6 presents these figures. In most of the months and for the year as a whole, seasonal underemployment is found to be more important than non-seasonal underemployment. About 8.6 per cent and 13.9 per cent of underemployment in Dhanbari and Parannagar respectively are due to seasonal factors, which are greater than the non-seasonal underemployment of 7.7 per cent and 9 per cent.

Table 7.6: Extent of Underemployment due to Seasonality

Months	% of Labour Underemployed due to Seasonality	
	Dhanbari	Parannagar
Baishakh	3.0	0.0
Jaishtha	0.0	2.3
Ashar	18.9	15.8
Shraban	13.4	14.7
Bhadra	20.1	27.0
Ashwin	22.0	26.7
Kartik	11.0	15.8
Agrahayan	3.8	12.6
Poush	2.1	15.3
Magh	6.1	16.2
Falgun	0.2	10.5
Chaitra	2.7	10.3
Total of seasonal + non-seasonal underemployment	16.3	22.9
Only non-seasonal underemployment	7.7	9.0
Seasonal underemployment	8.6	13.9

Source: Village Survey 1980.

It is also of interest to note that the seasonality of employment has different implications for poverty of different groups in the rural areas. In particular, seasonal unemployment can have different significance for the wage workers and the self-employed. Table 7.7 shows the monthly variation of wage employment and self-employment in agriculture for the workers of the two sample villages.

Table 7.7: Monthly Pattern of Agricultural Employment for Wage-Work and Self-Employment

Name of Months	Dhanbari (Days/Worker) Wage Employment	Dhanbari (Days/Worker) Self-Employment	Parannagar (Days/Worker) Wage Employment	Parannagar (Days/Worker) Self-Employment
Baishakh	15.4	7.3	14.5	10.5
Jaishtha	17.3	8.4	15.7	10.5
Ashar	12.1	5.8	9.6	7.6
Shraban	13.0	6.8	10.2	7.7
Bhadra	11.7	6.1	6.6	5.7
Ashwin	6.2	5.7	2.5	6.2
Kartik	7.7	7.7	4.4	8.5
Agrahayan	12.0	7.7	7.9	8.2
Poush	10.2	7.6	4.9	7.0
Magh	7.0	6.7	3.7	6.7
Falgun	7.5	7.5	3.8	9.0
Chaitra	6.7	7.3	2.9	9.3
All Year: Total	126.6	84.5	86.8	96.8
Standard Deviation	3.5	0.8	4.3	1.5
Coefficient of Variation	32.9%	11.4%	59.1%	18.6%

Source: Village Survey 1980.

Table 7.8: Monthly Employment of Landless Workers in two Villages in Savar

Months	Mandays Worked (All Types of Work) in Each Month Dhanbari	Mandays Worked (All Types of Work) in Each Month Parannagar
Baishakh	22.6	24.5
Jaishtha	22.6	24.2
Ashar	19.3	19.5
Shraban	19.8	20.3
Bhadra	18.4	17.2
Ashwin	17.2	16.6
Kartik	18.1	18.8
Agrahayan	21.2	21.3
Poush	21.4	21.5
Magh	21.0	20.7
Falgun	22.6	20.8
Chaitra	21.2	20.5

Source: Village Survey 1980.

It is clear from the data presented in Tables 7.7 and 7.8 that the wage workers face a much more serious fluctuation in employment compared to the self-employed. The average wage-employment is perilously low in some of the months. The problem is compounded by the fact that in periods of slack, the wage rates are also much lower (Table 7.9). Some respite is, of course, provided by alternative employment opportunities. Yet, as Table 7.8 shows, the problem of seasonal unemployment is not entirely removed.

Slack months of *Bhadra, Ashwin* and *Kartik* still offer less employment and low wage, resulting in poverty. Self-employment is much less seasonal. Still the farm households are adversely affected by the impact of seasonal agriculture on their income. Since income from agricultural produce comes at the end of a crop season, it can indirectly increase the risks of being in poverty.

Unemployment receives attention because of its implications for underutilisation of labour force and also for the consequent poverty. So a discussion of how such seasonal unemployment can result in poverty is pertinent. In the past literature on poverty, the seasonal dimension has been usually missing. Whether people are in a poverty situation is assessed by comparing the yearly income or consumption expenditure with a minimum requirement based poverty line. If people live below that norm for some months and go above in others, the yearly average may not show them as poor or undernourished. Yet seasonal undernourishment may have permanent implications for health and well-being. There is in fact evidence of loss of body weight due to seasonal malnutrition.

Although a detailed analysis of poverty incidence is beyond the scope of this analysis, a few aspects of the adversities faced by households who live close to the poverty threshold deserve attention. For many small and medium farmers, the amount of produce may be inadequate for the following season. Such a food shortage occurs just before harvest of the next crop, which may have adverse effect on efficiency as well, as this is the time for hard work. Thus the more uniform pattern of self-employment may in fact accentuate seasonal poverty related repercussions through seasonal nature of income rather than eliminate it. The seriousness of the problem obviously depends on the cropping intensity, which determines the periodicity of harvest. The scope of non-agricultural employment is also important in balancing the seasonal shortages.

Enquiry on food availability of households reveals that about 17.5 per cent of farmers with cultivated land of less than one acre face food shortage in Dhanbari. On the other hand, 33.3 per cent farmers in this group in Parannagar reported food shortage. Such shortages have been reported during the months of *Ashwin* and *Chaitra* in most cases. It may, however, be mentioned that food shortage in the sample villages are in most cases a seasonal phenomenon. Year-round shortage is faced by a small number of families in these villages.

7.4 Seasonality and Labour Allocation

Labour allocation, as it is guided by consideration of marginal product and wage rate, will be influenced by seasonal factors. Seasonality assumes importance in this context due mainly to the fact that the marginal product of labour input for a given crop is not the same in its various stages of growth. In other words, labour inputs in peak and slack seasons are not perfect substitutes.

Corresponding to the variation of marginal product of labour, there is also seasonal variation in the opportunity cost of labour. In the earlier description it has been mentioned that in some season there is a rush to complete the work, while in other months there is only a minimal amount of work. As a result, wage rates in different months show significant variation. Opportunity cost of family labour also varies depending on the scope for alternative use of time, which is clearly not the same in different parts of the year. In this context, three aspects deserve attention. These are: (a) whether the peaking of labour demand due to the seasonal factor makes the farmers face a labour constraint; (b) whether slack season labour input is related to peak season input and in that case how seasonality may influence variation of total labour input; and (c) how the characteristics of the rural labour market respond to such seasonal variations and how labour allocation in non-agricultural activities in rural areas is linked to seasonal agricultural employment.

7.4.1 Existence of a Labour Constraint

Densely populated Bangladesh with heavy pressure on arable land resulting in a low land-population ratio is often presented as a prime example of a labour-surplus economy. The discussion of a labour constraint may, therefore, sound irrelevant. But, given the seasonal factor, it may be useful to investigate the possibility of such constraint, which will be an important consideration for introduction of labour-intensive technology in either agriculture or modern sector.

Monthly figures of unemployment rate may be an indicator of labour constraint. The negative unemployment in some months, shown in Table 7.4, shows the possibility of such constraint. According to this indicator, a labour shortage in the months of Baishakh and Agrahayan prevails in some parts of the country. The constraint may be more acute for a shorter period and the nature of such constraint has been mentioned in the earlier section.

Shortage of labour would usually be felt by larger farmers who depend more on hired labour. In the peak season, there is a simultaneous demand for hired labour by all labour-hiring farms. On the other hand, some of the wage workers may be engaged in their own farms, which certainly comes first in their order of priority. If the wage-workers are observed to be fully employed in the peak month, then this would indicate the possibility of a shortage. In the present sample villages, landless workers on an average worked for 23 and 24 man-days in *Baishakh* and *Jaishtha*, which are above the full employment level (22 workdays) in a month.

On the other hand, labour constraint may be assessed more directly by asking the employers whether they faced any problem in getting adequate number of labourers when they needed them most. We can cite one study where such a direct enquiry was carried out. For a village in Comilla it was found that 20 per cent of the large farmers (cultivating more than 5 acres) faced problem in getting as much labourers as they wanted (Ahmed, 1981).

This is due to the nature of monsoon dependent cultivation practices described earlier. Some of the agricultural operations have to be performed simultaneously in all fields. Ploughing after the first few showers and harvesting of the crop are examples of such activities when a labour shortage in a situation of apparent labour abundance can be a reality.

7.4.2 Responses in Labour Market: From Casual Employment to Piece Rate Contract

Seasonality of agricultural operations thus causes seasonal unemployment as well as seasonal labour shortage. Even if there is no actual shortage, there is a fear of the same. This leads to different responses in the behaviour of the farmers. Apart from their own responses, the labour market tries to adjust to take care of the problem. The following aspects are relevant in this respect.

The nature of seasonality of agricultural work is such that sometimes it requires a large number of workers simultaneously on the field. It is not possible for permanently attached labourers to cope with this work. That is why there is always a dependence on casual labour. It may be difficult to contact a large group of workers within a short period of time. Sometimes there may be a problem of supervising the daily workers.

Table 7.9: Wage Rates in Harvesting Season

	Daily Earning		Average Hours Worked Per Day		Wage Rates of Eight Hours (One Manday)	
	Dhanbari	Parannagar	Dhanbari	Parannagar	Dhanbari	Parannagar
Boro HYV	28.2	*-	10.9	-	20.7	-
Aus	14.8	21.6	10.3	11.4	11.6	15.1
Aman	18.8	*-	10.5	-	14.3	-.

Note: *Only a small number of farmers grow these crops in Parannagar. So cases of contract harvest are very small.
Source: Village Survey 1980.

Terms and forms of labour hiring seen in the rural areas provide some answers to these problems. In busy periods, especially when the job needs to be done within a day or two, the workers are hired on contract basis to complete a piece of work within the specified period. So it is in the interest of the workers to complete the job quickly. They usually work for longer hours and more intensively. This type of contract is usually seen for harvesting a crop and for ploughing land. Such contract for harvesting is given to a group and not individually. The workers themselves form into groups and approach the potential employers. In the two villages studied, this sort of terms of labour hiring is a common practice. In the case of HYV boro, almost all harvesting is done by groups on contract basis. Same was the case with aman. Aus and jute do not necessitate such a hurry for completion. So the harvesting is mostly done on daily basis. In the cases of contract harvesting of different crops in these villages, the hours worked and wage rates are quite high. These are shown in Table 7.9. Daily wage rates are higher not only because they work longer hours, but the hourly wage is also higher than other periods. In fact, this provides the incentive of overtime work when the job is strenuous. Thus this form of contract reduces the problem of getting a large group of people simultaneously. Also, this helps to increase the supply of labour in the critical period by making the workday longer. This sort of arrangement attracts labourers from distant deficit employment areas to areas with high yield and employment opportunities. Such groups are reported to move long distances. This also helps to reduce regional imbalance in seasonal labour demand and wage.

7.5 Allocation of Labour in Non-Agriculture

Seasonal pattern of employment and underemployment not only influences labour allocation in agriculture, but also in non-agriculture. Many of the non-agricultural activities are seasonal by their nature, e.g., fishing, transport (in non-metalled roads and canals), etc. On the other hand, certain activities are consciously developed to take advantage of the surplus labour from agriculture in the slack season.

In this context, one should examine how far non-agricultural employment is seasonal and whether it counteracts the seasonal pattern of agricultural employment.

Non-agricultural activities in rural areas are most often supplementary to agriculture both in terms of employment and income. This is true especially for wage workers and their supplementary activities. These activities are likely to be seasonal and the pattern of seasonality is expected to counteract that of agriculture. Table 7.10 shows the pattern of employment in non-agriculture for the self-employed and wage workers in the sample villages. It is observed that the pattern is almost stable for the self-employed. For wage workers, it is quite seasonal and the pattern is such that it counteracts agricultural seasonality. Thus the agricultural wage workers get an opportunity to even out their employment pattern, at least partially.

The obvious policy implication of the observed pattern given in Table 7.10 is to develop non-agricultural activities to employ workers in the agricultural slack season. Planning of these activities has to take agricultural seasonality into proper consideration.

Table 7.10: **Monthly Pattern of Non-Agricultural Wage Employment and Self-Employment**

Months	Non-Agri Employment Days Per Worker			
	Dhanbari		Parannagar	
	Average Days of Wage Employment	Average Days of Self Employment	Average Days of Wage Employment	Average Days of Self Employment
Baishakh	9.2	16.4	12.5	11.4
Jaishtha	7.3	15.5	10.3	11.1
Ashar	6.9	15.4	11.5	13.3
Shraban	7.1	15.7	11.1	13.5
Bhadra	6.6	14.8	11.3	12.9
Ashwin	10.7	16.5	13.8	13.5
Kartik	12.4	16.1	15.9	11.7
Agrahayan	12.0	16.0	14.8	12.1
Poush	14.9	16.2	17.9	12.4
Magh	17.2	17.2	18.6	12.8
Falgun	17.6	18.4	16.9	13.9
Chaitra	17.6	17.9	16.9	14.5
Coefficient of Variation (%)	35.8	6.0	19.7	7.8

Source: Village Survey 1980.

More than 90 per cent of all workers of these villages are employed in agriculture for some part of the year. This implies that the use of rural labour in non-agricultural activities even within the location of their residence is not without an opportunity cost. If the opportunity cost of labour given by the shadow price is calculated from the rate of unemployment and prevailing wage rate, such cost will be different for peak and slack seasons.

In view of these considerations, it seems necessary that the scale of non-agricultural activities must be different in different periods of the year. Many of the construction activities are of this nature. These are done mainly in the winter. But a major problem of such activities is that it cannot fill the employment gap during the rainy season. The length of the slack season during late monsoon is less than two months. Even if suitable rainy season activities are developed, they may go beyond the slack season and cause problems in the harvesting of the main crop, namely aman. So a more practical approach is that policies should aim at increasing agricultural activity in such a way that the pre-slack employment is adequate to provide enough income to sustain the workers during the slack period.

7.6 Seasonality of Food Insecurity and Employment: Recent Evidence[4]

Food insecurity generally manifests itself in two forms: first, year round/chronic food insecurity and second, seasonal food insecurity. However, there is hardly any information on the extent of seasonal variation of food insecurity in Bangladesh. Household income may also serve as a proxy of household food insecurity. But data on monthly income of households are not available from any source. In fact, it will be difficult to estimate monthly income, especially among rural households engaged in agriculture and other self-employment where output may not correspond to months but are less frequent and lumpy in nature. In contrast, food insecurity data can be collected for each month of the year.

The Household Survey, conducted in some villages of Mymensingh (greater district) in 2008, collected month-wise data on food insecurity and on days of employment of all employed persons. The data show the link between seasonal variations of food insecurity and seasonal underemployment.

Seasonal variations of food insecurity are linked with seasonality in the labour market and the agricultural production cycles. The fluctuations of prices of foodgrains also play a role in this context. Therefore, the monthly variation of rice prices in these areas is also presented.

Table 7.11 presents data on monthly food insecurity. Data reveal large monthly fluctuation in the extent of food insecurity. The range is 7.3 days to 13.3 days for the area. Mid-October to mid-November (*Kartik*) and mid-February to mid-March (*Chaitra*) are the periods of most severe food insecurity. In fact, data confirm that the months of *Ashwin-Kartik*, traditionally known as Monga period, actually continue to be the periods of food insecurity even in recent years. Moreover, *Falgun* and *Chaitra* are also the months of extended food insecurity for the households in this area.

---

[4] This section draws from Rahman, Begum and Bhuyan (2009).

Table 7.11: **Monthly Employment and Food Insecurity in Villages of Mymensingh**

Month	Average Days of Employment Per Earner	Average Days of *Food Shortage
Baishakh	20.4	7.5
Jaistha	21.5	7.8
Ashar	15.9	8.2
Shraban	18.0	7.7
Bhadra	17.9	7.8
Ashwin	14.9	10.6
Kartik	14.6	12.9
Agrahayan	21.8	7.4
Poush	18.3	7.9
Magh	19.8	8.4
Falgun	16.8	9.4
Chaitra	15.1	13.3
Total	18.0	55.5

Note: *Average for households with food shortage.
Source: BIDS Food Insecurity Survey (BIDS-FISS) 2008.

Figure 7.1 shows the monthly fluctuations of the two variables, employment[5] and food insecurity. The extent (number of days) of food insecurity and employment shows an inverse relationship, as expected. There are two periods of low employment, extending over a period of about two months. In both low employment periods, food insecure days are high. The reverse is the case in months of higher employment.

Impact of days of employment on food insecurity actually operates through its links with income. Low employment implies low income in slack season/months, which leads to food insecurity.

In the case of self-employment, especially in agriculture, seasonal fluctuations of employment may not be directly linked to income flows. Both employment and income flows in this case are determined by the production cycle of agricultural crops. In these areas, aman and boro rice are major crops and the months in which these rice crops are sown and harvested in these villages are as follows:

Aman rice: Transplanted/sown in July-August, harvested in December

---

[5] These figures are based on total of paid and self-employment in both agriculture and non-agriculture. In fact, non-agricultural employment is likely to show less seasonal fluctuation. But total employment being dominated by agriculture shows considerable seasonal fluctuations.

Boro rice: Transplanted in February-March, harvested in May-June

Aus rice: Sown in April-May, harvested in July (not important in these areas).

Figure 7.1: Employment Days and Food Insecurity in Mymensingh

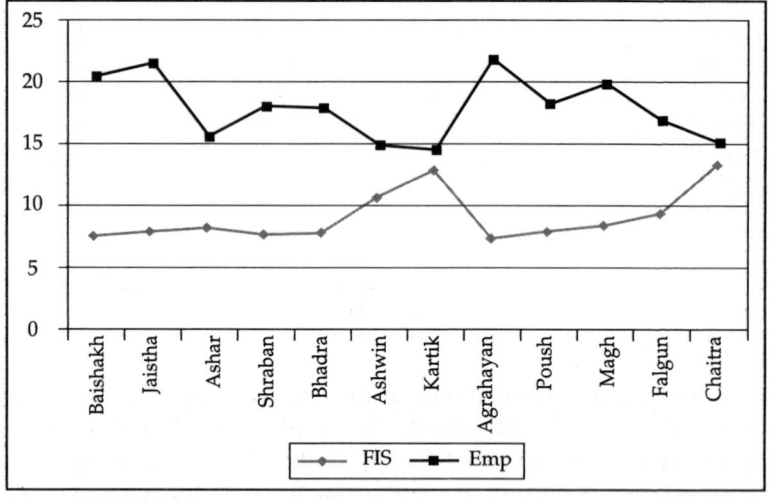

Source: BIDS-FISS data.

The months of low employment are September-October and March-April (Table 7.11). None of the major agricultural crops is harvested in these months. This implies that there is hardly any income flow during the slack employment periods. Therefore, in the case of self-employment as well, food insecurity is observed during the low employment periods. In both areas, April-June (*Baishakh-Jaishtha*) and November-December (*Agrahayan-Poush*) are the months of peak employment (Table 7.11). If 22 days of employment in a month is taken as the full employment norm, then these months show close to full employment and low food insecurity.

7.7 Monthly Variation of Wage

Wage data presented here has been obtained from the employers within the selected villages. This reflects the labour market in the space around their residence and within or neighbouring their own villages.

In contrast, wage data obtained from workers' responses will involve a mixture of wage obtained from various places as the workers sometimes go outside the village to seek wage employment in other villages and distant towns as well.

Data presented in Table 7.12 show a substantial monthly fluctuation of wage. A decline of wage during the slack period can be observed. The range between peak and slack wages is large (Tk. 110). In fact, in some villages employers did not report a wage rate for *"Kartik"* and *"Chaitra,"* because in these months they do not hire workers. Thus the slack season is characterised by decline of both wage and employment.

Table 7.12: Monthly Wage Rates in Agriculture and Rice Price in Mymensingh and National Average

Months	Average Wage Rate in Mymensingh in 2008 (Taka Per Day)	Price of Rice in Mymensingh in 2008 (Taka/Kg)	National Agricultural Wage, 2012 (Taka Per Day)	National Average Rice Price in 2012 (Taka/Kg)
Chaitra	98	22.0	247	28.3
Baishakh	191	22.5	274	28.5
Jaishtha	208	24.5	304	24.5
Ashar	166	25.0	271	25.6
Shraban	147	26.0	265	24.6
Bhadra	138	27.0	267	26.5
Ashwin	130	28.0	279	27.3
Kartik	115	29.0	286	27.5
Agrahayan	189	31.0	270	27.2
Poush	208	32.8	272	27.0
Magh	192	35.8	254	25.0
Falgun	165	35.8	254	27.3

Note: Wage rate reported by employers in the selected villages. Wage includes cash plus kind/food.
Source: BIDS Food Insecurity Survey (BIDS-FISS) 2008 (Rahman et al., 2009).

At this point, it should be emphasised that this type of survey and data analysis for small regions can be useful to focus on seasonality of employment and wage within a particular area. If such data is averaged for larger geographical regions, then the seasonal fluctuation will be less pronounced because the pattern in one area may counteract the pattern in other areas. This may be one of the reasons that the national average wage provided by *Monthly Statistical Bulletin* (BBS, various years) gives smaller monthly fluctuation of wage as shown in the last column of Table 7.12. It varies from Tk. 247 to Tk. 304 (a range of Tk. 57).

7.8 Monthly Variation of Rice Price

While employment plays an important role as a determinant of "entitlement" of the labour market participants, which, in turn, determines food security, the other side of the picture involves the supply situation of foodgrains. Although an analysis of the supply situation is beyond the scope of the present chapter, data on monthly rice price can demonstrate the role of price fluctuations in aggravating seasonal food insecurity in the survey areas.

Table 7.12 provides data on monthly rice price. During the twelve-month period, rice price displayed more or less a continuous increase. However, the incremental changes during *Ashwin*, *Kartik* and *Falgun* (the months with higher food insecurity) are not larger than the changes observed in other months. In the study year (2008) this may have been due to the rapid rise of rice price which has overshadowed the monthly fluctuations. The last column of Table 7.12 shows the national average rice price in 2012, which can be considered as a normal year. It shows very small monthly fluctuation. Thus, the link between monthly fluctuations of rice price and food inadequacy is not quite apparent.

7.9 Summary and Conclusions

It has been observed that labour use in agriculture is highly seasonal, showing large variation over the months and among different crop seasons as well as within a season. Most of the non-agricultural activities are also seasonal, but they often counteract the seasonality of agricultural employment and this type of occupational diversification helps reduce the seasonality of employment. But still the aggregate patterns of employment and underemployment show substantial fluctuation. When seasonal and non-seasonal components of underemployment are separated, the magnitude of seasonal underemployment is found to be much larger.

Seasonal underemployment means that there is substantial under-utilisation of labour force and at the same time they cannot be withdrawn to be employed elsewhere. Apart from implications of such underutilisation of labour force, the more important reason for concern about seasonal underemployment is that it causes food insecurity and poverty in certain periods of a year.

Data from the 2008 survey, which comes 27 years after the earlier survey, are quite illustrative of the severity of seasonality problem. After all these years of agricultural growth and achievement of higher cropping intensity, the problems of slack season underemployment and seasonal food insecurity remain quite pronounced. The range of monthly employment was 5/6 days in the earlier survey (lowest being 14.5 days and the highest being 20 days). These figures are more or less the same (14.6 and 20.4 days) in the recent survey. Data also show that even if there has been a reduction of poverty incidence, measured on the basis of poverty line expenditure, seasonal food shortage remains high. About 40 per cent of households faced food shortages to the extent of 10 to 13 days in each of the slack months of *Ashwin, Kartik* (September-October) and *Chaitra* (March).

The analysis highlights the other implication of such seasonal labour use. This involves the possibility of a seasonal labour constraint or fear of the constraint which may also influence total labour use on crops. Such constraint leads to various responses in the labour market, such as the use of contract labour, temporary inter-village migration of labour force, etc. Given the possibility of a labour scarcity at some point of time and seasonal unemployment at others, non-agricultural projects designed to absorb the seasonally surplus labour must be planned carefully.

CHAPTER 8

Modern Irrigation and Equity: Do Wage Labourers Share the Benefits?

8.1 Introduction

Modernisation of agriculture, consisting of modern irrigation, new crop varieties (especially of rice) and chemical fertiliser, has brought the promise of not only faster growth of yield and output but also of a higher wage and greater employment prospects in the rural areas of Bangladesh and in a number of other Asian countries. The distributional consequence of modern agricultural technology has been debated since the early years of its expansion. The distributional issue that has drawn most attention is whether the small farmers and tenant farmers could share the benefits through an access to the technology. This aspect has been discussed in Chapters 4 and 5.

The labour market issue, especially the question of whether the wage labourers benefit from new technology through higher wage rate and larger employment per worker, has not yet been resolved. For Bangladesh, this issue deserves particular attention because a large percentage of the wage labourers in rural Bangladesh live in conditions of poverty. An analysis of the equity implications of modern irrigation enables us to determine how far irrigation based agricultural growth can be relied upon as a strategy for poverty alleviation among the agricultural labourers.

In this context, it has been said that although theoretical arguments strongly suggest that labourers are likely to gain, there is growing evidence that "net gains to labourers from the process involving modern varieties in their total socio-technical setting are getting less clear" (Lipton and Longhurst, 1989: 177). The lack of clarity in this respect has been due to emphasis on some aspects of the relationship between labour and modern agriculture (e.g., demand for hired labour and wage rate for modern variety cultivation) without an integrated analysis of wage rate, employment of a labourer and household income of rural labourers. Studies have emphasised that wage rate is an insufficient indicator of poverty and welfare of rural wage labourers (Lipton and Ravallion, 1993). Yet, empirical research has concentrated mostly on wage.

The objective of the present chapter is to focus on the impact of agricultural modernisation on wage and employment of rural workers in Bangladesh. A direct analysis of the impact of irrigation on income has also been attempted. This is necessary because the impact on wage and employment may not be in the same direction and therefore these two cannot readily reveal the possible impact on household income.

Before entering into the discussion on wage labourer's benefits from modern irrigation and HYV technology, it will be useful to present data on labour input in crop production in irrigated and non-irrigated areas. Following section presents this data. The data set is based on a survey of households from 35 villages of Rangpur and Dinajpur districts. The survey was conducted in 1995. Although the data sets used in the analysis are from surveys conducted during the early 1990s, this chapter has been included in the present volume because other studies on impact of HYV technology in Bangladesh have not examined these issues and future studies may use this as a reference point.

8.2 Modern Crop Varieties, Irrigation and Labour Use

Increase of labour demand due to the cultivation of modern rice varieties come from two sources. First, the irrigated HYV rice uses a package of material inputs which require a larger labour input.[1] Moreover, the cultivation of modern varieties in the dry season is likely to increase cropping intensity, which, in turn, increases the total demand for labour over a year. In addition, when irrigated rice is grown in the dry season, it replaces either the rainfed aus paddy/jute or some low productive rabi crops. Therefore, the pertinent comparisons for understanding the impact of modern variety (MV) on labour demand are among labour use in these traditional crops and HYV boro paddy. Comparison of HYV and local varieties of the same paddy cannot reveal the full impact.

---

[1] These arguments have been mentioned in Chapter 4 of this volume. A number of early studies (e.g., Muqtada and Alam, 1986) have provided such comparison.

A comparison of villages within the same production environment can provide a better picture of the changes introduced by irrigated crops. Table 8.1 shows such data from the household survey in some villages.[2] Both irrigated and non-irrigated villages, covered by this survey, are in the greater districts of Rangpur and Dinajpur, in the north-west region of the country. Corresponding to each irrigated village, the survey covered a near-by village without irrigation but with similar soil conditions and ecological characteristics.

Table 8.1: Use of Labour in Different Crops in Irrigated and Non-Irrigated Areas

	(Man Days Per Ha)	
Crops	Irrigated	Non-Irrigated
Local T. Aman	117.4	134.6
HYV Aman	147.9	143.7
Local Aus	74.7	108.2
Jute	173.7	204.7
HYV Boro	166.2	226.9
Wheat	96.1	115.3
Pulse	87.9	55.2

Source: Data from BIDS-ESGKF Survey 1995, BIDS.

Data presented in Table 8.1 show that among the important crops in terms of area covered (which cover more than 5 per cent of gross cultivated area in either irrigated or non-irrigated villages), irrigated HYV boro is one of the highest labour using crops. When it replaces local aus paddy, the increase in labour demand is substantial. About 81 person-days more labour is used in HYV boro compared to local aus. However, in comparison to jute, labour use is lower in HYV boro. Moreover, it can be observed that labour inputs in the crops which are substituted by HYV boro are substantially lower in the villages growing HYV boro than the unirrigated villages which do not grow HYV boro. Thus, the labour co-efficient for a crop is not technically fixed and there are attempts to use more labour even in low labour using crops when there is no scope for growing more labour-intensive irrigated crops.

---

[2] Rahman and Saha (1995) include details about the sample.

Information presented above illustrates the need to take into account the overall picture while making predictions about the impact of irrigated crops on total labour use during a year. Even if an irrigated crop may not be the highest labour using crop, it may still lead to an increase in total labour use over the year through its positive impact on cropping intensity.

Data on labour use per hectare of cultivated area over a year in irrigated and non-irrigated land are shown in Table 8.2. The difference in average labour input is small (about 4 person days per hectare). In fact, Hossain et al. (1994) show that labour input per hectare is very similar between drought-prone land and irrigated areas. Thus there is no strong evidence that the initial optimism about the large increase in labour use associated with modern varieties has been realised.

Table 8.2: Labour Input in Crop Production Per Hectare in Irrigated and Non-Irrigated Villages

Farm Size (Hectare)	Irrigated	Non-Irrigated	Total
0.01-0.20	414.3	456.4	412.2
0.21-1.01	285.0	197.1	237.6
1.02-2.02	254.1	175.4	202.5
2.03 and above	215.3	195.4	209.6
All	262.1	257.7	259.6

Source: Data from BIDS-ESGKF Survey 1995, BIDS.

A further probing into the composition of labour use is necessary to arrive at conclusions regarding benefits of wage labourers. Not only total labour input, but also its composition in terms of family labour and hired labour can have important implications for employment and income of the households dependent on wage employment. Table 8.3 provides a breakdown of the pattern of hired labour use in the irrigated and non-irrigated areas and among various landowning groups. The larger demand for hired labour in the irrigated areas is clear from the data. Use of hired labour per hectare is about 68 per cent higher in the irrigated area. The greater use of hired labour contributes to the larger labour inputs by big landowners in irrigated areas, compared to such farm sizes in unirrigated areas, as shown in Table 8.2.

Table 8.3: Hired Labour Input in Crop Production Per Hectare in Irrigated and Non-Irrigated Villages

Farm Size (Hectare)	Irrigated	Non-Irrigated	Total
0.01-0.20	66.6	26.7	55.1
0.21-1.01	114.5	67.4	88.1
1.02-2.02	136.8	70.0	102.9
2.03 and above	181.7	126.6	153.3
All	101.5	60.6	86.4

Source: Data from BIDS-ESGKF Survey 1995, BIDS.

A number of studies show a significant increase in the demand for hired labour in the irrigated areas. In almost all studies, the difference in the use of hired labour is larger than the difference in total labour use between irrigated and non-irrigated areas (Hossain, 1989, Hossain et al., 1994).

Since the impact of the growth of irrigated agriculture on total labour use is ambiguous, the impact of such growth on the employment situation of a worker is even more uncertain. The differences in the total employment obtained by workers are blurred by the increasing mobility of hired workers between irrigated and non-irrigated areas. The opportunities of hired employment in the irrigated areas are likely to be shared by workers from non-irrigated areas. Moreover, they try to compensate the lower employment opportunities in agriculture through engaging themselves in non-farm activities. A number of studies (Rahman and Saha, 1995, Hossain, 1989) have demonstrated that areas with underdeveloped agriculture generate more employment in non-farm activities. Push factors also play an important role in this regard. But this also represents a boost in the demand for non-farm activities through agricultural growth in the neighbouring irrigated villages. Thus cross sectional comparison is unlikely to reflect the changes of employment situation of the labour force due to the introduction of new technology.

Empirical studies on this issue differ in their findings. One of the early studies observes a positive association between employment per worker/household and the extent of irrigation (Hossain, 1989).

Data from the survey quoted above show that the difference in average employment among labour force in the irrigated and non-irrigated areas is small (Table 8.4). During the harvesting season of the irrigated paddy, employment among workers in the irrigated villages is much higher.

Table 8.4: Employment Per Worker in Irrigated and Non-Irrigated Villages

Type of Village	Hours of Employment in a Month			
	Baishakh	*Bhadra*	*Ashwin*	Average Per Month
Irrigated	191	176	165	177
Non-irrigated	184	170	156	170

Source: Data from BIDS-ESGKF Survey 1995, BIDS.

8.3 Impact of Irrigation on Wage Rate, Employment and Income: A Framework for Analysis and the Hypotheses

A positive impact of irrigation on wage rate is expected through an upward shift in the demand for hired labour. Employment per household will increase unless there is a strong negative income effect of the higher wage, which is unlikely to be the case for agricultural labourers living in poverty.

The concern about a reversal of this positive impact on wages arises from the scope of mechanisation of some of the operations. This had happened in some of the Indian provinces where modern varieties of irrigated crops resulted in higher labour demand. In Bangladesh, large scale mechanisation may not be possible in the near future because of the physical features of land and its use, including fragmentation and scattered ownership. Therefore, with the expansion of irrigated agriculture, a wage increase would almost be inevitable.

Another possible dampening effect on wage rate may work through the inter-village migration of labour, as mentioned in the previous section. Labourers from non-irrigated villages migrate to the irrigated areas. This implies an expansion of the supply of workers. With such a shift in supply, there is a downward pressure on wage. In this case, employment among workers in the irrigated village may not increase because the increased demand is met by the supply from migrant workers. However, the inter-village migration of labour may not lead to complete equalisation of wage because of transport cost and higher supervision cost for unknown labourers.

A third possibility may be conceived where a reverse shift in the supply of hired labourers takes place. Supply of wage labour may decline with the introduction of irrigated agriculture, because some of the wage labourers also cultivate their own farms and there is an increased demand for their labour in their family farms. Therefore, the supply of wage labour in the village labour market may decline. An additional source of reduced supply of labour associated with irrigation is the possible income effect among the self-employed farmer-labourers whose income increase due to increased productivity of their own irrigated land. Such reverse shift in the supply of labour may counteract the in-migration of labour, providing additional reasons for wages being higher in the technologically advanced area.

The above points on the impact of modern varieties on wage have been based on a competitive framework. An obvious question arises as to the existence of surplus labour and its relevance for wage determination and the validity of the assumption of competitive market. Competitive wage determination would be valid for the peak season when there is little unemployment. The present study focuses only on wage rates for peak seasons. Slack season wage determination is not considered here in view of the fact that the slack period with substantial under-employment is short (about two months: September and October). The rationale behind wage determination in a situation with under-employment has been debated without a consensus being reached.[3] It is beyond the scope of the present chapter to enter into that debate.

Impact of irrigation on wage rates for only irrigated crops is not sufficient to capture the impact of irrigation on wage. The wage rates in non-irrigated crop seasons also need to be taken into account. In Bangladesh, the main crop season consists of unirrigated crops. The introduction of irrigated winter crops may reduce acreage of unirrigated crops, thereby reducing the demand for labour and dampening the effect on wage. Therefore, the present chapter also examines the impact of irrigation on wage in non-irrigated season.

The above framework can be used to identify the village level factors which influence either the demand or supply of workers and thereby influence the wage. The village characteristics included in the present analysis are: percentage of large landowning households (who own more than 5 acres), land per household, percentage of landless households and percentage of irrigated area. Percentage of area irrigated has been included to represent the extent of technological change in

---

[3] A review and critique of existing theories is provided by Rahman (1993).

a village.[4] An alternative indicator of technological change is the extent of adoption of modern rice variety. Both indicators cannot be included in the same equation because of their high degree of colinearity. Extent of irrigation is preferred because this involves not only a substitution of local paddy varieties by modern varieties but also the prospect of growing other irrigated crops like wheat. Price of rice, the main staple, may have an impact on wage through its effect on either the demand or the supply of labour. A higher price may induce a larger labour supply (to generate a subsistence income). On the other hand, higher rice price may increase demand for labour through higher profitability. However, such impact will depend on the factors associated with inter-village variations of rice price, which are often quite complex. The net impact on wage depends on the balance of these forces.

Individual's characteristics have also been included to explain worker level variation of wage. Age and years of schooling are two variables included along the line of traditional earnings function where these variables capture efficiency variation. Family characteristics may also influence worker's motivation directly as well as indirectly through their effect on family income. Number of dependent members and number of male working members in a family are two such factors. Size of arable land owned by a household can affect the efficiency of labour through an influence on the workers' experience in farm work as well as by enabling them to ensure better nutritional standards.

8.3.1 Determinants of Employment

The above analysis indicates that the rise in wage associated with increased irrigation may or may not be accompanied by an increase in employment per household. Moreover, rural wage labourer households derive employment and income from multiple sources. Employment in agriculture is often supplemented by non-farm employment which consists mostly of low productive family employment. Therefore, an analysis of the impact of irrigation on employment should take into account these two components separately.

Whether the household is an appropriate unit for labour supply analysis may be a subject of controversy. The tradition of estimating a household labour supply function for rural households has been

---

[4] In the sample villages, little area is irrigated by traditional methods. DTW and STW account for more than 98 per cent of irrigated area and thus the percentage of irrigated area represents modern irrigation.

followed in the present chapter without entering into the question of who takes the decision about household labour supply and the intra-household allocation of employment (Sen, 1966).

In addition to household labour supply functions, individual labour supply has also been examined. This may have implications for policies related to the scope for further expansion of irrigation and more intensive labour use as well as for welfare of workers. Separate analysis of the determinants of the employment of individual workers also serves to present an alternative estimate of individual decision based model of labour supply.

Labour supply is determined by individual and family characteristics which influence a worker's motivation behind the choice of income earning work vs. leisure. Such motivation influencing labour supply also depends on the return to labour and income from other sources. The return to labour is given by the wage rate or the marginal product. An increase in the return to labour may raise labour supply, depending on whether the price effect is larger than the negative income effect. Similarly, other sources of income may also exert a negative income effect on labour supply. It will be of interest to examine the impact of various productivity enhancing factors on labour supply. Irrigation also enters into labour supply choice through the effect on productivity.

8.3.2 Determinants of Household Income

A major part of income of landless labourers comes from wage sources and is determined by wage rate and the amount of employment. Therefore, the determinants of wage and employment reveal the factors determining income. However, it may be useful to directly examine the association between income and the variables which determine factor quantity and factor prices. The other variables determining household income are the resource endowment of a family and the village situation.

Household endowments consist of land owned and family labour force in comparison to dependent members. Characteristics of workers in terms of age, education and marital status may be considered as additional aspects of labour endowment. Village characteristics like extent of irrigation, presence of electricity, land per household, extent of landlessness, etc., may influence the wage/marginal products of labour and may be considered as important determinants of household income.

8.4 Findings from Wage, Employment and Income Equations

Data used in this analysis come from a household level survey conducted by the Bangladesh Institute of Development Studies (BIDS) in 1995. The survey was conducted as part of a study on the "Evaluation of Small Scale Irrigation Sector Projects." Nine projects were selected purposively so that they cover the entire country. To assess the impact of irrigation projects, households from four villages of the project thana were surveyed. A total of 36 villages were covered. Households from each village were selected on the basis of stratified random sampling, landownership being the criterion for stratification. Since the projects have been purposively chosen, it cannot be claimed that the sample represents the national picture. However, the sample size is reasonably large to capture sufficient variation of the value of the variables used in the analysis.

8.4.1 Results of Wage Equations

Two equations have been estimated to analyse the determinants of wage. Wage in the months of May and December have been used as dependent variables in the equations with the same set of explanatory variables as hypothesised above. Month of May has peak activity for the irrigated winter paddy. December is the month of peak activity (harvesting time) for the monsoon paddy, which covers the largest acreage in the country. Thus the equations can also show whether the wage in different paddy seasons is determined by the same set of factors and whether the impact of these factors is similar in direction and magnitude. To capture the impact of irrigation, the share of villages' cultivated area irrigated has been used as an explanatory variable.

The personal and household characteristics included as explanatory variables are: age (LAGE), educational attainment (last class passed: LCLP), Gender dummy (with a value = 1 for female) (GENF), size of farm owned (LFS), number of dependent members in the family (LDEP), and number of male workers in the family (LEARN). The village characteristics include: cultivable land per household (LCLV), percentage of area irrigated (IRRG), percentage of landless households (PLLS), percentage of large landowning households (PLLO), price of paddy (LPP), percentage of area under sandy soil (SAND), percentage of area under clay soil (CLAY), percentage of high land (PHLT), and percentage of very low land (PVLL).

The dependent variable and the explanatory variables (except those in the form of dummy or percentage) are in logarithms, so that the coefficients are easy to interpret as elasticities. The sample size in each equation consists of all employed persons from our sample who actually worked in agriculture in that particular month.

The results are presented in Table 8.5. Age is not significant in any of the equations. Education is insignificant in the wage equation for May but is significant and negative in the equation for December. Thus the variables of usual human-capital-earnings equation are not relevant in the present case where the jobs are essentially of unskilled nature. Gender dummy with a value of one for female workers has a significantly negative coefficient. Women receive a lower wage in each period.

The influence of village level characteristics on wage has expected signs. Irrigation deserves special attention. Percentage of area irrigated has a significant and positive impact on wage rate in May, but the coefficient is insignificant for the wage in December. It is not unexpected that the impact of irrigation on wage operates only in the irrigated season when HYV paddy covers most of the cultivated area but not in other months.

Table 8.5: Determinants of Agricultural Wage

Explanatory+Variables in OLS Regression	Dependent Variable: Log of Wage in May		Dependent Variable: Log of Wage in December	
	Coefficient	t-value	Coefficient	t-value
LAGE	-0.02	-0.52	-0.02	-0.45
LCLP	-0.02	-1.06	-0.03	-1.73*
GENF	-0.36	-5.05***	-0.29	-3.07***
IRRG	0.001	1.89*	-0.00003	-0.05
PLLS	-0.002	-2.67***	-0.003	3.52***
PLLO	-0.002	-0.31	0.002	0.49
LCLV	-0.005	-0.20	-0.03	-1.4g
LPP	-0.07	-0.46	-0.01	-0.06
LFS	0.007	1.21	0.009	1.64
LEARN	-0.006	-0.18	0.02	-0.52
LDEP	0.045	2.13**	0.04	2.09**
CLAY	0.001	0.79	0.001	1.85*
SAND	-0.002	-2.40***	-0.002	-2.13***
PVLL	0.001	2.14**	0.001	1.03
PUT	-0.002	-3.26***	-0.001	-1.84*
CONSTANT	4.08	5.18***	3.89	5.45***
Adjusted R^2	0.47		0.27	
F	16.89***		7.80***	
N	273		273	

Note: *, ** and *** denote significant at less than .10, .05 and .01 levels of probability respectively.
+ Description of variables used in Tables 1 to 5 is provided in Annex Table 8.1A.
Source: Village and Household Survey 1992.

Extent of landlessness raises the supply of labour and has a significant negative influence on wage. In contrast, the percentage of large landowners did not have any significant influence on wage. This variable was expected to increase the demand for labour in a village. Insignificant coefficient of this variable may be due to the fact that medium and even small farms are found to hire labour and thus the per cent of large landowners alone does not have a significant influence on the demand for labour. Arable land per household does not have a significant impact on wage.

An increase in demand for labour associated with higher profitability due to higher paddy price is expected to raise wage. The results show that this is not the case. This variable has an insignificant and negative coefficient. High price of paddy is likely to be associated with low productivity of land in an area. Therefore, if land productivity is not adequately captured by other explanatory variables, paddy price captures this impact and is inversely related to wage. The coefficient of paddy price in wage determination equation based on cross sectional data is found to be negative and significant in studies for India and Thailand (Ramaswamy and Kandaswamy, 1994, Isvilanonda and Wattanutchariya, 1994). The studies do not, however, provide any explanation for the observed relationship. It should be recognised that there may be other factors which lie behind cross sectional variation of price and thus causing both high paddy price and low wage, which remains to be explored.

Family's land ownership has a positive impact on its worker's wage. This can be explained in terms of greater efficiency of own-farm-operator-cum-wage-labourers. Experience in own farm may increase the demand for such workers. Landownership may also increase the opportunity cost and hence supply price of labour.

Larger number of male workers within the family is expected to increase the total family income. This has a potential for increasing the efficiency of workers. This effect is statistically insignificant in both equations.

The number of dependent members in the family has a significant positive impact on wage. This is contrary to the expected effect through the impact on labour supply. Dependency pressure should increase the labour supply to meet the consumption needs of larger family. Then the question remains, why "dependents" have this clear positive impact on wage. Possible explanations are that those who have a larger consumption need from a large number of dependents may take up more arduous tasks and the wage per unit of time for harder work is higher whereas the variation in the nature of work is not captured in this data. Another possibility would be that the employers of these workers may derive benefits from unpaid services by some of the "dependent" members of the workers, which is included in the wage of the worker. Our data is inadequate to capture this phenomenon. More intensive probing is necessary to test the validity of such inter-linkages in the labour market.

The adjusted R-square in the equations are 0.47 and 0.27 respectively. The percentage of variation explained for December wage is low. This may be due to lack of explanatory variables to represent the extent of crop activity in this period.

8.4.2 Impacts of Irrigation on Employment: Findings

To analyse the household labour supply of agricultural labourers, two equations have been estimated: one, with agricultural employment and the other with non-agricultural employment as dependent variables.[5]

Household characteristics have been used as explanatory variables to capture the preference patterns regarding income generation and leisure. Household characteristics include: number of adult males, number of dependent members, size of landownership, percentage of sharecropped land, amount of income from remittances, age, gender and education of household head. Wage, paddy price, electricity in the village and per cent of area irrigated are village characteristics used as explanatory variables. The results are presented in Table 8.6.

Number of dependents does not have a significant influence. Number of adult male workers in the household has a significant positive impact on employment in each equation because labour supply is defined on household basis. Female-headed households are less involved in agriculture and the dummy for such households has a significant negative impact on agricultural employment.

Farm size is expected to raise productivity and increase employment in agriculture. This variable has a significant positive coefficient in the equation on agricultural employment. Remittance has a negative impact on agricultural employment. It has a positive impact on non-agricultural employment, where it can provide a source of required

---

[5] In the sample there has been no household with adult male members who were completely without employment. Therefore, households could be classified into two categories: agricultural labourers and others.

capital. Percentage of sharecropped land (in ones total operated land) has a significant positive impact on agricultural employment. Thus the disincentive impact of sharecropping has not been operative.

Table 8.6: Determinants of Employment of Rural Households

Explanatory Variables in OLS Regression	Log of Agricultural Employment Coefficient	t-value	Log of Other Employment Coefficient	t-value
LCLP	-0.11	-2.40***	0.23	1.25
LFS	0.03	2.3**	-0.22	-3.62***
LADMC	0.54	7.52***	1.49	5.27***
GENF	-0.49	-2.94***	1.01	1.54
LIRHR	-0.01	-1.13	0.09	2.16**
CLAY	-0.005	-0.26	-0.007	-0.88
SAND	-0.004	-1.57	0.02	2.32**
PVLL	-0.006	-4.83***	0.02	5.14***
PUT	0.002	1.14	-0.02	-3.04***
ELECTD	0.14	1.29	-0.14	-0.32
LDEP	0.06	1.15	-0.02	-0.10
LAVLWR	0.36	1.80*	-4.84	-6.07***
IRRG	-0.003	-1.58	-0.003	-0.50
LPPMP	-0.26	-0.83	1.43	1.15
LP	-0.007	0.42	-0.006	-0.87
SP	0.003	2.0**	-0.02	-3.71***
Constant	5:74	3.16***	12.17	1.69
Adjusted R^2	0.31		0.26	
F	10.81***		8.63***	
N	302		302	

Note: *, ** and *** denote significant at less than .10, .05 and .01 levels of probability respectively.
Source: BIDS Survey, 1992.

Land characteristics in terms of soil type do not have a significant impact. Percentage of low land has a significant negative impact on agricultural employment and the reverse for non-agricultural employment. Percentage of area irrigated in a village does not have a significant impact on either agricultural or non-agricultural employment. It goes somewhat contrary to the expectation that increased productivity of modern agricultural technology is translated into increased employment obtained by wage labourer households. The influence of electricity in the village is also not significant. Paddy price has an insignificant impact on both types of employment.

Results of individual employment equations are shown in Table 8.7. These equations have been estimated for the heads of households. The reasons for using this set are: (a) information has been obtained from heads of households, and therefore information on their employment will be more reliable, and (b) criterion of employment decision of heads and others in a household may be different and the specific criteria used for two groups are not well formulated by current theories. Therefore, the use of data for only the heads of the households maintains uniformity of choice criterion.

Table 8.7: Determinants of Employment of a Rural Worker

Explanatory Variables in OLS Regression	Log of Agricultural Employment Coefficient	t-value	Log of Other Employment Coefficient	t-value
LAGE	-0.06	-0.06	-0.13	-0.23
LCLP	-0.08	-1.93*	0.36	1.88*
MHH	0.06	0.51	-0.33	-0.54
LFS	0.03	2.17***	-0.20	-2.99**
LADMC	-0.08	-1.08	-0.31	-0.82
GENF	-0.69	-3.25***	1.37	1.28
LIRHR	-0.02	-1:73*	0.11	2.50***
CLAY	0.003	1.51	0.01	-1.68
SAND	-0.005	-2.45***	0.02	2.22"
PVLL	-0.006	-6.33***	0.03	5.65'"
PHLT	0.002	1.86*	-0.006	-1.00
ELECTD	-0.09	-0.91	-0.48	-0.99
LDEP	0.04	0.74	-0.24	-0.98
LAVLWR	0.59	3.45***	-	-
IRRG	-0.007	-0.48	-0.003	-0.46
LPPMB	0.19	0.69	0.93	0.69
LP	0.007	0.51	-0.005	-0.67
SP	0.007	0.62	-0.02	-3.04***
Constant	2.61	1.64	-1.73	-0.23
Adjusted R^2	0.28		0.18	
F	7.51***		4.87**	
N	302		302	

Note: *, ** and *** denote significant at less than .10, .05 and .01 levels of probability respectively.
Source: BIDS Survey, 1992.

The results of the equations for this group show marked similarity with the household labour supply function. Most variables have the same type of influences. Two additional variables describing personal characteristics have been included. These are age and marital status. Both have insignificant coefficients. The variable "number of adult male" has implication for total earning capacity of a household and thus represents an income effect on labour supply. The coefficient of this variable is insignificant, which implies the absence of income effect. Impact of the extent of irrigation is insignificant.

8.4.3 Income Equations

Two separate equations have been estimated (Table 8.8) to analyse household income from agriculture and non-agriculture. The same set of variables as in the wage and employment equations are included as explanatory variables.

Table 8.8: Determinants of Crop Income and Other Income of Wage Labour Households

Explanatory Variables in OLS Regression	Log of Agricultural Income Coefficient	t-value	Log of Other Income Coefficient	t-value
LAGE	-0.05	-0.22	0.67	1.50
LGLP	-0.13	-1.63	0.26	1.64
MHH	-0.14	-0.58	-0.63	-1.25
LFS	0.14	5.23***	-0.05	-0.87
LADMC	0.66	4.32***	0.50	1.60
GENF	-1.06	-2.49***	-1.72	-0.82
IRHRD	-0.52	-3.56***	1.29	4.30***
CLAY	0.005	1.39	-0.01	-1.87*
SAND	-0.005	-1.43	0.006	0.72
PVLL	-0.007	-3.46***	0.02	4.37***
PHLT	0.002	0.77	-0.002	-0.34
PLLS	-0.01	-3.72***	-0.009	1.09
ELECTD	0.23	1.25	0.44	1.19
LDEP	0.21	2.16**	-0.02	-0.08
LCLV	0.06	0.65	-0.17	-0.95
IRRG	-0.001	-0.52	-0.008	-1.64
LP	0.006	2.35**	-9.99	-0:18
SP	0.002	0.83	0.002	0.36
Constant	9.10	10.60***	6.43	3.64***
Adjusted R^2	0.26		0.12	
F	6.99***		3.36**	
N	302		302	

Note: *, ** and *** denotes significant at less than .10, .05 and .01 levels of probability respectively.

Source: BIDS Survey, 1992.

Agricultural income is positively and significantly influenced by farm size, number of dependent members and number of working age members. Individual's characteristics in terms of age, marital status and education do not have any significant impact. Percentage of low land and sandy soil are observed to have negative influences; these variables work through their negative impacts on labour demand and wage rate. Electricity in the village has a positive but insignificant impact. The coefficient of the extent of irrigated area in the village is not significant for wage labour households (Table 8.8). For farm households (Table 8.9), "percentage of operated land of a household under irrigation" has a significant positive impact on agricultural income.

Table 8.9: Determinants of Crop Income and Other Income of Farm Households

Explanatory Variables in OLS Regression	Log of Agricultural Income Coefficient	Log of Agricultural Income t-value	Log of Other Income Coefficient	Log of Other Income t-value
LAGE	-0.05	-0.10	-0.29	-1.48
LCLP	-0.64	-4.61***	0.27	4.82***
MHH	-0.59	-1.11	0.51	2.34**
LFS	1.19	19.78***	-0.16	-6.38***
LADMC	0.96	3.68***	0.47	4.43***
GENF	-1.30	-1.88*	-0.09	-0.33
IRHRD	-2.68	-10.15***	1.13	10.46***
CLAY	0.02	2.75***	0.003	1.25
SAND	-0.002	0.21	-0.005	-1.04
PVLL	0.01	2.18**	-0.003	-1.70*
PHLT	0.03	3.72***	-0.004	-1.28
PLLS	0.01	-1.41	-0.002	-0.49
ELECTD	0.82	2.41***	-0.20	-1.43
LDEP	0.45	2.28**	0.21	1.57**
LCLV	0.52	2.46***	-0.12	-1.38
HIRR	0.008	2.64***	-0.001	-0.82
LP	0.05	4.76***	0.002	0.54
SP	0.04	6.78***	-0.007	-2.90***
Constant	-1.49	-0.67	10.48	11.42***
Adjusted R^2	0.54		0.25	
F	45.68***		13.21***	
N	676		676	

Note: *, ** and *** denote significant at less than .10, .05 and .01 level of probability respectively.

Source: BIDS Survey, 1992.

In the equation of non-agricultural income, remittance money has a positive impact, whereas landownership has a negative impact. Education of head of household and the number of adult male have positive influence on income. Extent of irrigation in the village has a negative impact, which approaches significance. This implies that irrigated villages have less scope for non-agricultural activities.

These finding confirm that modern irrigation helps to increase farm income and leave the question open as to whether the positive impact trickles down to the wage labourers.

8.5 Concluding Observations

The present study finds that the impact of the extent of irrigation on wage rate in the harvesting time in the non-irrigated season is insignificant and for the irrigated crop season it is significantly positive. Thus a consideration of the findings of wage equations alone provides grounds for optimism about the trickle down of the benefits of irrigated agriculture to the wage labourers.

This study has made an attempt to supplement the findings on positive changes in wage by direct evidence on impact on employment and income of labourer households. Irrigation has no significant impact on employment. Since wage rate increases in only one season and remains unchanged in other seasons, and there is no change in employment, income changes are unlikely to have been significant. The analyses show that the impact of irrigation on household income of wage labourers is insignificant.

The question remains why irrigation has no impact on employment. An increase in household employment through irrigation may have reached its limit because labourers in the irrigated villages are already working the maximum possible days during the peak season of the irrigated crop. These workers work 25 to 30 days during these months. Irrigation cannot remove underemployment during the slack periods of September and October and the present level represents a maximum employment that can be achieved with the use of irrigation in the winter season.

Part of the explanation lies in the use of migrant labourers. It has already been mentioned that the increased employment generated by irrigated agriculture is shared by labourers of the non-irrigated villages.

It actually implies that there are positive gains from irrigation and agricultural growth for wage labourers as a whole. A significant rise of wage in irrigated season is actually an indicator that labour productivity and labour demand has increased. The gain is not evident in the form of higher income of workers in the irrigated area, because it is shared by a larger number of wage labourers from both irrigated and non-irrigated areas. Moreover, a rise of agricultural wage, even if it occurs in the irrigated season, is likely to have a positive impact on non-farm wages, both in rural and urban areas. National wage data (MoF, various years) show that after the mid-1990s real wages in both agriculture and other non-farm sectors have risen. Such a rise demonstrates that an increase of wage in irrigated agriculture creates a chain of positive influence on non-farm wage.

Annex

Table 8.1A: Description of Variables used in Regression Analysis

LAGE	Age of the person
LCLP	Last class passed
MHH	Dummy for marital status (married = 1)
WF	Dummy for marital status (widow = 1)
GENF	Dummy for gender (female = 1)
LAVLWR	Village wage rate
LFS	Size of farm land owned by a household
LDEP	Number of dependent members
LADMC	Number of adult male members
LEARN	Number of working members
LIRHR	Amount received as rent, remittance, etc.
IRHRD	Whether receives rent, remittance (yes = 1)
CLAY	Percentage of clay type land in a village
SAND	Percentage of sand type land in a village
PVLL	Percentage of very low land in a village
PHLT	Percentage of high land in a village
LPP	Paddy price in a village
PLLO	Percentage of large landowners
PLLS	Percentage of landless
SP	Percentage of share cropped land in a household's cultivated land
LP	Percentage of leased in land in a household's cultivated land
ELECTD	Whether village has electricity (yes = 1)
IRRG	Percentage of irrigated area in a village
HIRR	Percentage of a household's cultivated area irrigated
LCLV	Cultivable land per household

CHAPTER 9

Youth Unemployment and Demographic Dividend

9.1 Introduction

The densely populated low-income countries of South Asia have experienced high rates of growth of labour force associated with high population growth during the last few decades. Prospect of utilisation of the growing youth labour force provides an important basis for their recent optimism about accelerating economic growth. The experiences of rapidly growing economies of Asia also illustrate the utilisation of demographic dividends for achieving high economic growth (Bloom and Williamson, 1998, Phang, 2003). The present chapter focuses on the "potential demographic dividend" in Bangladesh which takes the form of growing youth labour force.

In fact, the growing youth labour force has often been highlighted as the demographic dividend. It is expected to substitute other productive resources and help labour-intensive growth. Also, this segment is likely to be the more dynamic component of the labour market. In recent years the shortage of skilled labour for the modern sectors is being felt and in this context youth labour force can play an important role.

Younger labour force requires separate analysis because this group faces distinct types of demand which is likely to be generated by separate sets of employers. Youth labour force may face additional vulnerability because of their age. The transition of school to workforce is often difficult, especially for youth from low-income families, who are likely to enter the labour force earlier than others.

Youth labour force did not receive adequate attention in the context of analysis of Bangladesh's labour market. The assumption that they enter the labour market smoothly through family employment contributed to the lack of attention in the past. In an economy dominated by family employment, the entry of youth labour force is considered as an automatic process where they are first engaged as unpaid workers in family farm/enterprise. But this option may not be available for the youth labour force that receive education and aspire to move to new occupations and to paid jobs.

The objective of the present chapter is to examine whether a potential demographic dividend exists in Bangladesh and the features of youth labour market. The potential depends on the growth of youth labour force and the quality of youth population. It also depends on young persons' actual participation in the labour force and unemployment rates in this age group. This chapter presents an analysis of recent changes in these indicators. Although various policy papers including the Sixth Five Year Plan of the Government of Bangladesh have highlighted the role of "Demographic Dividend," research studies on this issue and on youth labour supply have been lacking. The present analysis can provide guidance for policies for future utilisation of youth labour force.

The chapter has been organised as follows:

Section 9.1 includes the background, objectives and rationale of the study and notes on data.

Section 9.2 examines the presence of potential demographic dividend in Bangladesh by analysing data on youth population and youth labour force.

Section 9.3 highlights a special feature of the youth population, i.e., under-enumeration of female youth population.

Section 9.4 discusses the age specific labour force participation rate (LFPR) and link between youth and old-age groups' labour force participation.

Section 9.5 discusses the quality of youth labour force and the sector and type of youth employment.

Section 9.6 focuses on youth unemployment.

Section 9.7 presents observations based on qualitative data on unemployment of youth labour force.

Section 9.8 provides a summary of findings.

9.1.1 Notes on Data

This chapter is based on secondary data provided by National Sample Surveys, in particular by Bangladesh Labour Force Survey (LFS) Reports of various rounds. Other secondary sources used in the study include various publications of the Bangladesh Bureau of Statistics (BBS), Planning Commission and various government ministries.

For a more in-depth analysis of the determinants of youth LFPR, unit record data from the latest round of the Labour Force Survey (conducted in 2010) have been re-analysed. In addition to national sample survey data, the views of some young job aspirants and young female employees of readymade garment (RMG) sector have been sought through case studies and focus group discussion (FGD) sessions.

9.2 Growth of Youth Labour Force and Size of Potential Demographic Dividend[1]

Table 9.1 shows that the sizes of youth labour force (aged 15 to 29 years) were respectively 14.5 and 20.9 million in 2000 and 2010. During this period about 6.4 million youth have joined the labour force in Bangladesh. During the two sub periods of 2000 to 2006 and 2006 to 2010, average annual growth of youth labour force was 3.48 per cent and 4.09 per cent respectively (Table 9.1). In 2010, 36.9 per cent of total labour force came from the youth group (15 to 29 years), which was higher than the share in 2006. This can be considered as a demographic dividend (of course in a potential sense) because this has resulted mainly from the growth of population and only a small increment resulted from the rise of labour force participation rate (considering no growth of youth population). Growth rates of youth population were 1.93 and 3.46 per cent per year during the 2000-2006 period and 2006-2010 period respectively. LFPR among youth increased from 51.7 per cent in 2006 to 53.2 per cent in 2010. Increment in youth labour force due to the rise of LFPR was only 0.45 million. Increment due to population growth was 2.65 million. During the 2010-2013 period, the growth of youth labour force and especially the component coming from the growth of youth population has gone through a decline (Table 9.1).

Bangladesh has reached the peak of the demographic dividend as population growth rate has significantly slowed down since the early 1990s (MoF, various years). Taking 18 years as the time from birth to entry into labour force, the rate of growth of youth labour force may as well decline in the coming years. Thus the potential demographic dividend will continue to exist but may grow at a decelerated pace.

---

[1] Sections 9.2 to 9.7 include edited version of parts of Rahman (2014).

However, a rise of labour force participation rate among women may help sustain the accelerated growth of youth labour force. With positive growth of youth population and labour force, it will be possible to continue human capital development for a part of the youth and still have a sufficient increase in growth of current youth labour force. This may not, however, be possible after a couple of years when the growth of youth population and youth labour force slows down.

Table 9.1: Growth of Youth Population and Youth Labour Force

Indicator	2000	2006	2010	2013
Youth Population (mill.)	30.6	34.3	39.3	43.2
Average growth of youth population (%) per year	-	1.9	3.5	3.3
Youth Labour force (mill.)	14.5	17.8	20.9	23.4
Average growth of youth labour force (%) per year	-	3.5	4.1	3.9
LFPR	47.4	51.7	53.2	54.1
Youth's Share in total labour force (%)	38.1	35.8	36.9	38.5
Increment of YLF due to population increase (between 2006 and 2010, in million)			2.6	2.1
Increment of YLF due to rise of LFPR (between 2006 and 2010, in million)			0.5	0.4

Source: BBS (various years): Labour Force Survey.

9.3 Youth Labour Force Under-enumeration: Missing Female Youth

Proper utilisation of the potential demographic dividend requires a correct enumeration of its availability. Therefore, it is important to ask whether we have counted the youth population correctly. It is well known that population census or large scale surveys suffer from age misreporting. Moreover, under-enumeration of female population is often substantial in the developing countries of Asia and Bangladesh is no exception. Apart from overall under-enumeration, this problem is more pervasive when one comes to certain special age groups: these are 10-14 years and 15-19 years aged women. Existing social taboo and violence against young women discourage reporting the presence of girls in these age groups. Another feature relevant here is that the marriage of women aged less than 18 years is prohibited by law. Therefore, data on married young girls are suppressed.

On the basis of the LFS 2006, sex ratios (number of male/number of female) in the three age groups 15-19, 20-24 and 25-29 were 1.31,

.88 and .79 respectively, whereas the overall sex ratio was 104.13. In 2010, these were 1.10, .82 and .86 respectively.

The sex ratio and the number of male and female population in these age groups reveal an interesting feature. In 2010, male population in the 15-19 age group exceeded female population by 687,000, whereas in the 20-24 years age group female population exceeded by 1328,000 (Table 9.2). Such a large jump cannot be imagined to occur due to any demographic or related reasons. This indicates age misreporting. Ages of women who were actually 15 to 19 years old were reported as higher. This may have been due to laws related to age bar on marriage and entry into labour force. The latter is even a more serious source of underestimation when it comes to labour force. In most surveys digit preference in age reporting is observed, but such large under-enumeration of young women (in comparison to men in this age group) reveals serious social bias against this age group. In 2006, under enumeration of 15-19 aged women was even more serious. In this age group, there were 1.455 million more men than women, the sex ratio being 1.31.

Table 9.2: Under-enumeration of Female Youth Population

Age	Share of Total Population (%)				2006			2010		
	2006		2010		Total Population ('000)			Total Population ('000)		
	Male	Female	Male	Female	Male	Female	M/F	Male	Female	M/F
15-19	9.3	7.3	10.1	9.4	6496	4941	1.3	7575	6888	1.1
20-24	8.0	9.5	7.9	9.9	5600	6379	.9	5929	7257	.8
25-29	6.9	9.1	7.1	8.5	4806	6096	.8	5353	6251	.9

Source: Calculated from the LFS 2006 and LFS 2010.

Such under-enumeration of female population and female labour force in the age group 15-19 can have serious adverse implications for appropriate policies and programmes for young women's health service provision and employment generation.

9.4 Youth Labour Force Participation: Trends and Implication

Youth LFPR is likely to depend on supply-side factors like school enrolment rates and its changes and the environment for investment on human capital. In addition, demand- side forces may act in either direction. Discouragement hypothesis predicts a decline of youth labour force participation rate during economic downswing. In the discussion of youth employment crisis during recent years, a recurrent hypothesis is that the economic downswing caused by the financial crisis in different parts of the world leads to high unemployment rate, which, in turn, discourages the young persons' entry into labour force.

Youth LFPR data for Bangladesh during 2000 to 2010 are shown in Tables 9.1 and 9.2. Data show that youth labour force participation rate has risen between 2000 and 2010. Gender disaggregated data, however, show that the picture is not quite comfortable. Labour force participation rate of male and female youth shows that the former has gone through a decline while female labour force participation rate has increased (Table 9.3). The rise of female LFPR has been, at least partly, due to better enumeration in recent LFS. The decline of male youth's labour force participation rate, to some extent, supports the discouragement hypothesis mentioned above. Rising school enrolment alone cannot explain the decline, because the decline has taken place in all three age groups, 15-19, 20-24, and 25-29, and in the last group enrolment in educational institution is negligible.

9.4.1 Age Specific LFPR

Next we proceed to compare the LFPR among youth and older population and the changes in the age group-wise LFPR.

Changes of LFPR among youth and older population may be linked through various socio-cultural features of our society. Before presenting the relevant data, it will be useful to highlight the related socio-cultural context.

In low-income countries like Bangladesh, state provision of old age care or financial support and pension schemes for the aged are provided only by formal sector employers, especially government. For the rest of the aged population, there is hardly any old age security. Society takes the pride that parents and elderly relatives are respected and cared for and the younger members of ones own family are in direct responsibility of such care. The distant relatives and society as a whole may oversee the matters and advise. A share of the actual provisioning and care may be borne by relatives and rich households.

Although these social relationships are supposed to be based on love and respect, economic and financial aspects are no less important. Parents spend their money and effort to raise the children, so it is natural to expect that when they are old the young children will look after the parents. Thus, it may be expected that with rising employment opportunities for younger persons, their LFPR will increase and as they take care of the aged, LFPR among the older groups will decline.

Changes of LFPR by five years age group show some interesting features. Data (Tables 9.3 and 9.4) show that the above mentioned socio-cultural expectations are, to some extent, borne out in reality.

Table 9.3: Labour Force Participation Rate among Youth and Older Population: 2000 to 2010

(Per Cent)

Age (yrs.)	2000	2006	2010
15-19	41.7	41.7	39.4
20-24	47.0	53.0	56.7
25-29	54.2	60.8	66.6
30-34	60.8	64.7	70.8
35-39	63.7	66.2	72.8
40-44	66.6	68.2	72.8
45-49	66.0	68.8	74.3
50-54	60.6	66.8	56.1
55-59	62.4	62.9	51.9
60-64	48.8	55.8	45.0
65+	37.4	38.7	34.8

Source: BBS (various years): Labour Force Survey.

Table 9.4: LFPR among Male and Female Youth and Older Groups

(Per Cent)

Age (yrs.)	Male 2000	Male 2006	Male 2010	Female 2000	Female 2006	Female 2010
15-19	55.8	62.9	48.4	27.3	13.8	29.4
20-24	74.0	80.4	75.9	26.3	29.0	41.0
25-29	91.3	95.3	92.2	27.1	33.7	44.7
30-34	95.7	98.7	97.3	26.5	34.9	46.6
35-39	98.2	98.8	98.3	25.7	34.8	47.6
40-44	97.8	97.7	98.0	26.6	35.1	47.7
45-49	97.6	97.7	97.4	23.4	32.6	46.2

Source: BBS (various years): Labour Force Survey.

A comparison of data for 2000, 2006 and 2010 shows a decline of LFPR among 55 years and above age groups, while LFPR among younger groups have risen (Tables 9.3 and 9.4). The other feature revealed by age-specific participation rates is that labour force participation rate is the highest among 40 to 50 years aged. There are important gender differences in the pattern of LFPR. During 2000-2010, male LFPR among age group 15 to 34 has gone through a decline and for the older groups it has increased. Female LFPR has increased continuously along all age groups.

9.5 Education of Youth Labour Force[2]

Prospect of youth labour force's contribution to growth depends on the quality of the youth labour force. Quality of labour force, reflected in education and skill development, determines the productivity of youth labour force and its contribution to the economy. Data on education of youth labour force have been presented below (Table 9.5). The share of youth labour force without any education has considerably declined and the shares with a few years' education have increased in recent years. The share with education above SSC level has not increased. These shares are likely to increase with a gestation gap and are expected to change within next five years or so. Studies reveal that there is significant inequality in access to education (Chapter 10 of this volume). Inequality between rural and urban areas and among income groups has been glaring and this may hamper the utilisation of youth labour force.

Table 9.5: Level of Education of Youth Labour Force (15-29 years): 2000 to 2010

(Per Cent)

Level of Education	2000			2006			2010		
	Total	Male	Female	Total	Male	Female	Total	Male	Female
Total	100.0	100.0	100.0	100.0	100.0	100.0	100.0	100.0	100.0
No schooling	38.6	34.3	49.4	27.75	25.87	33.17	26.9	27.4	25.9
Class i-v	26.3	28.0	22.2	28.90	29.54	27.04	27.4	29.4	24.1
Class vi-viii	15.0	16.8	10.4	17.56	18.06	16.12	19.2	18.5	20.5
Class ix-x	6.7	7.0	6.7	10.38	10.76	9.28	13.3	11.6	16.3
SSC/HSC & equivalent	9.4	9.6	9.1	11.72	12.06	11.75	10.7	10.3	11.5
Degree & above	4.0	4.3	3.2	3.44	3.47	3.37	2.5	2.8	1.7

Source: BBS (various years): Labour Force Survey.

---

[2] Section 9.5 and 9.6 are based on data from the LFS 2010. The LFS 2013 data have been released after the manuscript was finalised.

9.5.1 Structural Change of Youth Employment

Sector and status (type) of employment have been used as indicators for assessment of change of structure of employment. As discussed in Chapter 6, agriculture accounts for the dominant share of employment in Bangladesh. This is true for young workers as well as older ones. The labour market is characterised by preponderance of self and (unpaid) family employment.

Table 9.6: Distribution of Youth Employment by Status in Employment: 2000 to 2010

(Per Cent)

	2000	2006	2010
Total	100.0	100.0	100.0
Regular paid employee	19.8	15.1	17.0
Employer	0.1	0.3	0.1
Self-employed	32.0	27.6	18.4
Unpaid family worker	21.7	32.2	39.6
Irregular paid worker (agri., non-agri.)	26.4	22.2	24.4
Domestic worker/maid servant	-	0.7	-
Paid/unpaid apprentice	-	1.1	-
Others	-	0.7	-

Source: BBS (various years): Labour Force Survey.

Table 9.7: Distribution of Youth Employment by Broad Sector: 2006 to 2010

(Number in '000)

Broad Sectors	2006	2010	% Change
Agriculture	7170 (43.9%)	10057 (51.9)	40.3
Industry	3183 (19.5%)	3931 (20.3%)	23.5
Service	5958 (36.5%)	5361 (27.7%)	-10.1

Source: BBS (various years): Labour Force Survey.

Data on sector and status of employment among youth labour force have been shown in Tables 9.6 and 9.7. Agriculture accounted for 52 per cent of young workers in 2010. This share has risen substantially during the 2006-2010 period. The share of industry has slightly increased, while the share of service has been on the decline. The changes in the sectoral pattern are consistent with the changes in status of employment. Within agriculture self/family employment predominates and therefore with a rising share of agriculture in youth employment, it is no surprise that the role of unpaid family employment has increased.

Table 9.8 shows that during 2006-2010, number of young women in agriculture increased from 2,562 thousand to 5,068 thousand (by 98 per cent) while the number of young male workers increased by only 316 thousand (6.8 per cent).

In fact, a large share of women in the labour force actually is engaged in family's livestock raising activities. Therefore, with rising LFPR of young women, the weight of agriculture and unpaid family employment has been on the increase. However, the growing share of youth labour force in agriculture cannot be solely attributed to women's growing involvement in family's agriculture, especially livestock unit. Data show that the share of male youth employed in agriculture has also risen during 2006-2010 period. In fact, both share and number of male youth employed in non-agriculture have slightly declined during this period. Thus there has been a decline in the labour absorption capacity of the non-agricultural sectors. Otherwise, young workers show preference for jobs in non-farm sector, which is evident from the qualitative observations in the following sub-sections.

Table 9.8: Growth of Young Labour Force in Different Sectors of Employment

Sector/Status	2010 ('000) Male	2010 ('000) Female	2006 ('000) Male	2006 ('000) Female	% of Total Youth (2010) Male	% of Total Youth (2010) Female	% Change Male	% Change Female
Agriculture	4924	5068	4608	2562	40.3	71.0	6.8	98.0
Non-agriculture	7286	2065	7611	1530	59.7	29.0	-4.3	35.0

Source: LFS (various years).

9.6 Unemployment Rate among Youth

Youth labour force, who are new entrants in the labour force, are more likely to face unemployment than the older ones. Unemployment rate among 15 to 29 years old labour force was 7.5 per cent compared to 4.5 per cent for the entire labour force (Table 9.9). Higher unemployment rate among youth prevails not only in Bangladesh but also in most other middle-income countries (World Bank, 2007, Kapsos, 2008). Youth unemployment rate has increased to 8.1 per cent in 2013.

In Bangladesh, high rate of youth unemployment is actually due to higher rate of unemployment among educated youth. Table 9.10 shows that unemployment rate was higher among educated youth compared to those without education. This pattern, to some extent, reflects that the educated youth are from better-off families and can afford to remain unemployed. Nonetheless, it implies wastage of human capital. Educated unemployment tends to generate a vicious circle through its discouraging effect on future private investment on education. Young persons without education come from poorer households and can hardly afford to remain without employment. Unemployment rate in 2010 was only 4.3 per cent in this group. These workers usually engage in the casual labour market where continuous dearth of employment opportunity is rather unusual. Unskilled and uneducated workers seeking casual jobs do not therefore face continuous unemployment. Nonetheless, for the same reason they face greater risk of underemployment. Table 9.10 shows that unemployment rates were higher among youth with education of grades IX, X, SSC and HSC. It actually implies that the quality of education is such that these attainments do not make the young persons employable.

Table 9.9: Unemployment Rate among Youth Labour Force: 2000 to 2013

(Per Cent)

Sex	2000	2006	2010	2013
Male	9.5	7.2	6.8	7.0
Female	15.0	10.7	8.5	9.7
All	11.0	8.1	7.5	8.1

Source: BBS (various years): Labour Force Survey.

Unemployment rate among youth slightly declined during 2006-2010. Both male and female youth labour force experienced the improvement (Table 9.9).

However, the rate of unemployment among youth labour force in Bangladesh (and also among aged labour force as discussed in Chapter 6) appears to be incredibly low and it is lower than the current rate in many high-income economies. Therefore, a discussion of the factors contributing to such low rate is pertinent.

The very low unemployment rate has been largely due to the definition used by labour force surveys. The definitional problems arise from two sources. First, the question for identifying the unemployed is such that hardly anyone fits into it. It consists of two parts: whether one was without work for last one week and whether one was willing to work or was looking for work.

Being "without work" can be afforded only by persons from rich households. Moreover, only a fraction of an hour per day spent on income earning activities means that one has the status of "employed" and therefore the chances of being unemployed (without any work at all) is small in Bangladeshi labour market where self/family employment is predominant.[3]

Intergroup comparison of adult and youth labour force and those with various levels of education (as has been done in Tables 9.9 and 9.10) is still possible because underestimation affects all groups similarly.

Table 9.10: Unemployment Rate among Educated Youth

(Per Cent)

Level of Education	2010 Male	2010 Female	2006 Male	2006 Female	2000 Male	2000 Female
No education	3.3	6.1	3.7	5.7	3.0	4.9
Grade I-V	5.1	7.1	4.1	7.7	7.7	15.6
Grade VI-VIII	7.4	8.1	6.8	13.0	8.0	23.2
Grade IX-X	10.8	10.2	9.7	16.7	25.6	39.0
SSC, HSC Equivalent	15.4	13.9	16.9	21.3	23.0	39.8
Degree & above	7.6	15.4	18.6	21.4	20.8	28.5
All	6.8	8.5	7.2	10.7	9.5	15.0

Source: BBS (various years): Labour Force Survey.

9.7 Views of Unemployed Youth[4]

Employment prospects of educated youth, especially from poorer households, need special attention because of the special features of their labour supply. They are young, enthusiastic, and inadequately qualified.

FGD sessions and case studies were conducted among such boys and girls in the 17-22 age range.[5] Discussions centred on the questions

---

[3] The reasons of underestimation of unemployment have been discussed in Chapter 6, which apply to youth unemployment as well.

[4] This section draws from Rahman (2004a).

[5] Full fledged survey data is required for statistical test of hypotheses presented here.

of what type of employment (paid employment or self-employment) they sought, the experiences of job search and future plans. Apart from the information, the ways in which they approached the issue, the passionate views about why they cannot find jobs and still more, the determination and desperateness to do some earnings revealed the social wastage of youthful labour force. If appropriately manoeuvred, these unemployed persons are capable of providing an elastic supply of hired hands for local industries. The following insights may help adoption of short run and long run policies for this group (Case studies have been presented in Boxes 9.1 and 9.2).

a. There are two types of young persons: (i) those with poor school performance (was unsuccessful in SSC examinations or dropped out before sitting in the examinations) and the second is the better performers who crossed either the SSC or the HSC level. The difference between the two groups is not merely the certificate. The actual attainments of the groups vary to a significant extent. Those who dropped out without an SSC certificate claimed that the family's poverty has been the reason. After they wrote one or two lines in the small pieces of paper where they were requested to write about their future plans, it was evident that their Bengali

---

Box 9.1: Views and Wishes of Unemployed Youth: Results of FGD Sessions among School Dropouts

- I want any job. I do not get job because I do not have SSC level education. The reality is that without links with influential persons, one cannot find a job. In fact, our social system is not good and that is why I do not get a job (Zakir Hossain).
- I wish to go abroad. Yes, I shall go (Aminul Islam).
- I dream about getting a job (Masud Rana).
- It may be possible to get a job (Airin Parvin).
- If I do not get a job, I may do the work of an electrician and that can ensure survival (Ariful Shujon).
- I want self-employment and a solid ground to move forward (Shahriar Bhuiyan).
- I want to learn sewing and earn (Lipi Aktar).
- I dream about a job (Anjana Rani).
- I hope to set up a poultry farm if I get some seed capital (Anil Das).
- I want to get a job which gives enough income to run our family consisting of my mother and two younger sisters (Najmul Islam).

language skill is extremely poor. It can be assumed that other cognitive skills are poorer. With such levels of attainment, it is not surprising that they are waiting for periods ranging from one to four years without any employment opportunity.

They were asked whether they prefer paid job or self-employment. They expressed their desperate need to do any work and have independent earnings irrespective of the type of work. Some of them showed preference for self-employment. This may, to some extent, have been due to the already acquired knowledge that job market does not hold a promise of regular employment for job seekers with education less than SSC.

Box 9.2: Case Studies of Unemployed Educated Youth

Case Study 1
Md. Abdul Hakim, of village Bhringaraj in Kaliakair district was a young energetic man of age 21 with a HSC level education. He obtained second division in SSC and third division in HSC which he had completed two years ago. During these two years he could not get a job or did not even try for a job because he knew that he would not find a job with his poor grades in HSC. His plan was to learn driving at a local training school and then he could try to go abroad with a job.

Case Study 2
In case study 1 and in many other similar cases young persons expressed interest to go abroad with unskilled or semi-skilled jobs. But this may not be a permanent solution. They go with contracts for short periods. At the end of the contract period they return. Bashir (22 years age, SSC in 3rd division) went through such experience, worked for six months and then returned to Bangladesh. He was unemployed.

Case Study 3
Anjana Rani of Gazipur was unsuccessful in her SSC examination. She was engaged in private tutoring. She went to a well known hospital at Mirzapur to try for a "nursing" job. She thought that she needed right contacts (I do not have links with the right persons) for getting in.

Case Study 4
Sheikh Muhammad Hannan, a young person of age 24, obtained HSC degree but with a third division. He was trying for a job and for this purpose he took help of his maternal uncle, a lawyer. But Hannan preferred "business" (trading type self-employment).

---

b. Everyone in the group identified the economic condition of his/her family as "not good" and implied that their families have inadequate means for covering the basic expenses of the family. Since many of the boys and girls expressed their interest about self-employment, the discussion was geared to identify the barriers to their entry into such activities. The hypothesis with which the discussion initiated was that the availability of seed capital would be of foremost importance. In the course of the discussion, it became clear that the parents, brothers or other relatives could help with small amount of money and there would be scope for mobilising funds from microcredit institutions. The lack of experience and lack of relevant business skill emerged as the binding constraints in most cases. Most of them did not possess a specific or even a general skill for economic activities. One girl said that she had tailoring skill but not adequate for setting up a shop.

c. Having identified skill and knowledge about business techniques as the relevant constraints, probing was done about how they could improve the relevant endowments. They discussed the possibility of acquiring the skills and expressed their eagerness to undertake training. They were prepared to pay at least a part of the cost. When asked about their awareness about the supply of specific courses, it was found that such awareness was lacking. Various government organisations as well as training NGOs operate programmes for young job seekers. While most courses are offered to better performers among SSC/HSC holders, some courses may suit low performers. The FGD sessions were held in villages within 30 kilometres of Dhaka city and within 10 kilometres of the local district headquarters. Yet there was a lack of awareness about the availability of training programmes. The situation in more interior regions is likely to be worse. The lack of basic skills of arithmetic and language may act as constraints to entry into many training activities. Moreover, the younger persons can put technical training into use only if it is supplemented by management skill development. Both government and private facilities must also work towards establishing better links with the prospective clienteles. Therefore, to impart useful training the courses are likely to be of long duration and that would imply high cost per trainee.

d. For most of the young unemployed persons, a regular job was a dream. To bring them down to reality, they were asked whether they were ready to take up heavy work and long hours as required in many industries. Most of them did not mind except one or two (out of 14 in the group), although they qualified by stating that if they were remunerated adequately. This was then followed up by discussions on expected salary.[6] They were quite realistic, as no one mentioned above a level more than 30 per cent of the lowest salary of RMG employees. This was also comparable to the benchmark of what many unskilled wage labourers earned if they were employed for 25 days and it would be barely sufficient to maintain a family of two persons.

e. Even with such modest expectations, they were unable to find jobs. Most of them tried various means. Some of the case studies are in Boxes 9.1 and 9.2. The varied experiences reveal that there were valid reasons for frustration and many of them used harsh languages to voice such frustrations.

Some more unemployed youth with SSC/HSC education were asked a question on whether he/she considered undertaking skill training and if not, why. None of the respondents had gone through a skill training course. Neither they were considering one. Many of the young persons with SSC/HSC were unaware about the training facilities. In fact, they did not try to find out and they were not even interested about finding it out. Some of the young boys with secondary certificate and especially from non-poor households considered it a matter of embarrassment that they were required to look for opportunities of skill training to become technical hands. It would be more respectable if they could find jobs without having to undertake training.

Boys and girls from less well off or poor households showed enthusiasm about skill training. But again, they did not have any idea about what type of training they could enter into and how to use it for getting a paid job or for earning purposes.[7]

---

[6] At this stage, it was clarified that the researcher guiding the discussion does not possess "power" to create a single job and therefore, they had revealed the real baseline which they may accept.

[7] An ongoing study on unemployed youth shows slightly better access to training by secondary educated youth. However, the new set of case studies, conducted by the present author, show that the training obtained from private sources (often informal) is hardly adequate to help obtain expected employment.

Most of these young persons do not have definite plans about their future. They said that they prefer salaried jobs. But they are alert to the fact that with poor results in Box 9.3 presents recent case studies (conducted in December, 2015) of youth labour force or 'potential youth labour force'.

> **Box 9.3: Recent Case Studies of Young Job Aspirants**
>
> 1. Tarek aged 20 has been studying for a B.Com degree at a local college. Simultaneously Tarek has been continuing job search.
> 2. Hasan aged 19 could not cross the SSC examination hurdle and has been engaged in the family farm knowing that there was hardly any scope of paid regular jobs. His father owns a tiny plot of land and he has sharecropped more land so that two persons of a family can remain employed. Hasan would prefer a regular job because crop cultivation takes place during 6 to 8 months and rest of the period he has no work.
> 3. Kamaluddin aged 21 made an attempt to obtain overseas employment. The middlemen promised him the job of a supervisor which did not materialise and he has returned to his parental home. He is unemployed and is looking for a job. He may consider obtaining skill training to enhance employability.

Case studies of other young persons reveal similar stories. A common experience is that unemployed young persons resort to graduate level studies even though they are aware that the degree itself may not fetch a good job. The frequently observed phenomenon that young persons get enrolled into graduate studies shows an attempt to avoid the frustrations of being considered as unemployed. They should be given the opportunity of more job oriented higher studies and a scope of demand driven skill training.

9.8 Major Findings and Policy Recommendations

9.8.1 Summary of Findings

- Data on growth of youth population and LFPR substantiate the presence of "potential demographic dividend," i.e., youth labour force growth simply due to growth of youth population. The increments of such demographic dividend are likely to diminish in the coming years.
- Various survey and census provide under-enumeration of young women, which can affect enumeration and utilisation of youth labour force.

- Labour force participation rate among young men has recently declined, while it has risen among young women.
- Employment pattern among youth labour force shows that the desired pattern of structural change, i.e., from traditional to modern sector and from family worker status to paid jobs has not been taking place.
- Unemployment rates by age group show higher unemployment rate among the young workforce. Unemployment rates among young male labour force have declined, while unemployment rates among girls of young age have increased. Job seekers with SSC and HSC level education face high unemployment rate.
- Young job aspirants are quite realistic about expected salary, which is around what many unskilled wage labourers or lowest paid RMG workers get.
- The educated youth themselves have identified the lack of skill and knowledge about business techniques as the relevant constraints to self-employment.
- They are prepared to pay at least a part of the cost of training. When asked about their awareness about the availability of specific training courses, they have reported that such awareness is lacking.

9.8.2 Policy Suggestions for Employment Generation

Policy recommendations of this section are relevant for not only the youth labour force but also for total employment growth and improvement of the performance of labour market as a whole. These policies are based on analysis and findings of all relevant chapters of the present volume. In addition, specific policy suggestions for empowering women through faster growth of employment of women from poorer households have been presented at the end of Chapter 14 of this volume.

9.8.2.1 Choice of Appropriate Growth Strategies

A smooth transformation of the low productive, low earner, unskilled labour force into high wage earning workers in modern sector can be achieved through a combination of private sector growth and government investment in human capital and infrastructure. This can help achieve simultaneous progress of employment generation and acceleration of economic growth. For progress along this route, the incentive structure in the economy must be such that more labour-intensive modern sectors can grow. Macro policies must be geared to this end.

Policies for generating employment-intensive growth can be addressed at various levels. The first set consists of general economy wide policies. The second involves policies for improving the employability of the labour force, especially through training.

The findings of the earlier chapters of this volume including the sectoral pattern of employment growth, the trends of wage rate and the constraints and risks associated with self-employment imply that the strategy of poverty reducing growth must try to accelerate industrial growth with scope for using modern technology and for creation of regular jobs. This requires various forms of policy incentives.

Within large-scale industries, labour-intensive sub-sectors must receive emphasis and Chapter 2 has identified the sub-sectors with better prospects and has emphasised the need for diversification. Simultaneously small-scale industries need to be encouraged as these can be located in small towns and peri-urban areas. Policies should aim not only at raising present capacity utilisation of non-farm enterprises but new enterprises must be encouraged. Incentives must go to entrepreneurs of large as well as small- & medium-scale industry in locations other than the major cities. Chapter 2 has already suggested related policies. An enabling environment for development of local entrepreneurship can be created through easing the infrastructure problems. Microfinance institutions and private sector financial institutions should be encouraged to extend suitable package of financial services to the prospective entrepreneurs.

Regional dispersion of secondary and tertiary sector activities can also be an effective strategy for reducing inequality. Special schemes for depressed areas should be taken up. Activities for infrastructure building for linkage between semi-urban growth centres and rural hinterland may help direct and indirect employment generation.

Such regionally dispersed industrialisation strategy has scope of success because the entrepreneurs can thrive by drawing local labour force, especially the underemployed female labour force. In this context, it should be pointed out that at present the young persons who are neither in the labour force nor enrolled in educational institutions (termed as "inactive") may constitute a special source of labour supply. Among the young age groups, a large share is in this category. Therefore, policies should be geared to encourage them to enter the labour force and creation of employment close to their current residence can be one of the effective means in this pursuit.

The largest share of youth labour force is at present engaged in agriculture sector. This does not tally with the expectation that young workers demonstrate more dynamism and are likely to be employed in modern sectors. Moreover, a large share of young workers is employed as unpaid family workers. Therefore, paid employment generation in industry and modern service sectors should be a policy priority.

Employment creation in rural areas requires an emphasis on rural non-farm activities. The emphasis here should be on enterprises using hired labour. Purely family labour based activities have less scope for technology upgradation and expansion of scale. Incentive package for hired labour based non-farm sector in the rural areas should be appropriately planned.

Attention to industry and service sector employment generation at the cost of agricultural growth may be self-defeating and involves risks. In the short run, agricultural growth has prospects of generating demand for hired labour. In the medium term, policies should encourage non-cereal agricultural production, especially livestock, fishery, horticulture, etc. These can have linkage effects through agro-processing and service sectors development, which in turn requires proper incentives. Real wage may show a faster rise if non-farm sectors generate employment opportunity in activities with higher productivity.

9.8.2.2 Short-term Policies for Self-employment in Non-crop Activities

Self-employment can play an indirect role in poverty alleviation through generation of supplementary earnings and especially through creating opportunities of income-earning activities of women who are not able to join wage employment because of the burden of domestic chores.

Specific suggestions for expansion of family labour based employment for the poor households have been listed here:

i. Improvements of marketing channels and storage service and transport service can alleviate some of the constraints faced by poor.

ii. Skill training can play a critical role in generating productive self-employment.

iii. Such enterprises cannot solely depend on microcredit. Rate of interest on microcredit is quite high and many activities are not profitable at those rates. Microcredit is usually repaid in fortnightly instalments and thus do not allow investment on fixed capital which can bring returns after a few months. Microcredit institutions may reconsider their terms of lending to suit the poor borrowers' needs.
iv. Enterprises are vulnerable to risks and such risks are higher for poorer households whose current assets are inadequate to provide protection to the financial/physical assets. These enterprises therefore require microinsurance facilities at low cost.

9.8.2.3 Decent Work

Policies for growth of number of employment should not be viewed as the only goal of labour market policies. Ensuring progress along the path of decent employment and improvement of quality of employment in terms of freedom of association, better terms of employment, security and better environment at the workplace should receive due emphasis. Government has already accepted the decent work goals and has adopted a number of projects to reach the goals. Proper implementation of the projects and monitoring of progress should be given priority.

9.8.2.4 Training and Skill Generation

Policies for improvement of the quality of labour force and commensurate policies to create matching employment opportunities can reduce much of the wastage due to unemployment of educated labour force. Skill deficiencies and low educational attainment are also important factors behind low earnings. Given such deficiencies, policies for raising the employability of the labour force through skill training can be effective means for employment expansion. In this context, both long-term and short-term programmes need policy focus.

Programmes of short duration training can target the young unemployed persons and requires immediate implementation. Short-term programme will assume that it has to be based on the existing institutional facilities and current demand. The critical issue in this context is linking training with jobs. The past experiences reveal a lack of success of training activities of public institutions which offered traditional training and rigid and old curriculum which did not create enthusiasm among employers. Employability of trained personnel is a must for sustaining the demand for training services. This can be ensured through prior assessment of demand and identification of the sectors, and locations where demand exists.

Short-term policies should therefore give priority to generate self-employment which requires a combination of skill and management training. Training organisations should be reoriented to adopt practices for "getting the enterprise started" and supporting it for a minimum period. Such multi-input training facilities can be provided through flexible private training organisations if these are provided support by the government. Training NGOs may enter into collaborative programmes with microfinance institutions. Locations close to district headquarters may have better prospects for training organisations if a number of complementary activities can be targeted to meet local demand.

Another target group for short-term training is the prospective job seekers in overseas markets. Field of training for this group must be decided in consultation with the recruiting agents who send migrant workers.

9.8.3 Medium-term Policies for Training

The nature of medium and/or longer-term policies of skill development will depend on the pace of economic growth and the structure of growth. Therefore, the employment targets and the level of skill requirement cannot be precisely predicted. Assumption of a medium range of economic growth and accelerated pace of industrial growth rate will imply that gradually higher skills will be needed.

Effective policies for development of such skills require attention to the following issues.

　　a. Structural changes in the economy and projected medium-term sectoral growth with the associated change of demand for skill need to be monitored. Skill training must be diversified to cater to all types of users and various groups of labour force.

　　b. Training courses may be combined with mainstream schooling. Current capacity of "vocational group" in SSC may be extended and made more effective through imparting such levels of skill as would enable a student get a job. In addition, there should be scope for vocational degree holders' mobility into other tracks of studies. By imparting more in-depth courses, which can lead to good employment opportunities, better students may be attracted for vocational studies track.

c. Exclusion of underprivileged youth, school drop-outs and poor women is one of the important problems of the present system of the public sector technical and vocational education and training (TVET) system. This should be reversed and students from poorer families should be provided with special incentives.

d. Facilities must be created for upgrading skills of employed or retrenched workers from export sectors.

e. Public sector training facilities should give more emphasis on new skills. Thrust sectors such as computer-related services and new generations of leather goods may be encouraged. Government has recently announced its emphasis on IT skill generation and this should continue.

f. Expansion of training for women is of utmost importance. As shown in the analysis of labour market situation, a large percentage of women in the age group 15-18 are subject to unemployment and underemployment or remain outside the labour force. Incentives are required to draw them into the training schemes which can encourage them to seek employment. Special stipends for poorer women can be helpful. Women's vocational training institutes (VTIs) have been established. More efforts are needed to make the skills oriented towards market demand. In this context, more emphasis on increasing the number of female trainers may encourage young women to accept TVET.

g. Better quality of training requires better quality teachers. Training of teachers should be a priority and in this context the incentive system should receive attention.

9.8.3.1 Schemes for Dissemination of Labour Market Information

This aspect deserves attention because in the non-farm sectors there are possibilities of creation of jobs in new sectors and locations. In the suggestions for employment expansion, locational dispersion has been emphasised. But the question is, how it will be possible to disseminate such information. Private middlemen often extract excess charges for such services. Governments thana level offices may create some facilities for channelling information on vacancies. Local NGO branches may be used as well. Private sector agencies are emerging with facilities for dissemination of labour market information. Such agencies may be provided with guidance and other facilities.

Young school leavers do not have access to information on training facilities. Only way to access such information is through others who received training. In the urban areas, private training institutions are cropping up and information flow is better. In remote rural areas, spread of information is slower. Access to such information can help youth labour force.

Many of the school leavers aspire to take up overseas employment. While some of them may succeed, some may be trapped in debt due to fraudulent behaviour of middlemen. Lack of knowledge and experience coupled with unrealistic expectations make them vulnerable in the hands of unscrupulous middlemen/agents. Improvements in the dissemination of knowledge related to overseas migration require immediate attention.

9.8.3.2 Direct Employment Generation Programme

Employment polices for seasonal slack periods and disaster periods: government can provide effective safely nets for able bodied labour force members through well designed employment programmes and thus reduce the risk of poverty accentuation due to natural calamity like flood, etc. Active labour market programmes (ALMP) assume particular importance in years of severe floods, which cause damage to assets and crops.

Safety net employment is usually provided in schemes of infrastructure building. Such programmes can lead to effective infrastructure development if these are based on a comprehensive plan. Therefore, it is advisable that such a plan is drawn up with sub-components for various regions and districts and upon occurrences of calamities, chosen sub-components may be implemented and in normal years the components earmarked for normal slack season employment generation can be taken up. A large body of literature on this subject is available and therefore detailed suggestions have not been included here.

CHAPTER 10

Inequality in Access to Education and Employment[1]

10.1 Introduction

Education helps economic growth and overall development of a country through its impact on productivity of labour and through other channels of social benefit. Therefore, education is an important development goal of most low-income countries including Bangladesh (SFYP, 7FYP). In fact, the role of education in enhancing labour productivity and economic growth has been recognised by the developments in new growth theory.[2]

During the last two decades Bangladesh has achieved significant success in poverty reduction. But high income inequality still persists. Gini ratio of household income in Bangladesh is higher than its South Asian neighbours. Moreover, income inequality increased during the 1990s and has remained unchanged during the last decade.

In this situation, the processes contributing to income inequality must be immediately halted. More equal access to quality education is one of the few available means to halt the worsening of income inequality.

Inequality in access to education may lead to direct and indirect routes of further accentuation of income inequality. The prospects of poverty reduction through better employment opportunities may be hindered by lack of education among children of low-income households. This chapter therefore highlights the inequalities in access to education and analyses the impact of such inequality on the labour force from poorer households. The priority areas of intervention with scarce public resources can be properly planned if the differentials between income groups are properly identified.

---

[1] This chapter is an edited version of Rahman (2009).
[2] For example, Barro (1991), Barros (1993), Mahajan (2005).

10.1.1 Scope of the Study

One of the objectives of the present study is to examine the determinants of inequality in education. The analysis is based on identification of the nature and extent of such inequality. The chapter examines the inequality in access to education among income groups and geographical regions (represented by Divisions). Gender inequality also receives attention. Such analyses help identify the extent to which policy support can elevate the situation of the disadvantaged groups.[3] The chapter also examines the inequality in education through separate analysis of the primary, secondary and tertiary levels. Completion of secondary education (obtaining SSC) receives separate attention.

During the last one and a half decades government has undertaken various programmes for improvement of opportunities of education, particularly for primary and secondary education. Therefore, education sector and school enrolment should receive researchers' attention. Recent research on school education in Bangladesh includes CAMPE (2001, 2005 and 2006), Alam (2007), and Rahman (2006). These reports have focused on the social and other determinants of primary and secondary education. Some of these studies have examined the school level issues and determinants of quality of education. The present chapter focuses on issues related to inequalities in access to education and the implications of inequality which were not touched by earlier papers. It will be useful to mention the questions specifically covered by the present study and not by other recent studies on education.

Previous studies examined the determinants of school enrolment rates. But the primary level and secondary level studies were based on separate surveys (at different points of time) and therefore are not directly comparable. The present study looks at these issues on the basis of a single household survey. Constraints to the access to education and determinants of enrolment are likely to differ according to the level of schooling (i.e., primary, secondary and tertiary) and a comparison can provide useful insights. The study also examines the determinants of tertiary age enrolment and SSC completion, which are not covered by earlier studies.

---

[3] However, it does not imply that the removal of the inequality in access to education is sufficient to achieve balanced human capital development. Overall improvement of participation and coverage is as important as reduction of inequality.

Labour market provides the major routes for channelling the private benefits of education. Linkages between education and labour market operate through education's impact on labour force participation rate, unemployment and wage/salary. This chapter examines these linkages and tests the hypothesis that inequality in access to education creates a vicious cycle of poverty through its impact on labour market. The hypotheses have been elaborated in Section 10.2.

10.1.2 Organisation of the Chapter

The chapter is organised as follows.

The rest of section 10.1 provides notes on data used in the study and Section 10.2 elaborates on the linkages between education and employment. Section 10.3 examines enrolment rates disaggregated by primary and secondary age groups among the income quartile groups. Section 10.4 examines the links between the socioeconomic variables and the rate of achievements of SSC and beyond. Section 10.5 examines rural-urban difference in this context. Section 10.6 analyses the impact of education on labour force participation, unemployment and status of employment. It also analyses the impact of education on wage. Section 10.7 provides observations on how the highest income group's preference for separate channels of education may distort the pattern of development of the existing channels, including the curriculum and other aspects of quality of government-financed school education. Section 10.8 provides concluding observations on how the inequality of access to education and employment forms a vicious cycle which has negative implications for equity and development. This section also provides policy suggestions which are, directly or indirectly, related to the findings of the study.

10.1.3 Notes on Data

Data used in this chapter come from the National Labour Force Survey of 2002-03, conducted by the Bangladesh Bureau of Statistics (BBS). This survey provides data on both education and employment, which is not given by other surveys on education. The household survey questionnaire includes questions on each individual's education and labour market characteristics.[4] In addition, this chapter uses other published data from various reports of the BBS.

---

[4] The details of sampling methods and other methodological issues related to the survey are in the 2003 LFS report (BBS, 2003).

10.2 Access to Education and Employment: How the Vicious Cycle Works

Lack of access to education is an important factor behind household poverty. This, in turn, may act as a mechanism of intergenerational intensification of poverty. This has been highlighted by a number of studies (Moore, 2005). Studies have shown that in many Asian countries education has made direct contributions to poverty alleviation through a positive impact on prospects of employment and better type/status of employment (Islam, 2004).

A number of studies on poverty in Bangladesh have shown that certain types of employment accentuate poverty. Poverty incidence is the highest in the casual labour category, especially in agriculture (WB, 2002). This is linked with lower days of employment among casual workers. In contrast, regular salaried employment can lead to a lower poverty (Rahman, 2004a). Therefore, one should ask whether education can raise days of employment and provide access to "regular jobs." Such linkages can lead to a vicious cycle which deprives low income households of the opportunities of education and in turn reduces their access to better employment and higher income. Whether such a cycle operates in Bangladesh is an empirical question and the following sections of the chapter examine the evidence. The flow diagram in Figure 10.1 shows these linkages at a glance.

Figure 10.1: Interrelationship between Education, Labour Market and Household Poverty

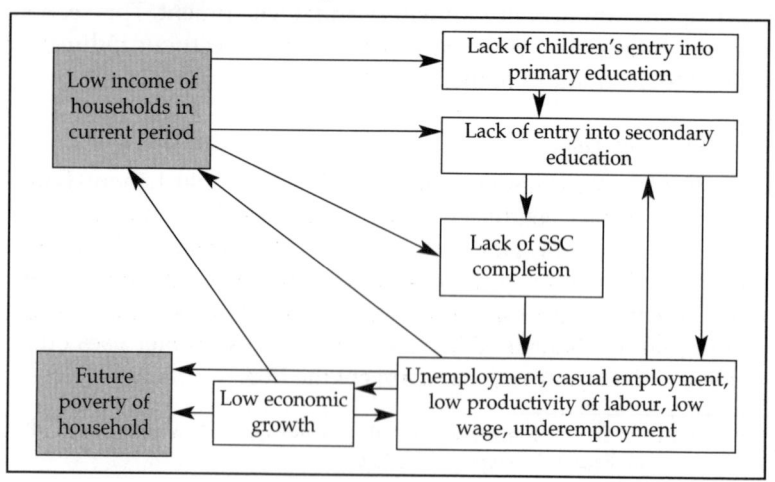

10.3 Access to Education: Impact of Household Income

10.3.1 Indicators of Access to Education

The enrolment rates for various age groups are presented for four income groups.[5] According to convention, primary enrolment rates are calculated for 6 to 10 years cut off points. Bangladeshi children often begin schooling later than 6 years age. Therefore, the estimates of rates of school enrolment are given for 8-12, 13-17 and 18-22 years age groups to capture primary, secondary and tertiary enrolment.[6]

It is being increasingly recognised that learning may not be adequately captured by years of schooling and suggestions have been made that the success at various levels should be directly measured through assessment of actual competence. CAMPE (2001) had undertaken a study on assessment of basic learning competencies of primary completed children. However, direct assessment of learning by outside researchers is not quite a practical proposition for the secondary level. Moreover, at the end of 10 years of schooling, which is the terminal year of secondary school, a public examination is centrally conducted (this is known as "secondary school certificate" examination). "Whether someone has completed SSC" can, therefore, be a yardstick of success at the secondary level. This chapter examines the determinants of SSC completion and the impact of inequality of income on this variable.

10.3.2 Primary and Secondary Enrolment Rates

Table 10.1 presents data on the enrolment rates for four income groups. The following observations can be made on the basis of these data.

- Primary enrolment rate is inversely related to income. The rates are 82.2 and 87.7 per cent among boys and girls of the lowest income group, while these rates in the highest income group are 93 per cent and 96 per cent respectively.
- Similar inequality is observed in the enrolment rates among secondary school age (13-17 years) children. However, the rates

---

[5] To measure the inequality of access to education, households have been classified into four income groups, of almost equal size. Most comparisons are made across these income groups.

[6] Alternative set of enrolment rate was calculated for each year of age beginning from 6 years. Enrolment rate has risen continuously from 6 years to 9 years. The estimates provided in this section are not directly comparable to those based on the conventional criterion.

are much lower than enrolment rates in 8-12 years group, as expected. The difference between lowest and highest income groups is larger for this age compared to primary enrolment rates. Among boys in the age group 13-17 years, in the poorest and the richest groups, 46 and 75 per cent are in school, and among girls the percentages are 64 and 85 respectively.

- Gender difference in enrolment rates deserves attention. A significant achievement of Bangladesh is the increase of school enrolment rate of girls. This has been borne out by the present data set. Girls' enrolment rates are higher than boys for both primary and secondary age groups. The conclusion holds for both low-and high-income groups. But one may wonder why the enrolment rate is not even higher since the girls are expected to get stipends. The reason is that some low-income families cannot afford the initial investment in the form of school books, suitable clothing, etc. Stipends are given only after girls are regularly attending school and therefore cannot help overcome the entry barrier. Moreover, certain conditions have to be fulfilled for receiving stipends.

Table 10.1: Enrolment Rate by Age Group and Income Group

Income Group*	Age 8-12 Years			Age 13-17 Years		
	Male	Female	All	Male	Female	All
1	82.2	87.7	84.8	46.2	63.8	53.8
2	84.3	90.8	87.4	52.2	68.0	58.8
3	87.3	92.7	89.8	59.9	76.6	67.1
4	93.5	96.5	94.4	75.4	85.0	79.8
All	86.5	91.7	89.0	60.1	75.1	66.6

Note: *Group 1 is the lowest, 2 is the second, 3 is the third and 4 is the highest income quartile group in all tables.
Source: LFS (2003), BBS.

10.3.3 Tertiary Age Group's Enrolment

Table 10.2 shows tertiary age group's enrolment rates in educational institutions. Only 0.8 per cent of the lowest income group and 14.2 per cent of the highest income group are currently enrolled. The rates are lower for women compared to men. Among women, 0.4 per cent of the lowest income group and 12.4 per cent of the highest income group in 18-22 years age group are currently enrolled.

Table 10.2: Enrolment Rate among 18-22 Years Aged by Income Group

Income Group	Male	Female	All
1	1.7	0.4	0.8
2	3.7	1.3	2.4
3	6.4	3.4	5.0
4	15.9	12.4	14.2
All	8.3	4.5	6.3

Source: LFS (2003), BBS.

Table 10.3: Distribution of Men and Women Aged 18-22 Years by Level of Education Achieved

(Per Cent)

Sex of Person	Income Group	Illiterate 0	Class I-V 1	Class VI-X 2	SSC 3	HSC 4	Others 5	Total
Male	1	49.3	21.7	20.7	5.8	2.1	0.4	100.0
	2	39.1	20.7	26.0	8.7	4.2	1.2	100.0
	3	28.2	18.6	31.9	12.6	7.1	1.5	100.0
	4	13.4	13.6	31.1	19.1	17.4	5.5	100.0
	Total	28.0	17.7	28.9	13.2	9.5	2.7	100.0
Female	1	59.1	18.8	19.5	1.7	0.8	0.1	100.0
	2	42.6	20.3	29.6	4.7	2.4	0.4	100.0
	3	26.1	18.1	38.7	10.6	4.9	1.5	100.0
	4	11.4	11.8	36.2	19.4	15.3	5.9	100.0
	Total	33.9	16.9	31.1	9.6	6.3	2.2	100.0
Male & Female	1	56.0	19.7	19.9	3.0	1.2	0.2	100.0
	2	41.0	20.5	27.9	6.6	3.2	0.8	100.0
	3	27.3	18.4	35.1	11.7	6.1	1.5	100.0
	4	12.4	12.7	33.5	19.3	16.4	5.7	100.0
	Total	31.1	17.3	30.1	11.3	7.8	2.4	100.0

Source: Computed from the LFS (2003) data of BBS.

10.3.4 SSC and HSC: Difference among Income Groups

Completion of secondary education takes place through obtaining SSC and HSC. Table 10.3 shows relevant data. The picture is not as bright as in the case of enrolment at secondary level.

- Only 13.2 per cent and 9.6 per cent of boys and girls among the 18-22 years age group have obtained SSC level education. The percentage is lower among girls compared to boys. This stands in contrast with the higher rate of secondary enrolment among girls compared to boys.

- The difference between the poor and non-poor is very large at these levels. The achievements of poor boys (about 6 per cent) and girls (3 per cent) in terms of this indicator (i.e., education level of 18-22 years aged) are, in fact, very low in the absolute sense. In the highest income group, 19.1 per cent and 19.4 per cent respectively of boys and girls have SSC.
- In the age group 18-22, 12.2 per cent male population and 8.5 per cent female population have HSC or higher education. In the lowest income group, HSC or higher achiever is only 1.4 per cent compared to 22.1 per cent in the highest income group. Differences between the lowest and the highest income groups are larger for HSC or higher level completion compared to SSC completion.

Although girls' enrolment rate at the secondary schools is higher than boys, their completion rate of SSC is much lower. The reasons behind the difference require further probing. An important factor discouraging SSC appearance of students is that sitting for SSC involves substantial cost. Such costs include examination fees, travel to test centres and the cost of private tuition. Parents are possibly less willing to make investment for daughters who are likely to get married soon and leave the parents' home. In contrast, sons are more likely to live with parents (or at least parents expect them to do so) and therefore are expected to bring a return to the investment on education. More intensive surveys on expenditure of each child's education and total household expenditure can throw light on the validity of this hypothesis (which is not available in the LFS). These forces have been observed to operate in the context of other South Asian countries as well (e.g., for Pakistan, see Aslam and Kingdon 2005).

A number of social and school level factors contribute to the obstacles to girl's SSC completion.

- When girls receive stipends at the secondary schools, it is alleged that girls without adequate competence are often promoted to next higher classes so that they can avail stipends (this is a condition for getting stipends). Such practice may be due to parents' request and the teachers' fear of withdrawal of girls from school. At present there is competition among schools to attract students.
- Newspaper reports suggest that the phenomenon of local "maastans" stands against girls' regular school attendance. The

number of girls actually harassed may not be large. But a small number of incidents may work as a discouraging factor and make a large negative impact. Negative social forces have larger impact on poorer households.
- Stipends may not ensure adequate quality of teaching. It may even adversely affect the quality because it requires diversion of teachers' time for administrative purposes related to disbursement of scholarship money.

10.4 Inequality in Education among Top Income Group

So far the inequalities among the quartiles income groups have been discussed. If one moves to the top 10 per cent income group, then inequality in access to education involves a number of new dimensions. Although the present chapter does not discuss these issues in details, these should be mentioned as agenda for further empirical research.

Children from families with top 10 per cent income have more choice about the type of education. A separate stream of private schools have emerged which charge very high tuition fees. A large number of private universities are in operation, again, in Dhaka and Chittagong. The fees are so high that only the top 10 per cent income earning households can afford it. Some of the good schools in this category offer similar standards as in high-income countries and use English as the medium of teaching. With degrees from these schools, students can obtain admission and scholarship in universities abroad. If they return to Bangladesh, they may avail the best jobs.

The above hypotheses are difficult to verify empirically. But the fact that the monthly tuition fee and other expenses for each student in private schools are often higher than the monthly salary of the high ranking government officials is sufficient evidence that these schools are only for the top income group.

This choice would be welcome to open new frontiers of education and skill development if it did not affect the other systems of education or if it helped to improve the normal channels through competitions (as envisaged by theories of private sector development). But the grave concern about the high cost stream arises from the lack of such competition. Rather, the upper strata being instrumental in policy making about education, they lose enthusiasm and motivation for improving the normal channels of education. The public schools at district headquarters were, once upon a time, institutions of excellence and many eminent personalities were educated there. Nowadays the standards of public schools located outside the two largest metropolitan cities have declined. In fact, studies have shown that in terms of performance in SSC examinations the schools in big cities are the best, next are schools in other urban areas and the rural schools are the lowest performing ones. None of the highest income decile families would send their children to rural schools. Even if some of them live outside the big cities, they have the means to arrange for children's education in the city schools. Thus there is a lack of motivation for improving the standards of the rural and peri-urban schools. There is also a lack of enthusiasm for improving the curriculum, the quality of teachers and the overall teaching methods.

10.5 Multiple Regression Results: Factors Affecting School Enrolment and Secondary Completion

Previous tables (Tables 10.1 through 10.3) in Section 10.3 have shown a gross difference of access to education among the income groups. Multiple regressions can provide more insights on the impact of relevant variables and identify the net impact of each factor. We have estimated separate logit regression equations for explaining "whether someone is currently studying" for 8-12-year, 13-17-year and 18-22-year old persons (Tables 10.1A to 10.3A). The discussion below presents the results in non-technical terms and can be meaningful even without going to the tables (presented in annex).

Among the determinants of primary school age enrolment, household's income has a positive impact. This impact is noteworthy even after controlling for a number of other poverty related variables: female headedness, landownership, head's education and spouse's education.

The equations provide evidence of strong intergenerational impact of education. Household head's and spouse's education have significant positive impact on enrolment among 8-12 and 13-17 years age groups. In this context, an interesting finding needs highlighting: household head's wife's education has a larger coefficient compared to head's education in the 8-12 age group's school enrolment. The impact is insignificant in the 18-22-years age group (Table 10.3A). Impact of landownership on school enrolment is positive and significant.

Larger number of school age children in a family implies a lower probability of enrolment. Since most families are of nuclear form, this implies a negative impact of higher fertility on education. Girl children have higher probability of enrolment than boys at both 8-12 and 13-17 age levels.

An equation on the "probability of having SSC level education" for the relevant (18-22 years) age group has been estimated (Table 10.4A). It has very similar results as the enrolment equations. As in the other equations, higher income groups have a large and positive impact. Positive impact of landownership of household and education of household head has been observed. Lower age group girls have an advantage over boys in terms of school enrolment, but the reverse is true for SSC completion.

10.6 Rural-Urban and Regional Difference

Table 10.4 shows rural-urban difference of enrolment rates. In the primary age group, rural-urban difference has been almost eliminated. For age group 13-17 years, enrolment rates for both boys and girls are higher in the urban areas. The same is true for 18-22 years age group. The urban-rural difference is the highest in this group. At this level, rural and urban enrolment rates are 4.1 per cent and 12.6 per cent respectively.[7]

Table 10.4: Enrolment Rate in Educational Institutions by Age Group and Location

Location	Age Group	Male	Female	All
Urban	8-12	86.6	91.9	89.1
Rural	8-12	86.4	91.6	88.9
Urban	13-17	66.1	78.8	71.8
Rural	13-17	58.2	73.9	64.9
Urban	18-22	15.2	10.4	12.6
Rural	18-22	6.0	2.5	4.1

Source: LFS (2003).

There are important regional differences in enrolment rates (Table 10.5). It is interesting to note here that Dhaka and Sylhet divisions have the lowest enrolment rates in educational institutions. This is true for all three age groups. The lower educational enrolment rates in Dhaka division, which includes the metropolitan city, are possibly

[7] Alam (2007) shows similar results.

due to the larger earning possibilities of school age children. Cultural norms may also influence education and may be at work behind the low enrolment rates in Sylhet division.

Table 10.5: Enrolment Rate in Educational Institutions by Division

Division	8-12 Years Male	8-12 Years Female	13-17 Years Male	13-17 Years Female	18-22 Years Male	18-22 Years Female
Barisal	89.6	93.6	68.6	77.5	23.4	17.4
Chittagong	87.1	90.7	64.6	73.9	24.8	13.2
Dhaka	85.4	90.9	57.0	74.4	23.9	15.5
Khulna	88.3	95.0	60.1	80.2	25.4	12.2
Rajshahi	86.7	93.7	60.8	79.1	28.5	14.1
Sylhet	79.9	82.6	59.8	64.1	21.2	12.2
Total	86.5	91.7	61.0	75.7	25.2	14.2

Source: LFS (2003).

10.7 Impact of Education on Labour Market

Households are expected to derive the benefits of education through various channels of the labour market. The most important ones are labour force participation rate (LFPR), wage, and type (status) of employment. This section examines how these are linked with education.

Whether the benefits of education are effectively derived depends not only on an individual's labour supply situation but also on the labour demand, which, in turn, is dependent on a number of macro-economic forces. The analysis of impact of education is complex because LFPR, hours of employment and wages are determined by a host of demand and supply-side variables. Multivariate analysis has been used to isolate the impact of education after controlling for other factors.

10.7.1 Education and LFPR

Table 10.6 shows LFPR of men and women aged 15 and above during the period of 1991 to 2010. Male LFPR has remained almost unchanged during that period (with some fluctuations). In contrast, female LFPR has gone through a significant increase. Therefore, a pertinent question is, whether this is linked with the rise of education.

Table 10.6: Labour Force Participation Rate (LFPR) in Bangladesh: 1991-2010

Period	\multicolumn{3}{c}{LFPR (Per Cent) among Population Aged 15 & Above}		
	All	Male	Female
1991	51.2	86.2	14.0
1996	52.0	87.0	15.8
2000	54.9	84.0	23.9
2003	57.3	87.4	26.1
2006	58.5	86.8	29.2
2010	59.3	82.5	36.0

Source: LFS (various years).

Logit regressions have been estimated to understand the impact of education on the probability that men and women are in the labour force (Tables 10.5A and 10.6A). The independent variables include a person's and his/her household's characteristics (age, square of age, own education, marital status, education of household head, land-ownership, family composition and location). The present discussion focuses on the coefficients of the variables representing education. A person's education is represented by four (dummy) variables: no education, primary or less, secondary (class six to ten) and SSC and above. "No education" is the excluded dummy.

In the case of female LFPR in urban and rural areas, primary and secondary level education has negative and significant impact. The impact is reversed in the case of SSC holders. SSC or above education has a positive and significant impact on chances of labour force participation in both urban and rural areas. Education has a non-linear impact on female LFPR: low education reduces LFPR, after SSC it raises LFPR. In the case of male LFPR, the impacts of primary and secondary education are not significant.

The negative impact of low education and the positive coefficient of SSC plus education in the LFPR equations are more likely to reflect the employers' preferences than the supply decisions. The rationale is that the employers are likely to show preference for the uneducated to low educated. Those with lower capability usually drop out before SSC and their actual attainment of basic competencies may be less than what is expected with these years of schooling. Moreover, salary expectations rise with the years of schooling and these expectations may not be commensurate with their actual learning or productivity advantage.

The SSC plus educated would be hired for jobs which cannot be satisfactorily performed by those with lower education. Moreover, those with SSC have a certificate to prove his/her attainment[8] while the employers cannot be certain about the competence of the lower educated ones.

10.7.2 Impact of Education on Wage

Investment on education is expected to raise productivity and thereby earnings. Educated workers have access to specialised jobs with higher productivity and higher salary. Moreover, with the expansion of school education, many jobs not requiring school degree may simply use education as a screening device for choosing better quality personnel and pay them higher wages. Therefore, all levels of education are expected to contribute to wage.

In addition to education, a number of other factors influence wage/salary. Region and age are among the important factors. Therefore, the impact of education on wage can be more distinctly shown through multiple regression analysis, which controls for the variation of other factors. Table 10.7A presents the results of wage equations. It can be observed that even after controlling for other determinants, wage rate increases with education. This is true for both urban and rural areas. This result is more or less expected. One feature of the results deserves attention-the impact of education increases at a faster pace for the higher levels of education.

The equation shows that daily earnings from salaried jobs are higher compared to those in casual jobs. Moreover, research (Rahman, 2009) shows that a higher share of those with education above SSC gets into regular jobs. A larger percentage of boys and girls from higher income group possess such education. Thus this links among high income, higher educational attainment and higher wage creates a cycle.

10.8 Summary of Findings and Policy Suggestions

The findings on factors related to access to education and inequality in the labour market can be summarised as follows:
- Analysis of school enrolment shows that children from households in the lowest income group have much lower school enrolment

---

[8] The data relate to early years when Junior Certificate Examination (JCE) system did not exist.

rate compared to the highest income groups. This is true for primary, secondary and tertiary education's age groups. In the primary education age group, 85 per cent and 94 per cent children respectively from the lowest and the highest quartiles are in school. In the age group of 13-17 years, 54 per cent and 80 per cent from the lowest and the highest income groups are enrolled in school. The enrolment rates in educational institutions are far smaller among 18-22-year-old persons, with large difference between income groups (0.8 per cent and 14.2 per cent in the lowest and the highest income groups respectively).

- When it comes to 18-22-year-old population who completed SSC, the differences between income groups are larger. In the lowest and the highest income groups, 4.4 per cent and 41.4 per cent have completed SSC respectively.
- Bangladesh has been successful in reducing gender gaps in access to education. Female enrolment rates are higher than male enrolment rates among 8-12 years and 13-17 years age groups. The pattern, however, reverses when one comes to 18-22-year-old group. In this group, enrolment rates among men and women are 8.3 per cent and 4.5 per cent respectively. In this age group, 25.4 per cent boys and 18.1 per cent girls have completed SSC or higher levels. The difference between boys and girls with SSC is even larger in the lowest income group (8.3 per cent boys and 2.6 per cent girls completed SSC or higher levels of education).
- The analysis of the chapter shows strong intergenerational impact on children's education (significant positive impact of parents' education). The intergenerational impact of education on children's schooling transmits the education-poverty link to future generations.
- Dhaka and Sylhet divisions have the lowest enrolment rates in educational institutions. This is true for all three age groups. The lower educational enrolment rates in Dhaka division, which includes the metropolitan city, is possibly due to the larger earning possibilities of school age children.
- The public schools at district headquarters were, once upon a time, institutions of excellence and many eminent personalities were educated there. Nowadays the standards of public schools

located outside the two largest metropolitan cities have declined. In fact, in terms of performance in SSC examinations, the schools in big cities are the best, next are schools in other urban areas and the rural schools are the lowest performing ones. None of the high-income families would send their children in rural schools. Therefore, there is a lack of motivation for improving the standards of the rural and peri-urban schools.

- Impact of poverty on school enrolment is reinforced through a lack of motivation to obtain schooling for children, which, in turn, is linked with the labour market. Inadequate motivation for education is rooted in the high rates of unemployment and low chances of getting salaried jobs, especially with education below SSC level. Workers from lower income group are engaged mainly in casual types of employment. Salaried job is the dominant mode of employment among labour force with education above SSC, who come mainly from higher income groups. Earnings function estimates show that salaried jobs are associated with higher earning, even after controlling for education. Thus, labour force from low income groups have lower educational endowment, which, in turn, keeps them confined to low wage casual employment and lower earnings compared to salaried employment.
- Girls with secondary education (but below SSC) are less likely to be in the labour force. This not only reduces their earning prospects but may discourage girls' schooling in future years. Data show that girls' enrolment in secondary level is higher than the boys'. But girls SSC completion rate is much lower. The observed pattern is at least partially due to the lack of prospect of girls' employment.

Thus the cycle of low current income, low education and adverse situation in the labour market may not only affect the young labour force but also the future cohorts of children's education prospects. Therefore, policies must be adopted to ensure access to quality education for all income groups so that worsening of income inequality is halted.

10.8.1 Policy Suggestions

- In most of the national policy documents the targets related to education have been formulated at the national level. The same is true for the education related MDG. The highly aggregative MDG related indicators of education cannot be meaningful when income inequality is high. Above analysis shows that the aggregate success indicators leave much to be desired. Government must adopt education related goals disaggregated by income groups, region and gender along with follow up strategies. Corresponding disaggregation of budgetary allocations and input provision strategies has to be worked out.

- Stipend and other support programmes for school education should give priority to poorer children. Here one may plan to channel higher cash benefits for new enrolment of the poorest students.
- Policies for motivating boys and girls to complete SSC may consider the following steps:
  - modify the secondary stipend for girls with provisions of allowances to cover initial entry expenses for class six entrants. Support for SSC examination fees of poor students can encourage SSC completion.
  - schools may be given the condition that a certain percentage of secondary stipend holder girls must sit at (and pass!) SSC. This may motivate teachers to provide free coaching for poor students who cannot afford to engage private tutors.
  - Similar support for covering poor boys' SSC examination expenses is required.
- It has been observed that the three rich areas, Dhaka, Chittagong and Sylhet, have lower school enrolment rates. In these divisions, poorer children have opportunities of employment. It is difficult to put sudden halt to child labour, especially in the informal sector. Therefore, policies and programmes are required for informal education among working children and for elimination of child labour.
- It has been argued that rich peoples' access to good quality of school may adversely affect the quality of schools in remote rural areas. A reversal of this trend demands that instead of establishing new schools, the existing schools' quality should be improved through training of teachers, etc.
- A strong intergenerational influence on children's education has been observed. Educated parents are more enthusiastic about education and also they may help children in the learning process

where school teacher's role (or private tuition) is insufficient. To make up for this deficiency among uneducated low-income parents, special teachers' services should be designed for such children.

- Job creation for young secondary educated persons should be a priority and with this objective industrial policy and infrastructure policies can be taken up in the medium term. Plans should be adopted for special skill training courses and informal learning systems to sustain the cognitive skills already obtained by class V to IX educated boys and girls who drop out. Modifications of the courses are required so that even without SSC completion, useful skills and knowledge are acquired which may enable them to seek wage employment as well as to engage in self-employment with higher productivity.

Above measures are not very resource-intensive and can be implemented through redirection of the current allocations. It requires a commitment to improve access to education among lower income groups. The vicious cycle of income inequality can be broken through interventions aimed at giving access to better quality education for children from lower income groups.

Appendices

Table 10.1A: Determinants of School Enrolment among 8-12 Years Old Children: Results of Logit Regression

Dep. Whether Studying in an Educational Institution

Independent Variables	B	S.E.	Sig
Sex of household head	-.16	.09	.08
Education of head	.13	.01	.00
Income group 2 dummy	.20	.06	.00
Income group 3 dummy	.30	.07	.00
Income group 4 dummy	.63	.11	.00
Education of female spouse of head	.14	.02	.00
Education of other 18+ male	.05	.01	.00
Education of other 18+ female	.03	.01	.01
Own sex dummy; 1=Male, 0=Female	-.58	.05	.00
Family land in decimals	.00	.00	.00
Area dummy; 1=Rural, 0=Urban	.33	.06	.00
Division dummy for Barisal	.28	.10	.01
Division dummy for Chittagong	.04	.07	.54
Division dummy for Khulna	.41	.09	.00
Division dummy for Rajshahi	.30	.07	.00
Division dummy for Sylhet	-.62	.09	.00
No. of persons in age group 1-17 years	-.09	.02	.00
Constant	1.83	.15	.00
Per cent correct prediction	89.0		
Sample size	25,413		

Source: Author's estimation based on the LFS 2003 data of BBS.

Table 10.2A: Determinants of Enrolment among 13-17 Years Old Persons: Results of Logit Regression

Dep. Whether Studying in an Educational Institution

Independent Variables	B	S.E.	Sig
Sex of household head	.19	.08	.02
Education of head	.11	.01	.00
Income group 2 dummy	.15	.06	.02
Income group 3 dummy	.31	.06	.00
Income group 4 dummy	.52	.08	.00
Education of female spouse of head	.10	.01	.00

Continued

Continued from Table 10.2A

Independent Variables	B	S.E.	Sig
Education of other 18+ male	.02	.00	.00
Education of other 18+ female	.02	.01	.00
Own sex dummy; 1=Male, 0=Female	-.70	.04	.00
Family land in decimal	.00	6.091E-05	.00
Area dummy; 1=Rural, 0=Urban	.14	.05	.00
Division dummy for Barisal	.32	.08	.00
Division dummy for Chittagong	.21	.06	.00
Division dummy for Khulna	.31	.07	.00
Division dummy for Rajshahi	.32	.06	.00
Division dummy for Sylhet	-.19	.09	.03
No. of persons in age group 1-17 years	-.02	.01	.11
Constant	-.21	.13	.10
Per cent correct prediction	70.6		
Sample size	19,227		

Source: Author's estimation based on the LFS 2003 data of BBS.

Table 10.3A: Determinants of 'Whether Studying' for 18-22 Years Aged Persons: Results of Logit Regression

Dep. Whether Studying in an Educational Institution

Independent Variables	B	S.E.	Sig
Sex of household head	.75	.11	.00
Education of head	.12	.01	.00
Income group 2 dummy	.49	.11	.00
Income group 3 dummy	.74	.10	.00
Income group 4 dummy	.65	.11	.00
Education of female spouse of head	.00	.01	.90
Education of other 18+ male	.03	.00	.00
Education of other 18+ female	.06	.00	.00
Own sex dummy; 1=Male, 0=Female	1.02	.06	.00
Family land in decimal	.00	5.335E-05	.00
Area dummy; 1=Rural, 0=Urban	-.20	.06	.00
Division dummy for Barisal	.00	.011	.98
Division dummy for Chittagong	-.00	.08	.96
Division dummy for Khulna	.08	.09	.34
Division dummy for Rajshahi	.36	.07	.00
Division dummy for Sylhet	-.22	.13	.09
No. of persons in age group 1-17 years	-.05	.02	.01
Constant	-4.74	.18	.00
Per cent correct prediction	84.4		
Sample size	20,138		

Source: Author's estimation based on the LFS 2003 data of BBS.

Table 10.4A: Determinants of Education Status, SSC or Above among 18-22 Years Aged Persons: Results of Logit Regression

Dep. Whether SSC

Independent Variables	B	S.E.	Sig
Sex of household head	.47	.13	.00
Education of head	.09	.01	.00
Income group 2 dummy	.63	.14	.00
Income group 3 dummy	.95	.13	.00
Income group 4 dummy	.83	.14	.00
Education of female spouse of head	.00	.01	.73
Education of other 18+ male	.02	.00	.00
Education of other 18+ female	.04	.00	.00
Own sex dummy; 1=Male, 0=Female	.43	.07	.00
Family land in decimal	.00	5.649E-05	.00
Area dummy; 1=Rural, 0=Urban	-.06	.07	.38
Division dummy for Barisal	-.06	.12	.64
Division dummy for Chittagong	.11	.09	.21
Division dummy for Khulna	-.02	.10	.88
Division dummy for Rajshahi	.23	.08	.01
Division dummy for Sylhet	-.35	.15	.02
No. of persons in age group 1-17 years	-.04	.02	.04
Constant	-4.55	.21	.00
Per cent correct prediction	88.8		
Sample size	20,138		

Source: Author's estimation based on the LFS 2003 data of BBS.

Table 10.5A: Determinants of Labour Force Participation (Results of Logistic Regression): Female

Variables	Urban B	Urban SE	Urban Sig	Rural B	Rural SE	Rural Sig
No. of children below 6 years	-.13	.02	.00	-.13	.01	.00
Worker age	-.01	.01	.41	-.06	.00	.00
Square of worker age	-.00	8.467E-05	.00	.00	5.781E-05	.01
Primary dummy	-.22	.05	.00	-.17	.04	.00
Secondary dummy	-.26	.05	.00	-.15	.04	.00
SSC + dummy	.31	.07	.00	.32	.07	.00
Education score of head	-.01	.00	.00	-.01	.00	.00
Head dummy	1.01	.07	.00	1.11	.06	.00
Land size in decimal	-.00	7.208E-05	.16	-9.4E-05	3.442E-05	.01
Whether married dummy	-1.09	.07	.00	-.74	.05	.00
Whether divorce/widowed dummy	-.67	.09	.00	-.38	.07	.00
Total no. of male earners aged 15+	-.02	.02	.39	.03	.01	.01
Barisal dummy	.12	.07	.08	-.07	.05	.20
Chittagong dummy	-.12	.05	.02	.11	.04	.01
Dhaka dummy	.04	.05	.46	-.15	.04	.00
Rajshahi dummy	.20	.05	.00	.07	.04	.06
Sylhet dummy	-.06	.08	.49	.23	.05	.00
Constant	.94	.13	.00	1.44	.10	.00
Per cent correct prediction	72.2			74.1		
N	18,764			34,206		

Source: Author's estimation based on the LFS 2003 data of BBS.

Table 10.6A: Determinants of Labour Force Participation (Results of Logistic Regression): Male

Variables	Urban B	Urban SE	Urban Sig	Rural B	Rural SE	Rural Sig
No. of children below 6 years	-.07	.03	.01	-.05	.04	.32
Worker age	.04	.01	.00	.10	.02	.00
Square of worker age	-.00	.00	.00	-.00	.00	.00
Primary education dummy	.03	.10	.77	.33	.14	.02
Secondary education dummy	-.02	.11	.88	.08	.14	.56
SSC + education dummy	.37	.17	.03	.12	.19	.53
Education score of head	-.02	.01	.05	-.01	.01	.51
Whether household head dummy	1.90	.10	.00	1.50	.13	.00
Family land size in decimal	.00	9.494E-05	.03	9.70E-05	.00	.56
Whether married dummy	1.05	.14	.00	1.10	.19	.00
Whether divorce/widowed dummy	.06	.20	.76	.20	.28	.49
Barisal dummy	.28	.14	.04	.33	.21	.11
Chittagong dummy	-.10	.09	.28	-.34	.12	.01
Khulna dummy	-.04	.11	.69	-.25	.14	.07
Rajshahi dummy	.12	.10	.20	-.03	.13	.80
Sylhet dummy	-.35	.13	.01	-.03	.21	.89
Constant	3.07	.23	.00	2.04	.32	.00
Per cent correct prediction	96.5	-	-	96.6	-	-
N	34,434	-	-	18,932	-	-

Source: Author's estimation based on the LFS 2003 data of BBS.

Table 10.7A: Determinants of Wage: Results of Multiple Regression

Dep: Log of Wage Per Hour

Explanatory Variables	Urban B	Urban t	Urban Sig	Rural B	Rural T	Rural Sig
Constant	2.67	35.74	.00	2.72	64.47	.00
Age of workers	.04	11.57	.00	.04	17.50	.00
Square of workers age	.00	-10.29	.00	.00	-17.37	.00
Primary dummy	.15	5.91	.00	.13	8.53	.00
Secondary dummy	.25	9.39	.00	.18	11.03	.00
SSC + dummy	.66	24.09	.00	.46	22.42	.00
Regular salaried employee dummy	.21	8.84	.00	.25	16.53	.00
Formal dummy	.16	7.03	.00	.14	9.69	.00
Public dummy	.08	2.68	.01	.21	7.72	.00
Land owned in decimals	.00	3.52	.00	5.E-05	3.58	.00
Head dummy	.17	6.65	.00	.11	6.92	.00
Whether received any training	.14	6.04	.00	.17	8.75	.00
Division dummy for Barisal	-.05	-1.27	.20	.02	1.22	.22
Division dummy for Chittagong	.10	3.77	.00	.12	7.87	.00
Division dummy for Khulna	-.16	-6.20	.00	-.11	-6.24	.00
Division dummy for Rajshahi	-.20	-8.59	.00	-.19	-13.41	.00
Division dummy for Sylhet	.04	.84	.40	-.08	-3.79	.00
Sex of workers dummy	.36	13.36	.00	.39	22.74	.00
Sample size	4,045	-	-	10,212	-	-
Value of F	245.13	-	.00	370.91	-	.00
Adjusted R-square	0.51			0.38		

Source: Author's estimation based on the LFS 2003 data of BBS.

PART 3
POVERTY, EMPOWERMENT AND SOCIAL CHANGE

CHAPTER 11

Poverty Reduction Experience: Hidden Questions

Bangladesh's achievement of accelerated poverty reduction during the last two decades has generated enthusiasm about research on the correlate of such poverty reduction. Many in-depth studies have been conducted on these correlates and the links between poverty trends and policies in social and economic spheres. However, a number of questions related to poverty trends still remain hidden behind the complex quantitative analysis. This chapter unveils some of these questions. Attempt has been made to identify three such questions which relate to (a) changes in poverty incidence in the different administrative Divisions, (b) changes in savings rate and its links with poverty trend, and (c) rural-urban difference in consumption and its implications for drawing poverty line.

11.1 Regional Poverty Decline: Fluctuations During 1996 to 2010

Regional inequality can be a matter of concern if some regions continuously experience slower income growth compared to other regions. Similarly, if regional inequality in poverty incidence persists over a long duration, it can have a disquieting impact on social and political processes of development of a country.

Data on poverty incidence of Bangladesh provided by Household Income and Expenditure Survey (HIES) contains disturbing features of regional inequality of poverty trends. The two rounds of the HIES (2000 and 2005) have revealed that there has been little poverty reduction in two divisions, namely Khulna and Rajshahi, and this feature has been highlighted by a number of studies. Remedial measures should, of course, be initiated to reverse this trend. However, the fact that poverty decline has been faster in the areas (Divisions) in the East can hardly be an adequate basis to propose the theses of East-West divide (WB, 2007). If this is based only on the experience of poverty reduction during the period 2000-2005, it may lead to misleading conclusions regarding the division-wise difference in development and may create inadvertent repercussions.

This section highlights the changes of poverty incidence of different "Divisions" not only during 2000-2005 but also looks at the changes during the longer time span of 1996 to 2010. In addition, this chapter presents division-wise data on a few other social indicators to see whether all indicators can be used together to come to a definite conclusion about backwardness of some regions (or East vs. West). To facilitate the adoption of remedial measures for reduction of regional difference in various spheres of development, the problem requires more in-depth attention.

The HIES 2000 and 2005 data show that poverty incidence is higher in Barisal, Khulna and Rajshahi compared to Dhaka and Chittagong (Table 11.1). Data from the four rounds of the HIES (1996 to 2010) show that during 1996 to 2000, poverty incidence has gone down in Khulna and Rajshahi. In the next period (2000-2005), Barisal, Khulna and Rajshahi have performed worse than Dhaka, Chittagong and Sylhet in terms of percentage point of poverty reduction. A reverse pattern has been observed during 2005-2010 when Khulna, Rajshahi and Barisal divisions have performed better. Thus, the conclusion emerges that the Divisions' performances in terms of magnitude of poverty reduction have not been similar in different periods. It is quite difficult to explain these upswings and downswings in divisional ranking of poverty reduction. This may, to some extent, have been due to deliberate policy efforts of the government which followed the dissemination of findings on poverty in any round of HIES. One would then wonder why the effects of policies were not sustained. In this context, data quality needs serious attention. Since a large part of consumption in rural areas is from self-production, accounting for such consumption expenditure may depend on the emphasis on its inclusion.[1]

The other point that deserves attention is that two divisions (Khulna and Rajshahi) about which there is a specific concern have shown very diverse pattern of poverty trend in urban and rural areas. Relevant data show that urban poverty has increased during the period 2000-2005, while rural poverty incidence has gone through a decline in Rajshahi. Moreover, one may be taken by surprise to note that rural

---

[1] There may be many routes through which non-sampling error may creep in a survey which involves a long questionnaire as is used by HIES.

Khulna's poverty rate was much lower than rural Dhaka in 2010. This observation suggests that if all rural and urban areas of Dhaka, Chittagong and Sylhet are aggregated to "East," then the need for policy targeting for the pockets of rural poverty within Dhaka Division may escape attention.

Table 11.1: Poverty Incidence by Division: 1996-2010

(% of hh, Based on Moderate Poverty Line)

Division	2010 National	2010 Rural	2010 Urban	2005 National	2005 Rural	2005 Urban	2000 National	2000 Rural	2000 Urban	1996 National	1996 Rural	1996 Urban
National	31.5	35.2	21.3	40.0	43.8	28.4	48.9	52.3	35.2	51.0	55.3	29.5
Barisal	39.4	39.2	39.9	52.0	54.1	40.8	53.1	55.1	32.0	49.9	50.2	44.4
Chittagong	26.2	31.0	11.8	34.0	36.0	27.8	45.7	46.3	44.2	52.4	54.0	40.8
Dhaka	30.5	38.8	18.0	32.0	39.0	20.2	46.7	55.9	28.2	40.2	48.5	18.4
Khulna	32.1	31.0	35.8	45.7	46.5	43.2	45.1	46.4	38.5	55.0	56.0	48.7
Rajshahi	35.7	36.6	30.7	51.2	52.3	45.2	56.7	58.5	44.5	61.8	65.0	36.8
Sylhet	28.1	30.5	15.0	33.8	36.1	18.6	42.4	41.9	49.6	-	-	-

Source: Bangladesh Bureau of Statistics: *Household Income and Expenditure Survey* (various years).

However, household income or poverty incidence is only a partial indicator of development. Therefore, data on two other indicators of social development have been presented below. These are school enrolment rates of children (Table 11.2) and infant mortality rate (IMR) (Table 11.3).

Table 11.2: Enrolment of Children Aged 6-10 Years by Division and Poverty Status

Division	Poor	Non-Poor
Barisal	88.1	94.0
Chittagong	75.5	87.1
Dhaka	77.3	89.0
Khulna	87.3	90.1
Rajshahi (Former)	78.7	91.6
Sylhet	64.2	82.1

Source: Bangladesh Bureau of Statistics: *Household Income and Expenditure Survey* (2010).

Sylhet and Chittagong have the lowest school enrolment rates of 6-10 years old children. Rajshahi division has the highest IMR. Dhaka and Sylhet have second and third highest IMR (44 and 39 per 1000 live births in 2008), while the figures for Barisal and Khulna are much lower (35 per 1,000 live births). Thus the positions in terms of income poverty reduction and in terms of social development do not match and various divisions' success in the two areas are somewhat contrasting. Therefore, policy responses must be alert to such differences.

Table 11.3: Infant Mortality Rate by Division

Division	\multicolumn{4}{c}{IMR (Number Per 1,000 Live Births)}
	2001	2008	Changes	Rank (in 2008)
Barisal	51	35	16	4
Chittagong	58	34	24	5
Dhaka	56	44	12	2
Khulna	51	35	16	4
Rajshahi	59	51	18	1
Sylhet	61	39	22	3
National	56	41	15	-

Source: BDHS (2008).

Although there are ups and downs in the rate of poverty reduction and relative position of Divisions in this respect, there can be no doubt that some divisions have substantially higher poverty rate and a lower level of economic development. There is need for policies for more balanced growth in various divisions.

Regional inequality may be examined at various levels, e.g., division, district, upazila, etc. Which level should be used for policies for generating more equal poverty reduction? Should policy actions be targeted to achieve fuller utilisation of potentials of growth and development for the country as a whole or to greater regional equality (at some chosen level of region) of growth and/or poverty reduction? Another alternative will be to accelerate poverty reduction in the pockets of acute poverty.

As has been mentioned above, Dhaka division's rural areas as a whole show higher poverty incidence compared to Khulna's rural areas (HIES, 2010). Some districts in Dhaka division are among the top ranking ones in terms of poverty rate. Therefore, poverty reduction policies should not adopt the simplified notion of "East vs. West" but should pay attention to the poorest spots in various districts and divisions.

One cannot always work at the same level of regional disaggregation for different types of policy choice. In the case of poverty reduction programmes, district or upazila may be relevant. Policies related to social development, especially education and health services, should target the divisions with lower achievement. For growth augmenting infrastructure building, divisional headquarters and port cities will be the most important physical spheres. For some environment related development projects, districts in the disaster prone coastal area will be the centre of action. Thus the labelling of a whole "Division" as poor may not enable proper targeting of various types of policies.

11.2 Poverty Reduction through Reduced Savings Rate?

Poverty incidence in Bangladesh went through a rapid decline during the period 2005-2010 (HIES, 2010). Poverty head-count ratio declined from 40 per cent in 2005 to 31.5 per cent in 2010. Obviously, this has injected a sense of optimism among both policy makers and development practitioners. The route through which the success has been achieved needs further probing. Many in-depth studies have been conducted to trace the factors associated with such poverty decline. This section takes a look at the changes of consumption expenditure, income and savings of households and thereby throws light on how these changes are associated with poverty reduction during the period 2005-2010.

HIES and all other analysis of poverty incidence are based on consumption expenditure data. It implies that poverty reduction may take place through rise in consumption financed by borrowing or reduced savings. Therefore, additional insights into poverty reduction can be obtained through a comparison of income and expenditure data.

HIES's estimates of poverty incidence in terms of head-count ratio have been based on a comparison of household expenditure and the norm of poverty line expenditure. An obvious question can be asked about how this expenditure is financed. The assumption is that a rise of income results in higher expenditure. Nonetheless, this assumption may not always be a perfect reflection of reality and one should look at concrete data to assess its validity. HIES provides both income and expenditure data which can be used to examine whether the two move concomitantly. HIES data of the last three rounds have been used to throw light on the pattern of consumption and savings rate (Tables 11.4 and 11.5).

Table 11.4: Growth of Consumption: 2000-2010

Period	% Change of Nominal Income	% Change of Consumption
2000-2005	23.3	31.3
2005-2010	59.4	84.5

Source: BBS: HIES (various years).

Table 11.5 shows that incomes were Tk. 5,856, Tk. 7,203 and Tk. 11,093 in 2000, 2005 and 2010 respectively. Consumption expenditures in those years were Tk. 4,556, Tk. 5,964 and Tk. 10,616. The difference between average income and expenditure provides the average household savings, which stood at Tk. 1,300, Tk. 1,239 and Tk. 477 in 2000, 2005 and 2010 respectively. Savings as a share of household income were 22.2 per cent, 17.2 per cent and 4.3 per cent in these three years (Table 11.5). Thus, according to HIES data, savings rate went through a substantial decline during the period 2005-2010 and a small decline during the period 2000-2005.

Table 11.5: Household Income, Consumption and Savings Rate: 1991-2010

Year	Income (Y)	Cons. Exp. (C)	Savings (Y-C)	Savings rate= $\frac{(Y-C) \times 100}{Y}$
1991	3,341	2,904	437	13.1
1996	4,366	4,026	340	7.9
2000	5,856	4,556	1,300	22.2
2005	7,203	5,964	1,239	17.2
2010	11,093	10,616	477	4.3

Source: BBS: HIES (various years).

Not only the share of savings out of household income declined, but also the absolute amount of savings (that again, in nominal terms) drastically decreased in the latest year of the HIES compared to the previous one. The figures of per household savings were Tk. 477 in 2010 and Tk. 1,239 in 2005.

During the entire period 1991-2010, per capita real household income increased. The usual hypothesis about savings propensity is that propensity to save out of increased income is higher and marginal propensity to save is expected to be positive. This has not been borne out by HIES data series and the drastic decline of savings rate during a period of rising income is difficult to explain.

An alternative data source (for 1997) showed savings rate of 16.3 per cent (Rahman and Mujeri, 2000), which was close to the HIES based estimates for 2000 and 2005. The 1997 data set was based on a nationally representative sample for rural areas only. Another micro-survey (in a microfinance programme covered village and a non-programme village) based study arrived at a savings rate of 9 per cent (Rahman, 2001).

Why did the savings rate decrease during the period 2005-2010 and what are the implications of such reduced savings rate? Rising inflation was perhaps a major reason behind the decline of savings rate. Low income groups and households close to poverty line try to maintain their consumption levels in the face of rising prices. They can accomplish this only at the cost of reduced savings.

Change of savings rate in various divisions and the extent of poverty reduction can provide useful insights into the links between the two. Data show that savings rates were negative (i.e., monthly average household consumption is higher than average monthly household income) in Barisal, Khulna and Rajshahi. The rates of poverty reduction were higher in these three divisions during the period 2005-2010. In 2005, they had much higher poverty incidence compared to other three divisions—Chittagong, Dhaka and Sylhet. With negative savings in 2010, the poverty situation may again worsen in the coming years. Therefore, policies for encouraging savings should be a priority.

However, the explanations offered here may not fully account for such a large downslide in savings. Difficulties in explaining the curtailment of savings may even lead to doubts about data quality.

Declining savings rate can have serious implications for future economic growth and sustainability of the poverty reduction process. Bangladesh's investment rate has been stagnating for the last few years (Chapter 1). Decline of household savings is a major reason behind such stagnation.

Poverty decline achieved through decline in savings rate may not be sustainable. Lower savings rate means lower investment growth, and it will result in slower income growth in future.

If income growth of poorer households is insufficient, in future they will not only reduce savings but may also sell their meagre assets. This will further worsen their vulnerability.

In fact, the decline of average household savings cannot result only from the reduced savings rate of poor households. Such a decline implies that higher income groups also curtailed their savings. This may have resulted from the lack of incentives for savings rather than from the squeeze due to rise in prices of essential goods.

Policies should be adopted to encourage household savings, especially in rural areas. Savings rate in rural areas was lower than that in urban areas. In 2010, savings as a share of household income were 2.2 per cent and 7.3 per cent in rural and urban areas respectively. Of course, an increase in income is required to raise households' savings propensity. Since a large percentage of households' have risen above the poverty threshold, in future they will possibly show interest in saving a part of income if suitable savings services are available through national commercial banks (NCBs).

11.2.1 Determinants of Savings Rate and Estimates of Savings Functions

Cross sectional savings function can help policy making for savings mobilisation. Two forms of savings functions are usually estimated: (i) the simple Keynesian function, and (ii) a more detailed function. Savings functions have been estimated on the basis of household level data of the HIES (2005 and 2010). Table 11.6 shows the results of the Keynesian savings function. According to the Keynesian hypothesis, marginal propensity to save (MPS) is expected to be less than one and the average propensity to save (APS) to be less than MPS (the intercept term to be negative). The values of MPS are 0.87 in 2005 and 0.72 in 2010 and the intercepts are actually negative as expected (Table 11.6). The regression coefficients are significant. The value of adjusted R-square and the F-values are high.

Table 11.6: Results of Savings Function (OLS Regression)

Explanatory Variables	Year	Dependent Variable; Household Savings	
		Coefficient	Value of 't'
Household income	2005	0.87	264.14***
Constant		-59487.9	-88.09***
Adjusted R-square		0.86	
Value of F		69772.1***	
Sample size		10080	
Household income	2010	0.72	135.5***
Constant		-111331.5	-100.8***
Adjusted R-square		0.60	
Value of F		18357.9***	
Sample size		12240	

Note: ***, **, * indicate significant at .00, .05 and .10 probability levels respectively.
Source: Estimated on the basis of HIES data.

In addition, an alternative equation has been estimated, which is based on a sample after the outlier values of the sample, i.e., 5 per cent from the upper and lower ends have been excluded. Other studies on savings functions followed this practice (Ahmed and Hossain, 1990, Sen, 1996). The rationale is that the extreme values of savings and dissavings take place due to unexpected earnings or unforeseen large expenditures arising from adverse incidents. In such cases, the savings/dissavings cannot be considered as a deliberate choice and will not be amenable to policies. However, for the present samples, the coefficients from these equations are very close to the original equation and have not been reported here.

The values of MPS may be compared with results obtained from similar studies in Bangladesh. Chowdhury (1987), Ahmed and Hossain (1990) and Sen (1996) may be mentioned in this context. Chowdhury (1987) uses group data from the HES and regresses saving on income per household for 1977-78 and later rounds of data. For these years, the MPS ranges between 0.23 and 0.19 for the rural areas. The figures are lower than the estimates of the present study. This is somewhat expected because of widespread poverty and low income during the 1970s. Moreover, during that period, the MPS might have been low due to low level of development of the economy as well as savings institutions. Alamgir and Rahman (1974) obtained a low value of MPS (0.11) by regressing per capita rural savings on per capita income. Ahmed and Hossain (1990) provide estimates of MPS in the range of 0.34 to 0.42. Sen (1996) arrives at a very low MPS because savings have been estimated from the investment account.

The other form of savings function has been estimated including the individual and household characteristics which may influence the returns to savings and has taken into account a number of variables to test the "life cycle" hypothesis and the hypothesis related to the effects of rates of return from investment. Table 11.7 shows the results of the expanded savings function. The coefficient of income in this equation is higher than the simple Keynesian version. The "life cycle" variable represented by age of the head of households has a significant negative coefficient. This is in conformity with the hypothesis. Agricultural land owned has a negative coefficient. This is due to the fact that land is a form of asset which can serve as insurance and thus reduce the need for saving from current income. The number of household members has a negative coefficient as expected, as it raises the consumption needs.

Years of schooling has a negative and significant coefficient, which is difficult to explain and the contrary would be expected. The dummy for receiving remittances has a positive and significant coefficient.

Table 11.7: Household Savings Function of Extended Form: Results of OLS Regression

	Dependent Variable: Household Savings		
Explanatory Variables	Coefficients	t	Significance
Constant	-25420	-4.190	.000
Total income	.92	317.752	.000
Age of head	-700.63	-3.135	.002
Square of head age	3.00	1.347	.178
Education of head	-3160.90	-25.794	.000
Household size	-9749.51	-35.616	.000
Whether receive remittances	8809.17	7.468	.000
Land ownership	-4960.37	-16.802	.000
Household has electricity connection (yes=1)	18184.1	14.945	.000
Urban dummy (urban=1)	7459.48	6.259	.000
Sex (1=male, 0=Female) of head dummy	10607.4	5.892	.000
Value of F	10300.1		.000
Value of adjusted R-square	0.91		.000
Sample size	10080		.000

Source: Estimated from the HIES 2005 data.

Access to electricity is likely to increase income and thereby increase savings. This factor also represents modernisation and, therefore, may directly influence household savings. The coefficient is positive, as expected. Adjusted R-square is higher in this equation compared to the simple Keynesian formulation. The value of F is also higher and significant.

11.3 Rural-Urban Differences in Calorie Intake: Implications for Poverty Line

Rural-urban difference in food and calorie intake can have implications for nutrition programmes as well as for conceptual and measurement issues. Therefore, it is of interest whether there are rural-urban differences in the calorie inadequacy.

Table 11.8 presents pertinent data. Within each poverty group, a larger percentage of households in urban areas are taking less than the recommended calorie. Rural-urban difference in calorie inadequacy is the highest among the middle group (i.e., the moderate poor). Table 11.8 also shows that among the non-poor households, a larger share (25 per cent) of urban households' calorie intake is below the recommended level.

Table 11.9 shows that average calorie intake is 1,950 and 1,863 kcal respectively among extreme poor in rural and urban areas. The average calorie in moderate poor group is 2,255 and 2,159 kcal respectively in rural and urban areas. Thus, the location factor has an independent influence on calorie consumption.

Table 11.8: Calorie Inadequacy among Poverty Groups in Rural and Urban Areas

(Per Cent)

Poverty status	Area Code	0-1805	1806-2121	2122+	Total
Extreme poor (EP)	Rural	47.8	29.1	23.1	100.0
	Urban	58.2	25.0	16.8	100.0
Moderate poor (MP)	Rural	20.3	25.2	54.5	100.0
	Urban	31.0	30.5	38.5	100.0
Non-poor (NP)	Rural	7.0	12.4	80.7	100.0
	Urban	11.7	13.6	74.6	100.0

Source: Estimated from the HIES 2005 data.

Table 11.9: Average Calorie Intake in Urban and Rural Areas

Poverty Group	Rural/Urban	Average Calorie Per Person Per Day
Extreme poor (EP)	Rural	1950.4
	Urban	1862.8
Moderate poor (MP)	Rural	2255.3
	Urban	2159.9
Non poor (NP)	Rural	2841.1
	Urban	2768.7

Source: Estimated from the HIES 2005 data.

11.3.1 Consumption of Different Food Varieties

Rural-urban difference in food consumption in fact extends beyond the total calorie intake. The intakes of different food groups have been shown in Table 11.10.

Although the focus of the present study is total calorie intake of poor and non-poor group, discussion of consumption of various food items can be useful to demonstrate the extent of nutritional inadequacy among poor and non-poor in urban and rural areas. This is particularly important because of the difference in prices of rice and prices of protein food the latter being costlier. Therefore, poor households are likely to consume more rice and less protein.

For the three poverty groups, extreme poor, moderate poor and non-poor, data examines whether they consume at least 50 per cent or more of the recommended weight of protein items. Table 11.10 shows the picture of adequacy of intake of some major protein items. The standard for comparison has been obtained from the list used by HIES official poverty estimation. A few studies have provided other standard recommendations for intake of various types of food in Bangladesh (Jahan and Hossain, 1998). However, these are not accepted for official purposes due to a variety of reasons including inadequate coverage of areas of the country, small sample, etc. Jahan and Hossain (1998) present requirement of nutrient and not weights of actual food items and therefore cannot be applied directly.

Table 11.10: Fish, Meat and Chicken Consumption by Poverty Status

(Per Cent)

Poverty Status	Location	<=29.55	29.55-59.10	>=59.11	Total
Extreme poor (EP)	Rural	63.7	32.4	3.8	100.0
	Urban	51.6	41.4	7.0	100.0
	Total	61.5	34.1	4.4	100.0
Moderate poor (MP)	Rural	31.1	51.7	17.3	100.0
	Urban	22.7	53.5	23.8	100.0
	Total	28.7	52.2	19.1	100.0
Non-poor (NP)	Rural	9.9	32.5	57.6	100.0
	Urban	5.8	21.8	72.4	100.0
	Total	8.5	28.8	62.7	100.0
All	Rural	28.4	35.3	36.3	100.0
	Urban	15.1	29.2	55.7	100.0
	Total	24.5	33.5	42.0	100.0

(Columns under "Fish and Meat Consumption Group (grams)")

Source: Estimated from the HIES 2005 data.

Recommended weight of fish and all types of meat is 59.1 grams per day. Only 4 per cent of extreme poor population consume this quantity or higher. About 62 per cent consume less than half of the recommended weight. The situation is worse in the rural areas compared to urban areas for all poverty groups. Among the extreme poor in rural and urban areas, 64 and 52 per cent are in this group respectively. Similar difference prevails in the moderate poor group.

11.4 Concluding Remarks

The presence of substantial rural-urban difference in calorie intake makes it evident that the formulation of poverty line on the basis of same calorie cut-off for rural and urban areas is questionable.

Urbanisation is likely to have a cultural impact on food habit. Availability of a larger range of non-food consumer goods in urban areas is likely to result in higher non-food expenditure in urban areas leaving less for food expenditure. Moreover, work intensities of rural and urban occupations are likely to differ. Future research should focus on decomposition of the rural-urban difference in calorie intake into three parts: difference in non-food essential expenditure requirement, occupational difference and the cultural practices.

Large fluctuations in savings rate calculated from income and expenditure modules of HIES data of various rounds raise questions about the reasons of such fluctuation. Moreover, the data from the latest round of HIES, which shows a high rate of poverty reduction and a substantial decline of savings rate, implies that a close scrutiny of this aspect is called for.

Above discussion highlights an alternating upswing and downswing in the divisional poverty incidences in various rounds of HIES. Attention to these issues can be useful for policy guidance for not only reducing poverty in the areas with current high incidence of poverty but also for sustaining the poverty decline over a longer time span.

CHAPTER 12

Children's Employment and Its Link with Schooling: Role of Poverty and Social Attitude

12.1 Objectives and Rationale of the Analysis

The welfare loss due to children's employment consists of private welfare loss faced by the working children and the long-term adverse impact experienced by the society as a whole. Children's involvement in economic activities can be the root of many forms of deprivation of children, especially in the low-income countries including Bangladesh. The major forms of such deprivations include lack of human capital development and inadequate development of social values. In a country like Bangladesh, where poverty incidence is high, children's economic activity may result in the perpetuation of poverty of the households.

Elimination or reduction of children's employment requires increased awareness of the causes of such employment and its impacts. Increasing commitment to enhance such awareness has resulted in a large body of research studies on working children in Bangladesh. The studies have contributed to improvement of data on the situation of children's work and have led to awareness among the policymakers, employers and international organisations. These studies have focused mainly on specific types of economic activities of children and provided analysis of working conditions, wage rates, and hours of work in some particular sectors.[1] Although a large number of studies on working children are available, there are a few gaps in the knowledge about child labour and its impacts.

First, there are few studies on the national level trends of child labour situation and factors influencing children's employment. Second,

---
[1] A review of the available studies is given by King and Knox (2002).

child labour as a phenomenon is intricately linked with the possibility of schooling. Such linkages have not been adequately analysed. Third, existing voluminous empirical literature on child labour has somehow paid inadequate attention to the question of type of employment of children. It is an important lacunae both in the context of monitoring the extent of child labour and in the assessment of the negative impact of employment on children's investment on human capital. Whether children are engaged in paid or family employment is expected to be linked to the extent of debilitating impact of children's employment.

A widely held view on the subject of child labour is that part-time employment may not be in conflict with their acquisition of human capital. This is reflected in the fact that some of the published studies (Basu, 1999) on child labour do not include part-time workers. It implies that active steps for eradication of children's employment should be adopted only when this leads to associated evils like loss of the opportunity of schooling. Even when one observes that working less than standard hours may not be harmful, the relationship may not actually be a direct one and may in effect be due to the link between type of employment and working hours in the child labour market.

In fact, children's employment, access to schooling, and household poverty are expected to be interlinked. Better understanding of the linkages among these three aspects can help more appropriate policy adoption for reducing the welfare loss which occurs through children's employment. This chapter examines these linkages. The study focuses on the reasons behind children's participation as labour force members and the effect of household characteristics on such participation. Paid employment and self-employment of children can have contrasting relationships with poverty and blur the net effect of poverty. The objective of the present chapter includes empirical verification of such hypotheses in the context of Bangladesh's child labour market.

12.1.1 Sources of Data

A major part of the present study is based on the Bangladesh National Child Labour Survey (CLS) data and Labour Force Survey (LFS) data. These national sample surveys have been conducted by Bangladesh Bureau of Statistics (BBS).

The changes of the type and characteristics of children's work have been traced through comparison of data from the National Child Labour Surveys (NCLS) conducted in 1995-96 and 2002-2003. Another round of Child Labour Survey of BBS has been underway. Intensive analysis of unit level data of the CLS 2003 supplements the data from published reports.[2] Data from other secondary sources including published studies have also been used (with references at appropriate places).

National sample survey data has been supplemented by data from a special survey of working children titled "Urban Working Children Survey." The survey covers fifty-three children from two slum areas of Mirpur (within Dhaka Metropolitan area) and information has been collected from the working children as well as their parents. In addition, case studies of employers of informal sector are conducted to highlight their attitude about children's economic activity.

12.1.2 Organisation of the Chapter

The chapter has been organised as follows:
- Section 11.1 includes the objectives of the study and provides notes on data used in the study.
- Section 11.2 examines the changes of number of children in economic activity in Bangladesh and children's labour force participation rate over the period 1984-2006. This section also examines the sector and status of employment of children with a focus on changes in the extent of their participation in paid work.
- Section 12.3 and 12.4 analyse the factors influencing children's participation in paid employment and family employment. Family characteristics, the role of location (urban-rural) and regional differences receive attention.
- Section 12.5 examines the compatibility of children's employment and schooling.
- The last section presents policy suggestions.

12.2 Children's Employment: Types and Trends[3]

12.2.1 Children's Participation in Economic Activity

In the present analysis, the terms "children in employment/economic activity" and "working children" have been used synonymously. The

---

[2] The Labour Force Survey 2005-06 does not provide much detail on working children. Therefore, more in-depth analyses of the present study make use of the 2003 CLS.

[3] This Section draws from Rahman (2005).

definition of working children spelt out in the CLS 2003 includes those who are working one or more hours for pay or profit or working without pay in a family farm or enterprise during the reference period (last 7 days) or have a job or business from which he/she is temporarily absent (BBS, 2003). Current status has been used in almost all analysis with a reference period of last one week. For defining working children, the present study uses the cut off age of 5 to 17 years. This is in conformity with the criterion used by the Child Labour Survey (2002-2003) of Bangladesh and the standards set by UN convention. The age cut off for defining child or child labour has not been accepted unanimously and some agencies use different standards. Previous labour force surveys of Bangladesh have used 5-14 years as the age range for defining child labour. Therefore, in the cases of comparison of different rounds of the LFS data, 5-14 years have been used in some tables. For defining economic activities, standard SNA activities have been included.

Table 12.1: Labour Force Participation Rates of Children (Age 5-14): 1983-84 to 2011

Year and Source	Number ('000) of Economically Active Children			Children's Labour Force Participation Rate (%)		
	Total	Male	Female	Total	Male	Female
1983-84 LFS	3782	3104	674	15.9	21.8	4.9
1984-85 LFS	3774	3098	676	13.3	21.5	4.7
1989 LFS	5979	3537	2442	19.3	21.7	16.6
1990-91 LFS	5923	3844	2079	19.3	22.9	15.0
1995-96 LFS	6455	3856	2599	18.7	21.6	15.7
2002-03 NCLS	4692	3372	1319	13.4	18.5	7.8
2005-06 LFS	3718	2829	889	10.1	15.0	5.0
2011 SPC	999	699	300	6.0	9.1	2.6

Note: The 1989 and 1990-91 data are based on the extended definition of economically active population, while the rest are based on the usual definition, usual status. The 2011 data are from Population Census.
Source: CLS, 2003, LFS, 2006; BBS, BIDS & UNICEF (2015).

Table 12.1 (and Figure 12.1a) presents data on children's labour force participation rate (LFPR). Children's participation in economic activity increased during 1984-1989. The percentages were 16 and 19.3 in 1984 and 1989 respectively.

CHILDREN'S EMPLOYMENT AND ITS LINK WITH SCHOOLING 215

Figure 12.1a: Economic Participation Rate of Children (Age 5-14) by Gender, 1983-84 to 2011

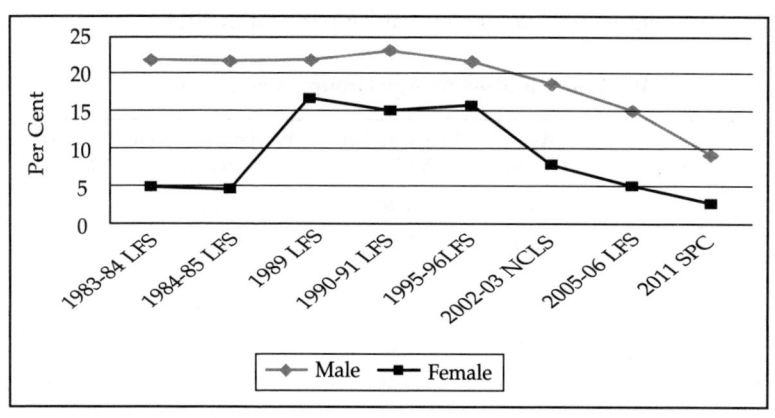

It remained unchanged in 1991. After 1991, the percentage of children in economic activity has been on the decline. It was 13.4 per cent and 10.1 per cent in 2003 and 2006 respectively. The 2011 data showed a large reduction in children's participation rate in economic activity, which stood at 6.0 per cent.

Figure 12.1b: Number of Children (Age 5-14) in Economic Activity by Gender, 1983-84 to 2011

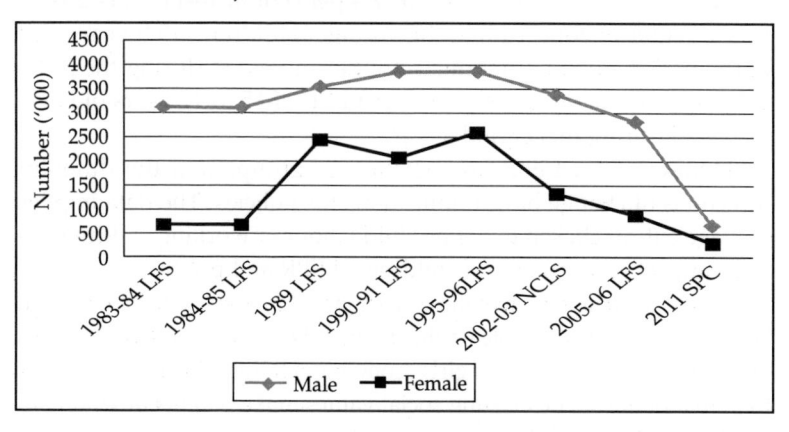

It should be highlighted that after 1995-96 not only the share of children but also the absolute number of children in economic activity declined (Figure 12.1b). The numbers of working children (age 5 to 14 years) were 6,4,55,000 and 3,7,18,000 in 1996 and 2006 respectively.

As shown in Table 12.1, the decline was larger for the girls compared to boys. Girls' LFPR declined to 5.0 per cent in 2005-06 from about 15.7 per cent in 1995-96. It stood at 2.6 per cent in 2011.

Table 12.2: Working Children by Age Group: 1996 to 2006

Year	Age (Years)	Total Children (Million)	Working Children (Million)	LFPR (Per Cent)
1996	05-09	17.40	.76	3.9
	10-14	17.06	5.82	29.2
2003	05-09	18.2	.36	2.0
	10-14	16.9	4.60	27.4
	15-17	7.32	2.91	39.8
2006	05-09	17.35	.66	3.8
	10-14	19.55	3.05	15.6
	15-17	5.89	2.80	47.5

Source: CLS (various years), LFS (various years).

Labour force participation rates of children in the age groups 5-9 years and 10-14 years have been shown separately in Table 12.2. In 2003, only 2 per cent children in the age group 5-9 years were engaged in economic activity compared to 27.4 per cent in 10-14 years group. It is a matter of concern that the younger children's (5-9 years old) participation rate in economic activities increased during the 2003-2006 period.[4] Table 12.2 shows that LFPR of 15 to 17 years old also increased during this period.

Differences in LFPR among the age groups and the different directions of change have implications for policies. The data implies that age cut-off chosen to define child labour or working children can have impact on estimates of children's LFPR and policies.

Data show that in each of these years girls' LFPR was much lower than boys'. In this context, a note on the quality of data for girl child deserves attention. Underreporting of girls economic activity is likely to be higher than that of boys. The existing social values make parents unwilling to disclose that girl children are engaged in income-earning work.

---

[4] The Urban Child Workers' (UCW) Survey (Rahman 2010) presents a figure on the basis of single year interval, which shows that the situation has worsened more for 7, 8 and 9 years old children.

12.2.2 Structure of Employment

This section examines the sector of employment in which children are engaged, their status of employment and type (formal vs. informal) of employment. Distribution of employment of children by formal and informal categories has been shown in Table 12.3. Data show that the number of children in both formal and informal employment went through a decline between 1996 and 2003. During this period working male children in formal and informal sectors decreased by 39 per cent and 6 per cent respectively. The informal sectors engaged 95.3 per cent of working children in 2003. The shares of formal sector were 4.6 per cent and 5.0 per cent among boys and girls respectively. Thus the difficult part of eliminating child labour consists of the informal sector employment.

Table 12.3: Formal and Informal Employment among Children: 1996-2003

Group	Number ('000)				Per Cent					
	Formal		Informal		Formal		Informal		All	
	1996	2003	1996	2003	1996	2003	1996	2003	1996	2003
Boys	270	164	3649	3400	6.9	4.6	93.1	95.4	100.0	100.0
Girls	120	71	2549	1357	4.5	5.0	95.5	95.0	100.0	100.0
All	390	235	6198	4757	6.0	4.7	94.0	95.3	100.0	100.0

Source: BBS, CLS (2003, 1996).

Table 12.4: Distribution of Working Children by Status of Employment: 1996-2003

(Per Cent)

Status	2003			1996		
	All	Male	Female	All	Male	Female
Self-employed	6.2	7.4	3.1	6.3	7.6	2.9
Unpaid Family Helper	56.6	49.7	76.0	56.7	49.5	76.7
Employee	9.1	8.6	5.8	8.3	8.6	7.6
Day Labour/Casual Labour	23.5	28.6	10.3	23.7	28.6	10.2
Paid Apprentice	1.7	2.2	0.4	3.3	4.2	0.7
(All Paid)	(34.3)	(39.4)	(16.9)	(35.3)	(41.4)	(18.5)
Others	2.9	2.1	1.1	1.7	1.6	1.9
Total	100.0	100.0	100.0	100.0	100.0	100.0

Source: BBS, CLS (2003, 1996).

Distribution of children's status of employment is shown in Table 12.4. Since the 2006 LFS does not provide data on working children's status/mode of employment, changes during 2003-2006 cannot be captured. Table 12.4 shows that about one-third of working children were engaged in paid employment in 2003. Between 1996 and 2003, there was hardly any change in the share of working children engaged in paid employment (35 per cent and 34 per cent in 1996 and 2003 respectively). Since children's participation in economic activity has fallen during this period and the share employed in paid employment has remained almost unchanged, it can be concluded that children's participation rate in paid employment has also gone down.

12.2.3 Sector of Employment

Table 12.5 shows that the sector composition of working children has changed over the inter-survey period. The percentage of working children employed in agriculture declined from 65.4 per cent in 1996 to 56.4 per cent in 2003 and to 39 per cent in 2011. This has been accompanied by increases in the percentage of children in non-farm sectors, especially services and manufacturing. This is consistent with the fact that child workers share in "regular employee" category increased between 1996 and 2003, and service and manufacturing sectors usually depend on regular employees.

Table 12.5: Working Children's Distribution by Sector of Activity

(Per Cent)

Sector	1996 All	1996 Male	1996 Female	2003 All	2003 Male	2003 Female	2011 All	2011 Male	2011 Female
Agricultural	65.4	67.1	63.0	56.4	55.5	59.1	39	45	16
Manufacturing	8.2	9.7	7.0	17.7	15.9	22.5	20	18	29
Transport	1.8	3.0	0.1	4.5	5.9	0.7	41*	37*	55*
Other Service	10.3	14.4	4.2	16.8	19.3	10.1			
Others + Household service	14.4	6.8	25.7	4.4	3.3	7.7			

Note: *Total of all services.
Source: BBS, CLS (2003, 1996), BBS, BIDS and UNICEF (2015).

12.3 A Framework for Analysis of Children's Participation in Economic Activity

Children's employment is usually viewed as a decision of the parents and thus the supply side dominates the analysis of children's labour force behaviour. The present analysis also focuses on the supply-side factors. It examines the compatibility of children's employment and schooling and both are supply-side decisions in the present context. An understanding of the factors affecting children's participation in economic activities can also serve the purpose of generating insights into factors underlying their participation (or lack of it) in schooling. However, the analytical context integrating both supply and demand side factors affecting children's employment provides the context even for an empirical analysis which focuses mainly on the supply related factors.

Figure 12.2: Factors behind Children's Employment

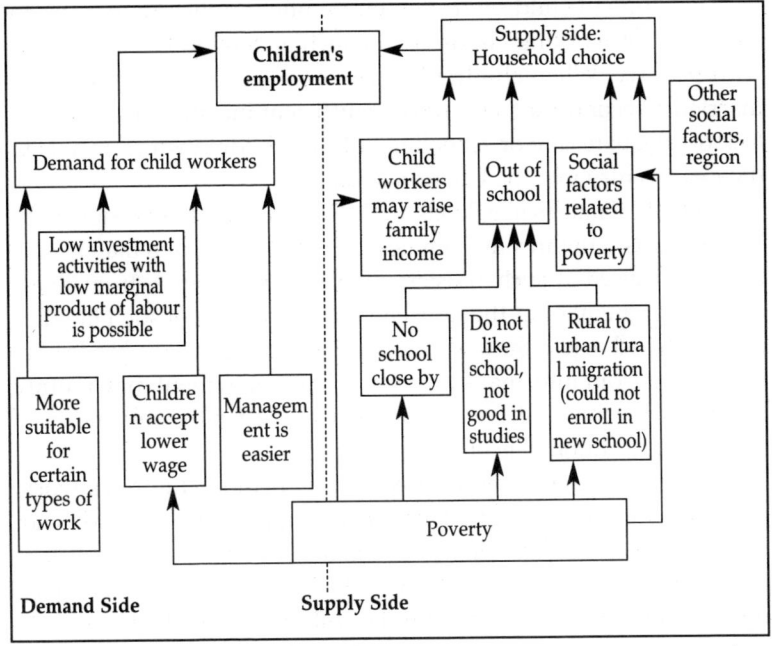

These forces are shown in Figure 12.2. The immediate factors on the supply side work through some intermediate forces. The figure shows how the immediate first layer of factors and the second layer of factors are linked. Poverty is a common block operating behind most factors and it can be argued that in the absence of poverty, the immediate causes may not lead to children's employment. Following discussion elaborates on the processes through which poverty can contribute to child labour.

Internal migration of poor households and settling in new homestead, especially in urban slums, often create processes which push children to work. Lack of security of young girls living in the urban slums of Bangladesh often compels the working mothers to allow children work. It may be safer that the girls spend their time at the place of work rather than staying alone in the shack in the slum. With growing problems of drug addiction and violence, similar concern holds for boys as well. Parents, therefore, want that boys enter employment if they are not going to school. These forms of vulnerability and insecurity are intricately linked to poverty.

Alienation of children from their families implies an increase in the extent of working children and such alienation has close links with poverty. When children's own parents are not alive or have married a second time and have insufficient income, there may be lack of adequate care or schooling of those children which results in their early entry into the labour market.

Natural calamities like floods, cyclones and riverbank erosion cause loss of assets. Low-income families have little margin to manage the problems caused by such disasters. Similar situation arises from illness of an adult member of the household and children of such families are compelled to join the labour force. Such emergencies often lead to borrowing from informal sources and loan repayment may require additional income. Children's employment is often the only means of generating additional income.

Poverty also acts as an indirect reason behind children's work, especially their wage employment. For example, when a child is not good in studies, parents will allow him/her to repeat a class or engage a house-tutor if they can afford one. If there is no school in the vicinity, not-so-poor parents usually send the children to a distant school. In contrast, if the parents are poor, any of the above situations will mean non-enrolment/dropout. The next step is that parents try to engage the children in income-earning activities.

Some social factors may lead to children's work in the case of both poor and non-poor households. Non-poor households can afford to send children to school and engage hired labour in family farm/enterprises. Even then some of the families may encourage children to work in the family enterprise, at least on a part time basis, so that they learn the work. Imperfect functioning of the labour market also provides the motivation for mobilising more family members including children.

12.3.1 Demand-Side Factors

Even if the supply side factors dominate the discussion of causes of child labour, the demand-side factors must be present to translate the willingness of parents into actual involvement of children in economic activity. Demand related questions of child labour use did not receive attention in recent researches because of the implicit assumption that child labour and adult labour are more or less perfect substitutes.

Lower wage rate of the child workers is the strongest motivation behind the employers' preference for such workers. A child worker is usually categorised as helper and accordingly paid a lower wage although some of them may have equal productivity as adult workers. Low wage of children is also linked to the low bargaining power of low-income families. Moreover, children are not usually employed by formal enterprises and therefore the demand is limited. Legal restrictions on employment of child labour are complied only by formal enterprises. Such restrictions limit the scope of bargaining by child workers' parents. Poor parents who are in urgent need to generate income accept low wage for their children. Chandrashekhar (1997) observes that some of these factors are relevant in the context of some Indian enterprises.

The working children are provided less facilities at their work places and thereby they contribute to lower non-wage costs of employment. Advantage of employing child workers includes non-economic factors as well. One major attitudinal factor is that children are much less aware of their rights. They accept orders and carry out monotonous work for many hours because of their lack of awareness about workers' rights. For the employers, another attractive feature of child workers is that they cannot become members of organised trade unions. Many employers are averse to trade unionism.

Discussion in the following section attempts at empirical examination of a combination of both demand and the supply-side factors. In addition, case studies have been conducted to highlight the attitude of employers. These are presented in Section 12.5.

12.4 Factors Affecting Children's Participation in Paid and Family Employment

This section analyses the impacts of household level factors, especially the roles of poverty and asset in the choice of children's paid and self-employment. This provides a basis for the analysis of Section 6 which examines the reasons why working children do not simultaneously pursue education.

Table 12.6: Parents' Response on Reasons of Children's Employment

(Per Cent)

Parent's Opinion: Why a Child Works?	Paid	Self/Family	All
To enhance family income	71.2	69.1	69.9
Repayment of family loan	4.1	3.9	3.9
To run family business	.9	3.3	2.4
No school close by	.3	.3	.3
For future of the child work is good	3.7	2.9	3.2
Unable to bear the educational expenses	5.5	3.0	3.9
Child's unwillingness to learning or unsuccessful in studies	4.5	5.0	4.9
Others	9.9	12.4	11.5
Total	100.0	100.0	100.0

Source: NCLS (2003).

The reasons mentioned in the above scheme (Figure 12.2) can be verified through direct enquiry and interview of the parents. The following discussion presents parents' direct responses and is supplemented through analysis of data on family situation. Table 12.6 presents the NCLS data on reasons behind children's employment as stated by the parents. A large majority (about 70 per cent) stated "to increase household income," while some of the other responses are also manifestations of household poverty.[5] For example, "cannot bear expenses of school" means that due to inadequate income, the child stops going to school and after the children drop out of the school system, the parents usually consider that their involvement in income-earning jobs is the best available option. About 4 per cent cases reported the need for loan repayment as the cause of children's work. This is also a reflection of household poverty. Lack of school in close proximity

---

[5] These responses were provided in the questionnaire. The response "to increase family income" is, however, almost definitionally true.

was the reason for only 0.3 per cent households. Five per cent parents considered the unwillingness of the child to attend school (or to learn) as the reason for child's employment.

Since children's involvement in income earning is usually viewed as derogatory, it is understandable that parents will try to emphasise their "lack of means for supporting child's education" as the major reason behind child's employment. Therefore, a follow up question was asked about how serious is the need for generating income through engaging children in economic activity (Table 12.7). About 9 per cent households said "survival would be difficult" without the child's income. For another 69 per cent households "standard of living would decline." Since most families with child labour are living in poverty, a further decline may accentuate poverty for those households.

Table 12.7: Consequence If a Child Stops Work

(Per Cent)

Consequence if a Child Stops Work	Paid	Current Status Self/Family	All
Standard of living will decline	67.4	69.2	68.6
Survival will be at stake	15.6	5.4	9.1
Running business of the hh impossible	0.8	3.1	2.3
Running family farm difficult	1.4	3.8	2.9
Others	10.0	12.5	11.6
Total	100.0	100.0	100.0

Source: NCLS (2003).

Tables 12.8 and 12.9 show the impact of family's land asset and its current income on incidence of children in employment.

Table 12.8: Share of Children in Self/Family and Paid Employment by Household's Landownership

(Per Cent)

Land Group (in Acres)	Paid	Self/Family	None	Total	All Employment
0.00-0.49	9.1	10.2	80.6	100.0	19.3
0.50-.099	5.9	13.1	81.0	100.0	19.0
1.00-2.49	3.3	14.1	82.6	100.0	17.4
2.50-5.00	2.1	15.3	82.6	100.0	17.4
5.00+	1.8	15.2	83.0	100.0	17.0
Total	6.6	12.0	81.4	100.0	18.6

Source: NCLS (2003).

When one looks at the aggregate of all status of employment of children (last column of Tables 12.8 and 12.9), a continuous negative relationship over the entire range is not apparent. However, the highest income group has much lower incidence of children's employment compared to lower-income groups. The incidence of children's employment is the highest in second and third income quintiles. An interesting feature of the data presented in Table 12.9 is that incidence of paid employment of children declines monotonically with household income, whereas among self-employed the relationship is not continuous. As a result, when the two status of employment are lumped together, the association with income gets blurred (last column).

Table 12.9: Households with Children in Economic Activity by Status of Employment of Head of Household by Income Group

(Per Cent)

Income Group (in Tk.)	Paid (1)	Self/Family (2)	None (3+4)	Total	Children in any Employment
0-2000	8.5	10.8	80.8	100.0	19.3
2001-3000	7.7	13.3	79.0	100.0	21.0
3001-4000	7.1	13.7	79.2	100.0	20.8
4001-6000	5.1	12.5	82.4	100.0	17.6
6001+	3.3	9.1	87.6	100.0	12.4
Total	6.6	12.0	81.4	100.0	18.6

Source: NCLS (2003).

However, what appears to be a selfish endeavour to improve family's standard of living may as well be motivated by human capital development in an indirect manner. The earnings made by one child may be used to cover the expenses of education of other children in the family. This can be tested empirically by looking at the effect of the number of children in a family on the probability that one child works. This hypothesis has been tested through logistic regression analysis. If such link prevails, it can have important implications for policies related to fertility decline as well as for elimination of child labour.

The relationship between income and incidence of child labour (Table 12.8) shows that children are employed in a large percentage of non-poor families as well. This implies that policies for complete ban on children's employment should be implemented with income support only to families which were entirely dependent on child's earning as the source of income. Nonetheless, the observed behaviour is likely to be influenced by associated social forces as well.

When one looks at children's employment as a whole, irrespective of type of work, relationship with household's landownership is not strong (last column of Table 12.8). When the link between paid and family employment is dealt with separately, paid employment has a strong negative association with landownership while the incidence of self/family employment of children rises with ownership of land. The contrasting relationship demonstrates that the two types of employment are considered to have distinct implications for social status of a household and therefore for their choice of use of family labour in economic activities. In fact, larger landownership (which is often associated with larger numbers of livestock in the family farm unit) generates demands for labour, which cannot be always met with hired labour and all members of the family may share the work.

12.5 Attitude towards Poor Working Children's Education: Parents' and Children's Views[6]

12.5.1 Transition from School to Work

In the survey of poor slum households with working children (Rahman 2010), questions were asked to generate information on whether children's employment directly causes them to dropout from school. The questions have been phrased as follows:

a. Did the child drop out from school before or after she/he started work and how long after or before work?
b. Whether the child dropped out through a clear decision implemented in one step or it was done gradually by being absent now and then.
c. Whether the child's parents kept school fees outstanding for a considerable period before she/he dropped out.

Table 12.10 shows that only 8.1 per cent of the working children left school after they started to work or simultaneously, 51.3 per cent left 1 to 12 months before they took employment and 41 per cent left school one year or a longer period before they started work.

---
[6] This section draws from Rahman (2010).

Table 12.10: Time Gap between Leaving School and Joining Work

(Per Cent)

Time Gap between Leaving School and Joining Work	Male	Female	Total
After joining work	4.3	14.3	8.1
1-6 months before joining work	13.0	14.3	13.5
7-12 months before joining work	34.8	42.9	37.8
13 months+ before joining work	47.8	28.6	40.5
Total	100.0	100.0	100.0

Source: Rahman (2010).

Table 12.11 shows that 17.2 per cent of those who are not studying dropped out in one step. The rest (82.8 per cent) became irregular in attendance and then stopped going to school.

Table 12.11: School Dropout Children's Experience

(Per Cent)

Process through which Child Left School	Male	Female	All
Suddenly absent one day	15.8	20.0	17.2
Slowly absent	84.2	80.0	82.8
Total	100.0	100.0	100.0

Whether any School Fees were Outstanding before Leaving School	Male	Female	Total
Yes	54.2	43.8	50.0
No	45.8	56.3	50.0
Total	100.0	100.0	100.0

Did it happen that Child Could Not Complete Home Task for School?	Male	Female	Total
Frequently	14.3	4.0	9.4
Occasionally	75.0	72.0	73.6
Rare	3.6	8.0	5.7
No	7.1	16.0	11.3
Total	100.0	100.0	100.0

Source: Rahman (2010).

Fifty per cent of working children, who are not currently studying, went through a phase when school fees remained outstanding (Table 12.11). Home task for school remained frequently incomplete for 9.4 per cent cases and occasionally incomplete for 73.6 per cent cases (Table 12.11). Data thus show that dropping out of the school system was a gradual process. The process began when the parents without lack of means could not pay school fees, and children were unable to complete "home work" for the school. The children then started disliking school and remained occasionally absent. Then ultimately they stopped attending school.

The above description does not mean that children's employment prospects had no role to play in the process of discontinuation of studies. Such prospects played an indirect role through offering an attractive alternative to studies. In this context, the following case study is quite illustrative.

Case Study: Hamida's Sons

Mrs. Hamida and her husband Nasim and two sons (10 years and 6 years old) lived in a village in Rangpur, a northern district. Nasim used to work as a seasonal agricultural labourer and also tried petty trading in vegetables. But the earnings were not enough for four persons. So they left the village home and came to Dhaka. Nasim has rented a rickshaw van and transports heavy loads. Hamida has got a temporary job in the kitchen of a cafeteria of an office. The earning is now enough.

After they came to Dhaka, Hamida sent her older son to a "Madrasa" close to her house where the fee is nominal. But after a few months the child started to remain absent from school. In spite of all persuasions, he did not attend regularly. Sometimes, he would go to different places in the city with his friends. For enjoyment, they needed money. The older son began collecting things from garbage bins and other places and made a few takas. He may have done odd jobs in the market places, but his parents did not know exactly what type of work it was. Eventually, he stopped going to school. Since he was spending most of his time with his friends, his parents became worried. One of Nasim's relatives worked in a factory about 30 km away from Dhaka. That relative did a great favour to Hamida and Nasim. He requested his employer to employ this boy. But the boy did not like the routine job and whenever he came to his parents' home on weekends or on other leave, he would overstay and go back only reluctantly.

Hamida has been careful with the second son. She has put him in a government primary school. Here the pressure is less. The boy is continuing his studies.

"We have learnt from the experience with our elder son. Quality of school is very important. My younger son likes this school." Responding to a question as to why she failed to do this in the case of the first son, she said that they did not have much experience about the difference in the type of school and they could not pay full attention to this because they were busy finding suitable work for themselves to earn enough for the family. Now she wishes that the younger son gets good education and a good job.

12.5.2 Parents Attitude about Working Son's/Daughters' Education

The purpose of seeking opinion of parents of working children about son's/daughter's education was twofold: first, to get an idea about their general attitude towards educating children and second, to obtain an idea about what they feel about the child's prospects after she/he started work. These details about attitude of parents can provide insights about how to design the awareness programmes to eliminate child labour.

Table 12.12 shows that parents were not averse to education of children; 79 per cent parents thought that they should study at least upto age 15. Only 4 per cent said a straight "no" to this question; 17 per cent expressed doubts with "what will be the benefit of such education!"

As shown in Table 12.13, 10.2 per cent parents were of the opinion that if the children do not want to go to school, they should engage in earning, while about 80 per cent believe that persuasion could be the strategy to send them to school.

Table 12.12: Whether Son/Daughter Should Study upto at least Age 15: Parent's Opinion

(Per Cent)

Do you think that Son/Daughter should Study Upto Age 15	Parent of Working Son	Parent of Working Daughter	Total
Yes	82.1	76.0	79.2
No	3.6	4.0	3.8
What will be the benefit?	14.3	20.0	17.0
Total	100.0	100.0	100.0

Source: Rahman (2010).

Table 12.13: If Children Do Not Go to School What Should be Done?: Parent's Opinion

(Per Cent)

What is to be done if they do not go to School	Parent of Working Son	Parent of Working Daughter	Total
Send them forcibly	3.8	8.7	6.1
Send them by persuasion	76.9	82.6	79.6
Engage them in earning	15.4	4.3	10.2
Others	3.8	4.3	4.1
Total	100.0	100.0	100.0

Source: Rahman (2010).

Table 12.14 shows answers to supplementary questions on poor parents' attitude to schooling. About 78 per cent answered "yes" to the question "Do you think you should consult the teacher if the child wishes to leave school."

Table 12.14: Parents' Views on Children's Schooling and Work

(Per Cent)

	Parent of Working		Total
	Son	Daughter	
Is it necessary to consult with teacher if the child wants to leave school			
Yes	70.4	84.0	76.9
No	7.4	.0	3.8
Consultation will be of no use	22.2	16.0	19.2
Total	100.0	100.0	100.0
Do you think that your child can earn more if he studies 2 or 3 years more			
Yes	78.6	76.0	77.4
No	21.4	24.0	22.6
Total	100.0	100.0	100.0
Was it an unwise decision to stop child's school?			
Yes	19.2	29.4	23.3
Sometimes	15.4	.0	9.3
No	65.4	70.6	67.4
Total	100.0	100.0	100.0
Child is learning something which will help him in future			
Yes	19.2	4.0	11.8
Slightly	23.1	48.0	35.3
No	57.7	48.0	52.9
Total	100.0	100.0	100.0

Source: Rahman (2010).

While 77.4 per cent parents considered that 2 or 3 years more schooling would enable the child to earn more, 33 per cent parents felt (answered straight "yes" or "sometimes") that it was not a wise decision to stop studies.

Parents were not happy about scope of skill acquisition of working children from their present jobs. Only 12 per cent thought that children are acquiring useful skills. Another 35.3 per cent responded to this question as slightly or to some extent and about 53 per cent said the children were not learning anything useful.

Parents' as well as children's views were sought on the future of working children. Parents were asked two questions: first, 'what do they wish the child to do' and second, 'how this can be achieved'? Parents "wishes" about what the child should do were limited, because the child was already working. The answers are not presented in a table, as most of them said, "the child should do well in their work."

12.5.3 Working Children's Attitude

12.5.3.1 Problems Faced by Working Children who are Studying

The interview of working children who were also studying included a question on the problems they faced in combining the two. The constraint that was apparent to the outsider was that the children did not get adequate time to study. A realistic description of this incompatibility came out through the responses of children. For example, they said:

"If I am late at school, the teacher scolds
If I am at work, I forget about school and reach the school late
If I go late, I sit in the 'last bench'
If I am late, the teacher marks me 'absent'
I cannot learn my studies because I do not have time.
I cannot answer the teacher's question."

In this list, lack of time for learning studies was not one of the major concerns of the children. The matters which troubled them were the immediate outcomes. These are usually no less important for sustaining children's interest in school.

When parents were asked about why children left school, they focused mainly on lack of means for continuing school and the need for family expenses and "not good in studies" in general terms.

Children's responses to the question "what is the main reason for not continuing studies" have been presented in Table 12.15. About their lack of interest in school, as mentioned above, parents described it in general terms as "not good in studies." In contrast, the children were more specific. Not good in studies, no interest in studies and beating by the teacher, these three responses accounted for 21 per cent cases. Forty-one per cent said in various terms that lack of means for bearing school expenses was the reason. Family dislocation (in the form of quarrel, death, migration, etc.) was the next frequent reason. Children's responses demonstrated their feelings about studies and why they dropped out from school.

Table 12.15: What are the Major Reasons for Not Studying: Children's Response

Response	Per Cent
No parents	9.1
Eldest son's duty	2.3
Lack of means	40.9
No interest in study	9.1
Not good in study	9.1
Father separated	4.5
Quarrel in family	2.3
Father wanted it	6.8
No other earner	4.5
Mother ill	2.3
Mother only earner	2.3
Teacher beats	2.3
Migration	2.3
Total	100.0

Source: Rahman (2010).

12.6 Policy Suggestions

12.6.1 General suggestions

Polices related to elimination of child labour are undoubtedly desirable steps in the social development of a country. It is desirable from the perspective of human rights and child rights. However, the adoption and implementation of such steps are not easy. Policy adoption in this sphere often faces some dilemma. The major difficulties underlying policy-making in this area must be understood before appropriate steps are taken. Only a few obvious factors have been mentioned below:

- Households in which children are only/major earners will face survival problem if sudden steps are taken to stop all types of child labour. For some households, even if bare survival is possible without child's earning, it may lead to drop out of other children from school because the expenses cannot be met.
- Children who are "not good in studies" or "does not like school" and therefore drop out from school education will sit idle for a considerable period of time and this may not be the most desirable situation for building human capital.
- The currently employed child workers who are released as part of implementation of ban on child labour cannot easily restart schooling.

The first difficultly may be dealt with through provision of safety net for such families. This is especially important in times of unforeseen food scarcity. For example, in the period of escalating rice price in 2007-08, parents reported that one of their responses to high rice price was to send children to work (Rahman, Begum and Bhuyan 2009). The second problem needs to be approached through systematic alternative modes of human capital development for out of school children. However, as the number of school dropout children is very large, it will be extremely difficult to absorb all of them in skill development programmes. Therefore, the elimination of children's employment requires improvement of the school system so that drop out is reduced to a minimum. Policies must be adopted to retain children in schools. With the above perspective, some specific recommendations have been listed below.

12.6.2 Improvement of the System of Education and Reduction of Drop out

Keeping children in school is the most effective way to eliminate child labour. To retain children in schools, the system of education must be made attractive and school education must demonstrate its relevance for employment. The curricula and teaching methods must improve. Scholarship programmes already taken up by the government have proved to be useful in this context. But this is not sufficient to generate enthusiasm among the students.

12.6.3 Programmes for Skill Training

Training policies for the prospective child labourers, especially from low-income groups, should include scope for programmes for their useful engagement in non-formal education. This may take various forms, ranging from informal schooling to various types of social work and voluntary work under the guidance of NGOs, private schools, etc. Skill upgradation programmes can be useful for some of the children who are currently working. Skills should be chosen with the objective that in future they can move to jobs with higher productivity and higher remuneration. Skill training must be carefully planned to include both full time training and part-time training, especially evening or early morning courses suitable for children who are engaged in part-time work.

Some of the children who show aptitude for self-employment should be provided relevant skill training along with management training. This may be viewed as a package and should be followed up by a monitoring team. There should be provision for giving them access to inputs needed for setting up enterprises. Since these young people begin without much experience, they require some sort of "incubation" facilities for their enterprises.

Children who receive training suitable for wage employment should be linked directly with employers. The employers may help in such training and may be encouraged to give part-time employment to the children in the relevant enterprises.

12.6.4 Need for Awareness Raising

As has been mentioned above, the adverse implications of children's work are often not so obvious and many employers of children consider this as a favour to the children and their poor parents. However, child labour should be viewed as a special dimension of deprivation and should not be overshadowed by the concern about family poverty (Saith and Wazir, 2010).

Campaign should be taken up to discourage employment of child labour in both formal and informal sectors. Society's awareness about the harms done by children's work must be improved. This is especially relevant for the informal sectors where the ban on child labour cannot be monitored properly. Campaign should be taken up for parents as well, which can target the poorer households willing to send their children to work. The indirect harmful effects should also be emphasised. The electronic media can play a role in this context.

It has been demonstrated that a variety of reasons work together to make the use of child labour more profitable. As a result, ban on child labour goes against employers' interest. Ban of child labour may not be against the interest of parents or teachers. These two groups will happily accept the ban if government, in addition to the ban, takes steps to keep the children in the learning process and makes provision of income support for at least the poorest families.

12.6.5 Some Immediate Steps

Child labour and children's work cannot be completely eliminated in the short run, because many children without adult family earners need to ensure their own livelihood. The state may not be able to take full responsibility to provide support to all such families.

Does it imply that children who remain out of school may be allowed to join the labour force after some time? Even though one is sure that a group of children are not going back to school, they should not be allowed to join the child labour force. If they are allowed, then other parents will be encouraged to take children out of school.

Then the question is what types of work should be immediately banned and how the quality and quantity of work done by children can be monitored. Strong monitoring mechanisms should be established to help eliminate overwork, harmful and immoral work and the worst forms of child labour. Therefore, it is necessary to identify specific types of activities which should be eliminated in phases.

Data have shown that a large share of working children is toiling for long hours and they do not receive additional compensation for working longer than the standard hours. Economic work for more than 20 hours a week can be extremely harmful for the development of children and their attitude. Data show that only a small share of these children (working long hours) is engaged in schooling. A much higher share of paid child employees compared to children in family employment belong to this group.

Therefore, children's employment above certain duration should be prohibited. This cut-off line can be chosen in the range of 14 to 20 hours a week, which can still allow children attend school. This may be implemented in phases for various age groups, beginning with paid workers in 5-12 years age group immediately and covering 10 to 14 years aged in the near future.

The next phase would be to ban all types of employment and all lengths of weekly hours for 5-12 years age group. They are expected to complete their primary school during this age. It is preferable to choose this option even as the very first step. In the third phase, even part time paid employment is to be eliminated for 13 to 14 years age group followed by elimination of part-time self/family employment for this group.

In addition to the ban on children's employment in phases, steps should be taken to assist parents in putting children to school at the right time. This will be especially relevant for parents in urban slums, socially disadvantaged groups and for those in remote places and areas affected by natural disasters. In addition, each step of ban of child labour must be accompanied by scope of learning activities for children who are not in school.

CHAPTER 13

Microfinance and Development: Emerging Issues

13.1 Introduction

Microcredit (MC) has played an important role as an instrument for enhancing income and employment of the poorer households in Bangladesh. Microfinance Institutions (MFIs) in Bangladesh have developed innovative mechanisms for providing collateral-free loans to the poor and asset-less households. During the three decades of operation, MFIs have used innovative strategies to solve many problems which could not be foreseen initially. As MC has been expanding, new challenges are emerging. The present chapter analyses the following issues which are important for the future of microfinance in Bangladesh and may pose as key challenges for the MFIs.

    a. Expansion of microfinance (MF) will depend on the scope of profitable investment by the borrowers and on the rates of return from MC financed employment. So one must analyse the returns to labour and capital of MC recipients' enterprises.

    b. A related question is what range of rate of interest can help in this endeavour and whether rate of interest on MC is high;

    c. Another aspect of MFI activities which did not receive much attention so far is whether MFIs should include mostly women as their credit recipients, as is presently being done.

13.2 Return from Economic Activities Financed by Microcredit

Whether MC helps income growth of recipient families have been analysed by a large number of researches on the subject. A direct assessment of the impact of MC on income growth or poverty is difficult. Past studies of impact of MC on income growth adopted a number of alternative approaches and sophisticated econometric techniques. But such assessment is time consuming and resource intensive.

Most studies on assessment of impact of MC on poverty are based on household consumption expenditure. Such assessment may not, however, fully reflect the impact of MC on income, because MC may be directly channelled to consumption and get reflected as poverty reduction even without an impact on income.

An analysis of rates of return from economic activities pursued through use of MC can provide some idea about the possible impact of MC on household income. From the early days of the expansion of MFIs, the skeptics have put forward the view that MC-financed activities bring a low return and MC cannot therefore be instrumental in raising household income. A deep-rooted apprehension is that, given the low rate of return from most of the existing rural activities, investment opportunities will soon be exhausted and the scope for further expansion of MC will be limited. The decline of rate of return is likely to discourage the participation of the family labour force in these activities.

Table 13.1: Return Per Hour of Labour Input in Activities Financed by MC

Activity		Rate of Return Per Hour (Taka in 1996)
Rickshaw Plying	Case 1	5.4
	Case 2	5.3
	Case 3	1.4
Oilseed processing	Case 1	5.3
	Case 2	3.5
	Case 3	2.5
Food processing	Case 1	2.5
	Case 2	2.9
	Case 3	2.8
Bamboo craft	Case 1	2.9
	Case 2	3.2
	Case 3	3.5
Paddy husking	Case 1	2.9
	Case 2	2.8
Tailoring	Case 1	6.0
	Case 2	6.2
Livestock	Case 1	0.9
	Case 2	0.8
Peddling	Case 1	8.7
	Case 2	1.8

Source: Rahman (2004b).

A direct analysis of whether the return from MC-financed activities is low and therefore inadequate for loan repayment at the current rate of interest is pertinent and data from studies conducted during the 1990s as well as case studies conducted in recent years are presented below. Among the past studies Hossain (1984) and Rahman and Khandker (1994) confirm that the returns to labour from many activities are high and only for some of the activities returns are lower than the market wage rate. However, the return may be considered sufficient for loan repayment as long as it is positive after taking into account the payment of interest on capital. Some of the spare-time activities such as livestock raising may generate low returns, whereas skill-intensive activities yield a higher return as shown in Table 13.1. Rural male wage rates in that year has been in the range of Tk. 4.8 to Tk. 5.5 and many cases of tailoring, peddling and rickshaw pulling show higher hourly return. Some activities generate lower return, but it is still worthwhile to pursue the MC-financed activity if it is not taken up at the cost of other activities with higher returns or higher wages. This is likely to be the case because adequate wage employment opportunities are not usually available, especially for female workers.

The point of concern in this respect is the opportunity cost of labour in alternative uses. It has been widely recognised that such opportunity cost is low, especially among women who are not engaged in directly productive activities. Many of the male borrowers undertake the MC-financed activities through extra hours of work during unemployed days in slack seasons or as an extension of existing self-employment. The opportunity cost of labour is low in such cases and it can be worthwhile to pursue the MC-financed activities even if the returns from such activities are lower than the prevailing wage rate.

One should also look at the rate of return to capital, to examine whether the return per taka of investment is positive at the current rate of interest. The above discussion on the opportunity cost of labour, however, points towards the difficulty of calculating the net return to capital after accounting for labour cost. Imputing family labour cost, either at market wage or at zero opportunity cost of labour, can result in negative or extremely high rate of return respectively. Both can be misleading and cannot provide guidance for setting rate of interest within a realistic range. Recent examples from specific cases can illustrate this problem.

13.2.1 Rate of Return to Non-Farm Activities: Recent Evidence[1]

At the very beginning, it must be clarified that the entire return to a MC-financed activity cannot be attributed to MC. Value of capital in an enterprise consists of investment financed by MC as well as other sources of loan and own savings. But one cannot partition the return to each source of fund in proportion to the amount invested. In fact, money is fungible and one cannot be sure whether one source of fund would be available for investment if other sources were not present. In this sense, even consumption expenditure financed by MC may have contributed to investment. Therefore, a simple method is used here whereby rate of return to the entire capital has been calculated after accounting for all current cost including cash wage. The rate of returns to sub-sectors and to activities with various size of capital within each sub-sector have been calculated to draw conclusions on which activities can or should grow through further allocation of MC.

Table 13.2: Returns to Labour and Capital: Case Studies of Poultry Farms

Inputs/Return		Poultry Farm Case 1 (Large)	Poultry Farm Case 2 (Medium)	Poultry Farm Case 3 (Very Small)
Family labour	Male	2	2	1.0
	Female	-	-	0.5
Hired labour	Male	2	1	-
	Female	-	-	-
Salary per month per labour		3,562	3,000	-
Fixed capital (taka) with land		450,000	344,100	12,000
Working capital (taka)		225,000	121,400	54,000
Land used in the enterprise (taka)		10 Dec.	4 Dec.	1 Dec
Total land owned		18 Dec.	8 Dec.	3 Dec.
Yearly net income of the owner of the enterprise		3.0 Lac	1.56 Lac	0.13 Lac
Return as % of capital		44.4	33.5	20.7
Sources of capital		SELF	BRAC	ASA
Women's participation as labour (%)		0	0	33
Total capital (fixed plus current) per labour		168,750	155,166	44,000
Fixed capital per labour (taka)		112,500	114,700	8,000

Source: Khalily and Rahman (2011).

---

[1] This section draws from Khalily and Rahman (2011) and Rahman (2004b).

Table 13.3: Returns to Labour and Capital: Case Studies of Rice Mills and Paddy Processing

Inputs/Return		Rice Mill (Big)	Rice Mill (Med.)	Paddy Processing (Very Small)
Family labour	Male	2	4	1.5
	Female	-	-	0.5
Hired labour	Male	20	3	-
	Female	5	10	-
Salary per month per labour		4,750	2,375	-
Fixed capital (taka) with land		20,000,000	2.5 Lac	5,000
Working capital (taka)		51 Lac	15 Lac	16,500
Land used in the enterprise		150 Dec.	100 Dec.	0.5 Dec
Total land owned		250 Dec.	125 Dec.	6 Dec.
Monthly net income from the enterprise (taka)		14 Lac	3.5 Lac	3,780
Return as % of capital		57.7	303.5	211.0
Sources of capital		KRISHI BANK	KRISHI BANK	BRAC and ASA
Women's participation as labour (%)		18.5	58.8	25.0
Capital per labour (taka)		930,000	102,900	10,750

Source: Khalily and Rahman (2011).

Case studies presented below help answer some of the questions on scope of scaling up the current activities. Rural non-farm (RNF) enterprises of poor and non-poor households are usually of different nature. The linkages between self-employment and return to labour can be understood through detailed data on labour input and capital used in poor and non-poor households' enterprises.

Data for a number of enterprises from two sub-sectors have been presented in Tables 13.2 and 13.3. These are poultry production and paddy processing. In both tables, the first few columns show enterprises of non-poor households and the last column provides data on a low-income household.[2] The contrasts between the smallest enterprise and the larger ones are:

- In the smaller enterprises of poor households, capital-labour (family + hired) ratios are much smaller compared to the larger ones. Total capital in the poor household's enterprise is very small.

---

[2] The enterprises were selected purposively to represent various sizes. These are located in various parts of greater Mymensingh districts.

- Returns to capital from the smaller enterprises are unusually high. Returns to capital in the larger enterprises are also high. The returns are many times higher than the rate of interest.
- In the mini enterprises, the monthly earning per family is close to the monthly salary of paid workers.

These findings raise some questions relevant for policies for microfinance-based firms' growth. If the rate of return to capital is so high, why these enterprises cannot expand? Why the banks and MFIs do not extend credit to new and existing enterprises? The answer is that other constraints which do not appear in the tables may be binding. Such constraints operate in the form of shortage of land/house, managerial labour, etc.

Another observation is that the poor households' self-employment enterprises earn as much as full time wage labourers. Why more women from poor households cannot engage in self-employment and add to family earnings? Case studies on paddy processing provide some answers. These enterprises require labour input from family's male workers as well, which may not be available. Moreover, the high workload, which results from the combination of economic activity and domestic activity of women, is another discouraging factor.

13.2.2 Comparison of Returns to Male and Female Workers' Enterprises

There is a common notion that the return to self-employment is lower for women compared to men. It is difficult to test this hypothesis because both men and women from the same family are usually engaged in an activity. Moreover, there is also job segmentation within an economic activity and between activities. Women contribute more labour in certain activities, e.g., livestock raising, production of small handicraft items, etc. In livestock raising, women perform the feeding, shed cleaning, etc., which are located in the premises of the household.

Average return to labour in female and male dominated activities has been presented in Rahman et al. (1994). Rahman et al.'s study shows variations across activities and in some cases return is lower in enterprises using a higher share of female labour. Lower return in some of the female dominated activities is due to two factors: the norms of women's involvement in traditional activities, and the use of smaller amount of capital.

More recent case studies are also presented to illustrate the difference in return to male and female labour using enterprises in some sub-sectors. The case studies of paddy processing business include enterprises based on male and female family labour (Table 13.3). In this sector, female labour takes various forms: entrepreneurial cum physical labour, hired labour and family labour. The case studies[3] focus on the following aspects of gender differences in employment in this sector:

   a. Difference in the type of work performed by hired persons and family's male and female labour force.
   b. The size of capital and the links between this factor and the role of women.
   c. Earnings and rate of return to labour for different combinations of male and female labour.

Traditionally, women's role in productive activities in the rural areas of the country has been confined to activities performed within the vicinity of the homestead. Paddy processing in *"dheki"* is performed within the household premises and therefore is within the spatial sphere of women's activity dictated by the societal norms. Such manual processing of paddy results in low productivity and intense drudgery of female workers. Therefore, it is not surprising that power driven large scale rice milling machines have replaced the *"dheki"*. Such automation has important implications not only for productivity but also for women's employment in this sub-sector.

Before the introduction of commercial rice mills, the major source of poor women's employment has been paid employment for paddy husking and processing. The introduction of rice mills has taken away this job from female wage labourers. Rice mills are usually located close to the market centre and/or close to the road links. Therefore, the family's women do not participate in this activity. To run the business, male members of the owner's family usually perform the managerial and supervisory roles. In addition, male workers are hired to perform the major tasks in the mill: measuring, operating the machinery, packaging of finished products, etc. Before husking the paddy, it is parboiled and dried. This work is performed in the open space of the factory unit. Female wage labourers are usually hired for some of these activities, especially for winnowing for separating the

---

[3] It should, however, be mentioned that the case studies can highlight the nature of gender related differences in this sector; but the conclusions cannot be quantitatively established on the basis of such case studies.

broken rice. Thus women who lost the paddy husking job, which they performed in their houses, now find an alternative employment.

The case studies on rice mills confirm this practice. One mill has hired 20 men for work with the machine and to do the marketing. Five women have been hired to do the drying and winnowing. The owner, of course, works full time. In another smaller rice mill business, only three men have been hired, who, along with 10 women and the owner, perform all jobs. Following the mechanisation process another type of small-scale paddy processing and trading business has emerged. This is a home based activity. Paddy is purchased and taken home where it is parboiled and dried by family's women (sometimes with a few hours of part-time female wage labourers). Then it is husked in rice mills on payment of a charge and the finished product (rice) is marketed by the family. This business makes value addition through the initial processing and through performing the marketing function. One case of such business has already been presented (Table 13.3). Such small paddy processing business has been dominant among poor households who obtained MC, especially during the early phase of MC. Since the profitability of such activities is low, this business is losing popularity and MC is being channelled to other activities.

The salient features emerging from these cases deserve attention. The big paddy processing mills with large capital are usually managed by men. Family's women do not have a role in such business. In contrast, paddy processing business without the ownership of a rice mill can be managed by women or jointly by men and women. In these businesses, families' women contribute a major part of labour. Features like use of machinery, larger size of capital and location outside home result in women's deprivation of the managerial role. Rural women usually manage a business when the size of investment is small. Due to smaller size of investment, income per month and the rate of return to labour are smaller in the firms with female family workers, although the percentage return to capital is not very different. In the rice mill, the hired male workers perform the tasks of operating machines and other processes related to marketing. These jobs require some skill, experience and numeracy. Therefore, the salary of the male workers is much higher than the salary of female workers. In some other mills where women work outdoors (in drying and boiling), the wages of unskilled men and women do not show much difference.

13.3 Rate of Interest[4]

During the last few years, a major criticism against MC has centred on its high rate of interest. It is often alleged that rate of interests on MC is so high that some of the MFIs may be considered similar to the traditional money lenders who charge exploitative rates of interests. This section endeavours to discuss various issues raised in the context of the rate of interest on MC and its links with profitability of activities.

Before a discussion of the prevailing rates of interest of MFIs, clarification of the notion of rate of interest in this particular context is required. Rate of interest of MFIs and commercial banks cannot be used in the same sense. The latter is motivated by profit maximisation. Although MFIs interest charges may include a component of profit, these institutions are not being run with the objective of profit only. Still they need to charge a rate of interest because they have to cover the cost of operation and if there is no interest charge, loans may flow to activities of low profitability or even for consumption.

To provide an opinion on the appropriateness of the level of rate of interest of MFIs, one needs an idea about the prevailing rates, which have been shown in Table 13.4.

Table 13.4: Interest Rate of Microcredit

(in Per Cent)

	Effective Interest Rate (Usual Range) Considering Deduction for Savings and Insurance during Loan Disbursement
General microcredit (Rural & Urban)	28-70
Micro-enterprise Loan	28-65
Ultra poor Loan	22-28
Agricultural Loan	28-65
Seasonal Loan	28-55
Disaster Management Loan	2.46-21

Source: MRA (2009), *NGO-MFIs in Bangladesh*, Vol. 16, June 2009.

According to data (Table 13.4), provided by Microcredit Regulatory Authority (MRA),the effective rate of interest on MC ranged from around 28 to as high as 70 per cent in 2009. Data on rate of interest currently charged are not available in the same format. MRA source

---

[4] Sections 13.3 and 13.4 draw from Rahman (2004b) and Rahman and Rashid (2011) along with new analysis and inclusion of new data.

reports much lower figure of rate of interest on MC provided by its licensed MFIs. In fact, MRA has announced a ceiling (27 per cent) on the effective rate of interest to be charged by licensed MFIs. Whether the MFIs actually comply with this restriction should be monitored by independent organisations/researchers. Even if it is assumed that all MFIs charge this rate, it may be considered as high, since it is much higher than the interest rate charged by commercial banks of the country.

If such rates can be accommodated by the borrowers and still return per hour of labour is higher than the relevant wage rate, then it means that there is no serious objection of the borrowers to these rates. This can be used as an argument to justify that the current rates are not high as these are accepted willingly by the borrowers.

Before one accepts this conclusion, rethinking of the relevant issues is necessary. A high dose of family labour input brings down the hourly return to labour and results in high rate of return to capital (as shown in the above analysis). If a family can eke out a subsistence living through such a combination, then it accepts the rate of interest charged by MFIs. There always remains the possibility that the interest rate be lowered and the poor borrowers receive greater benefits, and poverty alleviation is achieved at a faster pace.

In this context, the exchange of views with some NGO executives is worth quoting. One executive mentioned that their NGO believes in a philanthropic motive and the rate of interest is very low (less than 10 per cent). This view needs to be supplemented by arguments that philanthropy may be consistent with a higher rate of interest if the interest earned is used for expanding loans among a larger number of poor households and for covering the poorest borrowers, which may involve larger operational costs. Thus MFIs must strike a balance between helping a small number of the poor with larger benefits per borrower through a low rate of interest, and expanding their operations to a larger number of the poor by generating funds through charging a higher rate of interest.

The other question on rate of interest is a comparison of MFIs and commercial banks. The average rate of interest for poor borrowers is much higher than the rate of interest charged to the richer clients of commercial banks who pay 16 to 18 per cent interest on their loans. Such a difference involves an obvious inequity and therefore, the reasons behind this difference should be examined.

The rate of interest charged by the financial organisations depends on the cost of funds which they lend and the cost of intermediation. MFIs' cost of funds is lower than the cost of funds for the commercial banks. The cost of fund for the MFIs is lower because many of them obtain funds from cheaper sources, including international donors. Sources of funds for MFIs are shown in Table 13.5. Palli Karma-Sahayak Foundation (PKSF) and donors provide funds at lower rates of interest. Members' savings are likely to be less expensive for MFIs, because they pay their savers a lower rate of interest than the commercial banks and the savings are not easily accessed by the members.

Table 13.5: Sources of Funds for the Provision of Microcredit by MFIs: 1999, 2012

Source	Per cent from Each Source	
	(December 1999)	(December 2012)
Members' savings	25.4	33.6
PKSF	23.8	15.0
Local Bank	11.3	14.6
International donors	18.8	3.2
Service charge on loans/cumulative surplus	12.4	29.3
Others	8.3	4.3

Source: CDF (2000), MRA (2012).

MFIs' access to cheaper sources of funding does not result in a lower rate of interest on loans because of the high costs of loan operation among the poor and illiterate clients. This, in turn, is due to door-to-door services provided by most MFIs and the small size of the loans. Moreover, the difference between MFIs and commercial banks' usual investment finance loans would be much higher if the cost of intermediation by commercial banks could be lowered through a more efficient banking environment.

If the high rate of interest is due to the cost of door-to-door services, then the MFIs may make an endeavour to reduce the cost through modification of these practices. If the cost of banking among the poor is high because of their illiteracy and because they are not capable of dealing with the usual banking practices, then this is to some extent a legacy of the deprivation arising from the lack of access to education and due to the prevailing social system and attitude. The incidence of such backwardness falls disproportionately on the poorer section through the high rate of interest charged for the small loans they obtain and thereby a double deprivation is imposed on them. Moreover, the gap between the rates paid to savings of MFIs clients and the service charge on loans is high.

The rates of interest of MFIs have been more or less stable during recent years. More vigorous competition among the MFIs (often in the same location) may have contributed to this stabilisation. Stabilisation of rate of interest can be helpful in the overall development of the MFI environment, rather than a vigorous price competition leading to frequent changes in clients' affiliation. Smaller NGOs charging high rates of interest should be motivated to bring down the rates to the modal level. Large MFIs can take initiative in this context and set examples by cutting down their rates.

13.4 Gender Dimension of Targeting and Women's Empowerment

From the time of initiation, female members constituted a large share of microcredit recipients of MFIs. The share of women borrowers increased rapidly and from the early 1990s, women have dominated the membership of the MC programmes. Data presented in Table 13.6 show that in all the major MFIs, more than 80 per cent of current members are women. Many MFIs allow only women to receive MC.

Table 13.6: Female Share of Borrowers in Major MFIs

Name of Organisation	Number of Borrowers			Share of Female in Total (%)
	Female	Male	Total	
BRAC	6,765,514	288,284	7,053,798	95.9
Jagoroni Chakra Foundation	256,951	8,584	265,535	96.8
Shakti Foundation	158,763	0	158,763	100.0
Padokkhep Manobik Unnayan Kendra	147,498	19,452	166,950	88.3
ASA	4,751,543	924,241	5,675,784	83.7
Thengamara Mohila Sabouj Sangha	560,354	3,276	563,630	99.4
Peoples Oriented Programme Implementation	166,844	1,655	168,499	99.0
RDRS	236,275	44,076	280,351	84.3
BURO	371,180	105	371,285	99.9

Source: MRA (2008), NGO-MFIs in Bangladesh.

Access to credit has helped women generate self-employment, which has enhanced their earnings. Access to credit leads to empowerment of women, which includes increased mobility, more decision-making power and greater control over their lives. MFIs are acclaimed for their endeavours in empowering women. Poor women receive appreciation for being bankable.

Even if MFIs provide useful services for women and on balance lead to an improvement in women's status, MFIs' approach of lending only to women may require revision and give way to more balanced targeting. Even if initially this was motivated by a genuine concern about women's need for financial services, the concerns about adverse repercussions necessitate a rethinking of the strategy of targeting "only" female clients.

One of the major concerns is that the funds borrowed by women are being used by their husbands or other male members of the household. Apparently, the use of MC for investment in family enterprises can be quite acceptable and such a contribution to family investment may enhance women's status.

However, the total shift towards a system of MC channelled through female borrowers contains a number of routes through which tensions may accumulate from various angles. There are pressures for obtaining credit for use by the husband alone and there can be discontent of husbands about the small size of loans. Even when the loan is used by the husband, the repayment is the responsibility of the women who have taken the loan. If the husband does not contribute to the payment of instalments, the wife may have to resort to various types of employment to make the repayment. Such tensions may even lead to quarrels and ultimately to violence.[5] In this context, it may be mentioned that empirical studies suggest that MC leads to improvement of women's decision-making power about small expenditures but not about large investments.

Since the MFIs' success in banking among women has been overwhelming, they are eager to continue to see such success without drastic changes in their strategies. Nonetheless, now it is time to reassess the gender related targeting strategies of MFIs so that women can have adequate access to financial services but are not used as bearers of the burden of repayment of loans, which are being used solely by the male members of the household. There is a risk in such reallocation: a disproportionate share of the credit may be channelled to the male

---

[5] A woman from a village said "previously I was beaten once, now it is twice: the additional one is for not being able to bring NGO loan as others did."

borrowers. This may, however, be easily prevented by setting a limit of share of male and female borrowers in an MFI.

Some of the MFIs' field level officials reported that men are usually outside the home during daytime. Therefore, they cannot attend borrower groups' meeting. If they default on payment of instalments, it is difficult to catch them. However, a mechanism must evolve to solve this problem of accountability without overburdening family's women with the risk of financial obligation resulting from the male members' use of borrowed fund.

It is somewhat unusual that such an important issue did not receive attention in the discussion and debates on MC. The prospective male borrowers do not protest their deprivation, because they may access MC through their wives/daughters and conveniently escape the responsibility of repayment and put the entire burden on women.

It has already been mentioned that NGO executives also find it easier to provide loans to women, and to organise women's group meetings and to secure repayments. Thus the convergence of willingness among the two groups resulted in the absence of discussion or debate on this issue.

Among the feminist groups' and those concerned about women's empowerment, a standard notion is that access to finance has a positive implication in this context. Here one has to think beyond the prevailing notion and take into account the fact that loan disbursement in the name of women is not sufficient for women's empowerment. Rather one should look at who uses the loan, who has access to income from loan financed activities and who bears the brunt of repayment responsibility. In this context, if loan is disbursed only in the name of women, then the MFIs should, at the time of disbursement of loan, make it clear to both the borrower and her husband that loan repayment responsibility bestows equally on both. This can be initially done at an informal level and subsequently through formal consent.

The problems related to the modifications of targeting and the inclusion of both men and women need more intensive probing. The views of MFI leaders on the subject must be sought and the clients' and prospective clients' opinions should also receive attention.

13.5 Concluding Observations

Like any growing institution, MFIs in Bangladesh are facing new challenges. Evaluation of the impact of microcredit on poverty and household income and the assessment of success of targeting reveal a number of emerging problems for MFIs. The challenges are often critical because they involve certain dilemmas. A few examples can make it clear.

To increase the size of operations, MFIs must enhance their resources, which may require that interest rates on loans are high; this may discourage the poorest clients and encourage the borderline poor and thus lead to a compromise in targeting success. MFIs may resort to larger loan sizes which help increase the degree of financial sustainability. Such steps may lead to worsening repayment performance and exclusion of the poorest.

Achievement of financial sustainability of an MFI branch requires an increase in the number of clients in a branch. This may imply investment in less profitable activities, and reduce the return on investment and demand for loans.

Similarly, with limited resources it may be difficult to cater to the credit needs of both men and women. But the current practice of targeting only women must ultimately give way to more balanced gender composition of membership of MFIs.

These problems are not insurmountable and an early identification of these trade-offs may enable the MFIs to adopt suitable strategies. The remedies involve an appropriate balancing between the conflicting objectives.

MFIs made significant progress in providing collateral-free loans to asset-less households and achieved impressive loan repayment by members. MFIs solved the problems that baffled the traditional commercial banks who could not reach the poor. Institutions with such innovative approaches to banking can also be expected to succeed in facing the emerging challenges. Balancing will be required to achieve proper combinations of the poorest and less poor among the target group, between small and medium loans, and between male and female clients. MFIs should seriously pursue strategies of reduction of cost of operation, which can help reduce the rate of interest charged on loans.

CHAPTER 14

Women's Economic Empowerment: Gender Inequality in Poverty, Labour Market and Decision Making

14.1 Introduction

Improvements in the sphere of political, social and economic empowerment of women are desired development goals in both advanced and developing countries. Nonetheless, economic empowerment of women in most of the developing countries is much behind the level desired and is also less impressive than the progress in economic growth. Bangladesh is no exception in this respect. Bangladesh's aspirations to make progress towards inclusive development require reduction of gender inequality which in turn will depend on women's economic opportunities.

Empowerment implies control over one's own life, access to opportunities which can enhance such control and the ability to contribute to the quality of life of others in the society. Therefore, economic empowerment consists of opportunities in the economic sphere which enables women to become independent of other's control and to use that independence to contribute to economic progress of the society. In a resource poor low-income country like Bangladesh, the major components of economic empowerment are: (a) access to income or its mirror image, ability to rise out of poverty, (b) access to good quality employment, (c) access to productive assets and services, and (d) control over ones income and resources. Each of these consists of sub-components which receives attention in the course of the discussion.[1] This chapter discusses

---

[1] Of course, the components may be different in the case of advanced economies where market forces operate more freely and poverty and unemployment are not pressing concerns. In those economies, regional difference, occupational segmentation, access to consumption loans, etc. can be important indicators.

the gender inequality in each of these aspects on the basis of empirical data, both quantitative and qualitative. Women's economic empowerment can influence their social and political empowerment as well. Past studies on gender inequality in this country focused mainly on social and political aspects. Therefore, this chapter intends to look closely at the components of economic empowerment listed above.

Although Bangladesh has made significant progress in reducing poverty rate, the number of households living below poverty threshold is still rising. Implications of household poverty are likely to be different for men and women. The burden of poverty is likely to be heavier among female-headed households compared to male-headed households because of various social constraints that prevent women from pursuing various strategies for rising above the poverty threshold. This chapter examines the extent of feminisation of poverty.

Economic vulnerability of women and a larger burden of poverty on them are likely to arise from the structure of social relationship as well as the disparity in the access to asset. These are reinforced by unemployment, underemployment, discrimination and job segmentation in the labour market. The situation of female labour market therefore deserves in-depth analysis, which is one of the major objectives of the chapter.

Whether poor women are deprived in terms of access to asset and to other services needs special focus. Women's access to education and health services not only reflects their access to the benefits of economic development, but also contributes to their human capital as well as their capability to contribute to the process of development and overall empowerment. The prevailing inequalities in these areas reinforce each other. An analysis of these forces can shed light on the causal factors behind women's poverty and lack of empowerment.

Understanding of female empowerment and female poverty should ideally consist of two types of analysis. These are: first, the difference between female-headed households and male-headed households and second, the difference in empowerment of male and female members as individuals. This chapter attempts to discuss both issues as far as possible, within the constraints of limited availability of data. Women's economic empowerment is a vast subject; therefore, within the limited scope of the discussion, the situation of poorer women receives greater attention.

This chapter is organised as follows. Sections 14.2 and 14.3 focus on the linkage of female headship with poverty of households. Section 14.4

examines the gender inequalities prevailing in the labour market. The analysis of male-female difference in the labour market has been based on the Labour Force Survey of BBS. The quantitative data have been supplemented by qualitative information based on case studies and FGD (focus group discussion) sessions. Section 14.5 provides an in-depth analysis of the determinants of employment with a special focus on prospects of employment of poor women. Section 14.6 focuses on women's decision making role in spending their income. Section 14.7 provides some suggestions for empowering women, especially through employment.

14.2 Poverty among Female-headed Households: Results Based on Conventional Definition

Female-headed households in South Asian countries are faced with many social barriers which reinforce the constraints of poverty. The patriarchal society's norms make it difficult that they rise out of poverty. A discussion of the difference in poverty incidence among female-and male-headed households is therefore pertinent at the very outset.

Data on poverty incidence obtained from HIESs cannot actually play a useful role in this context. Data for all three years, 2000, 2005 and 2010, show lower poverty incidence among female-headed households, which stands in sharp contrast to the experience of neighbouring countries and the social reality in Bangladesh.

Poverty estimates for female-headed households, provided by the HIES, therefore, require closer scrutiny. The problem, in fact, lies in the definition. Female headship in a household usually takes place due to absence of adult male members. When this is associated with male overseas migration and receipt of remittances, the female-headed households are likely to be living above poverty threshold. In contrast, female-headed households which do not have male earners in the household or remittance senders living abroad are likely to be poor.

Econometric analyses can help isolate these effects. Multiple regression analysis (regression results are presented in annex Table 14.1A) has been conducted on the basis of unit records of data from the HIES, 2010.

Multivariate analysis examines the determinants of household income. Explanatory variables include household's resource endowments, head of the household's age and education, dummy variables for region (administrative division), a dummy variable for remittance receiver and a dummy variable for male-headed households. The coefficients reveal that all types of assets and human capital have positive and significant effects. Male-headed households have higher income even after controlling for assets and human capital.

Other studies have arrived at similar results. World Bank (2006) has used the HIES 2005 data and conducted a logit regression analysis for determinants of being non-poor, which shows that the coefficient for female headedness is negative, implying that female-headed households' probability of being poor is higher.

Such analysis implies that the earnings of female workers are usually lower and female-headed households depending mainly on female earning members are likely to be poor. Nonetheless, isolation of impact of female headedness after controlling for education, landownership, etc. cannot fully reveal the deprivation of women, because lower endowment of education, asset and employment prospects, etc. are actually the results of gender related deprivation. Therefore, the next step in understanding female poverty and deprivation of women is to look directly at women's earning prospects, not only for female household heads but for all women. This will be linked to inequalities in the labour market. These aspects receive attention in Section 14.4.

14.3 Income, Asset and Human Capital of Effective and Nominal Female-headed Households

This section proceeds to obtain a clear understanding of the situation of effective female-headed households as compared to effective male headed households. The discussion is based on the analysis of unit records of data of the HIES 2010 and provides a comparison of income, expenditure, asset ownership and access to human capital.

With an increasing concern about the definition of effective female-headed households and the overlap between female-headed household and residential female households, it is pertinent to work out consistent and distinct definitions of these categories and to compare the intensity of poverty among effective female-headed households and the male-headed households. A finer distinction of the effective female-headed households and nominal female-headed household is, therefore, necessary.

This section is based on a classification into two major categories of female-headed households: first, those who receive remittance income and are actually "residential female-headed households," (RFH) and here the male head does not reside within the same village/city. The other category has been termed as "effective female-headed households" (FHH), who do not receive remittance. This category is thus distinct from the RFH. To make the FHH comparable with similar social strata of male-headed households, all male-headed households have been divided into two groups: those who receive remittance inflow (RMH) and those who do not (MHH).

14.3.1 Comparison of Four Types of Households in terms of Poverty, Income, Expenditure, and Asset

Current income provides a picture of flow of the means of survival and therefore various categories of households have been compared in terms of the previous year's income and expenditure.

Table 14.1: Income and Expenditure of Male- and Female-headed Households

Type of Household	Income Per Month (Tk.)	Expenditure Per Month (Tk.)
Male headed without remittance (MHH)	10,458	10,556
Male headed with remittance (RMH)	15,174	12,573
Female headed without remittance (FHH)	6,850	7,339
Female headed with remittance (RFH)	12,516	10,175

Source: HIES, 2010.

Income of FHHs is 65.5 per cent of the mean income of MHHs (Table 14.1). This has been reflected in poverty incidences as well, which are 36.5 and 34.0 per cent among FHHs and MHHs respectively (Table 14.2). Among the male- and female-headed households who receive remittance, average incomes are Tk. 15,174 and Tk. 12,573 respectively. Similar differences in expenditure have been observed, as shown in Table 14.1.

Table 14.2: Poverty Incidence among Male- and Female-headed Households

(Per Cent)

Type of Household	Below Poverty Line	Above Poverty Line	Total
Male headed without remittance (MHH)	34.0	66.0	100.0
Male headed with remittance (RMH)	20.2	79.8	100.0
Female headed without remittance (FHH)	36.5	63.5	100.0
Female headed with remittance (RFH)	16.5	83.5	100.0

Source: HIES, 2010.

14.3.2 Ownership of Land

Economic opportunities for poor households in a low-income economy consist mostly of traditional employment opportunities and traditional productive assets. In the rural areas of Bangladesh, agriculture is the main productive activity and agricultural land constitutes the main productive asset. In a land scarce country like Bangladesh, where the land frontier has already been reached, land values are absurdly high and poor landless households can hardly expect to get ownership of land through purchase.

In the rural area, apart from arable land, the homestead area and the dwelling house may also serve as important productive assets. Many of the non-farm activities (e.g., paddy processing, other food processing, handicraft, poultry raising, etc.) are carried out in the household premises. Therefore, whether or not the house and the adjacent land is owned by a family will determine the choice of economic activities open to it. If a poor family is allowed to live in the unused part of the house of a richer person, whether as a matter of charity or in exchange for domestic services, the benevolence is not usually sufficient to allow them to use the premises for carrying out economic activities like poultry raising or paddy processing.

Data on landownership are presented in Table 14.3. Average homestead land owned by the MHHs and FHHs are 7.9 and 6.1 decimals respectively. Data also show the amounts of cultivable land owned by various groups of households. Male- and female-headed households (without remittance) own respectively 54.3 and 32.2 decimals. However, ownership of land by a FHH does not mean that ownership belongs to women. In most cases, young children are likely to be the owners and data on which member of the household owns the land are not available.

Table 14.3: Ownership of Land among Male- and Female-headed Households

Type of Household	Cultivable Land Owned (Decimal)	Homestead Land Owned (Decimal)
Male headed without remittance (MHH)	54.3	7.9
Male headed with remittance (RMH)	79.0	10.9
Female headed without remittance (FHH)	32.2	6.1
Female headed with remittance (RFH)	47.0	8.3

Source: HIES, 2010.

Table 14.4: Literacy Rate and School Enrolment Rate among Male- and Female-headed Households

Type of Household	% of Adults who are Literate	% of Boys Aged 6-15 Years Currently Studying	% Girls Aged 6-15 Years Currently Studying
Male headed without remittance (MHH)	56.6	77.8	85.8
Male headed with remittance (RMH)	60.2	80.2	85.9
Female headed without remittance (FHH)	48.0	64.4	74.6
Female headed with remittance (RFH)	60.8	86.8	87.8

Source: HIES, 2010.

14.3.3 Access to Human Capital

FHHs fall short of in terms of human capital acquisition. Literacy rates among adults in FHH and MHH are 48 and 56.6 per cent respectively. School enrolment rates among both boys and girls (aged 15+ years) are lower among FHHs compared to MHHs. In these respects, the nominal female-headed households who receive remittances are again better off. However, the situation is expected to improve in the near future with increasing school enrolment of girls in both primary and secondary age groups and among both poor and non-poor groups (HIES, 2010, 2005).

14.4 Gender Inequality in Labour Market, Type of Employment and Wage

Involvement in productive employment is a major route for enabling women to contribute to the economy. However, gender inequality in the labour market acts as an impediment to the process. Such inequality may act through the extent of participation in labour force, employment rate, unemployment or underemployment, type of employment and wage rate. These aspects receive detailed attention in the present section.

14.4.1 Women's Share in Employment and Labour Force Participation Rate (LFPR)

Women's share in the total employed workers in Bangladesh has risen during the last one decade (2000-2010). Table 14.5 shows that in 2010, women contributed 30 per cent of employed workforce. Although it is currently lower than other fast growing Asian countries and advanced economies, it may get closer in the coming years if the rising trend observed during the last decade (from 21 to 36 per cent) continues. During this period the rise in the share of women in total employed persons has been associated with a decline of male employment rate and increase of female employment rate. Apparently, this change implies a feminisation of labour force. Whether such feminisation can be helpful for women's empowerment depends on the type of employment of the growing female labour force and their earnings. Following sections probe into these details.

Table 14.5: Employment Rate and Share of Women in Total Employment by Sex: 2000-2013

Year	Sex	Employment Tate (ER) (%)	Share in Total Employment (%)
2013	Female	33.5	30.0
	Male	81.6	70.0
2010	Female	36.0	29.9
	Male	79.1	70.1
2006	Female	27.2	23.8
	Male	86.7	76.2
2000	Female	23.9	21.1
	Male	83.8	78.9

Source: BBS, LFS (various years).

Data already presented in Chapter 6 (Table 10.6) show that female LFPR has gone through a continuous rise during the period 2000-2010. Male LFPR has decreased from 87.4 per cent to 82.5 per cent, while female LFPR has increased by 10 percentage points, from 26.1 to 36.0 per cent, during this period.

The rise of female LFPR during the period 2006-2010 stands in contrast to the scenario of other Asian countries like India. To some extent, this has been due to the initial low value of female LFPR, 16 per cent in 1996 when many of the developing countries of Asia had female LFPR above 40 per cent.

However, the positive trend of female LFPR has been recently reversed. The value of FLFPR has fallen to 33.5 in 2013. Future growth of labour force requires its reversal again. A rise of female LFPR will not only lead to women's empowerment but will also help accelerate GDP growth.

Table 14.6 presents the values of rural and urban LFPR. Female LFPRs in both rural and urban areas have risen during the period 2000-2010. Female LFPRs in urban areas were 26.5 and 34.5 per cent in 2000 and 2010 respectively. During the same period, female LFPR in rural areas have risen from 23.1 to 36.4 per cent. Urban and rural female LFPRs are thus quite close and both have risen over the 15 years. Therefore, the pace of urbanisation or growth of either the rural or the urban economy cannot be singled out as the reason behind the changes of LFPR of women. In 2010, female LFPR was higher in rural areas than in urban areas. In 2000, the pattern was reverse.

Table 14.6: LFPR by Sex by Location

Year	Location	Male	Female
2000	Urban	83.7	26.5
	Rural	84.0	23.1
2006	Urban	83.2	27.4
	Rural	88.0	29.8
2010	Urban	80.2	34.5
	Rural	83.3	36.4

Source: BBS, LFS (various years).

Table 14.7: Age Specific Labour Force Participation Rates by Sex: 2006-2010

Age Group	2010 Male	2010 Female	2006 Male	2006 Female
15-19	48.4	29.4	62.9	13.7
20-24	75.9	40.9	80.4	29.0
25-29	92.1	44.7	95.3	33.7
30-34	97.3	46.6	98.7	34.9
35-39	98.3	47.7	98.8	34.8
40-44	98.0	46.2	97.7	35.2
45-49	97.4	47.6	97.8	32.6
50-54	94.1	10.3	95.4	31.1
55-59	88.5	11.2	92.4	27.7
60-64	77.2	6.6	82.7	22.6
65 +	57.9	8.3	59.3	14.8

Source: BBS, LFS (various years).

LFPRs among the younger age groups are likely to be influenced by school enrolment rates. During the last one decade school enrolments increased both among boys and girls and by similar magnitude (HIES,

2000, 2010). Therefore, school enrolment alone cannot explain the differences in LFPR.

Data on age specific LFPR (Table 14.7) show that during 2006-2010 women's LFPR has increased in all age groups and the rise has been higher among younger age groups (20 to 34 years). In contrast, LFPR has fallen among young men aged 15 to 30 years.

Labour force participants include both employed and unemployed persons and therefore the changes in LFPR depend on both components. Data show that female LFPR has increased through increase of employment rate and despite a decline of unemployment rate (Chapter 6).

14.4.2 Problems of Definition of Female LFPR

The interpretation of data on female LFPR must take into account the definition and data quality. LFPR depends on the criterion for being counted as a labour force member. One encounters problems in the criterion used by the LFS.

LFSs 2000 to 2010 use the following definition of labour force: Economically active population or labour force is defined as persons aged 15 years and above, who are either employed or unemployed during the reference period of the survey (preceding week of the day of enumeration). It excludes disabled and retired persons, income recipients, full time housewives and students, beggars and other persons who did not work for pay or profit at least one hour during the reference week' (LFS, 2010).

Inclusion of a person in the labour force thus depends on what is "work for pay or profit" (and there have been changes in the definition of economic activities).[2]

---

[2] Production for own consumption and fixed capital formation for own use which are economic activities are include:
    a. all production of primary products for own consumption covering the characteristics products of agriculture, hunting, forestry and logging and mining and quarrying.
    b. the processing of primary commodities by the producers of these items in order to make goods such as butter, cheese, flour, oil, cloth or furniture for their own use whether or not they sell any of these products in the market.
    c. production for own consumption of other commodities only if they are also produced for the market by the same households.
    d. all production of fixed assets for own use that is own-account construction of building, roads and similar works as well as fabrication of tools, instruments containers and similar items which have an expected life or use of one year or more (LFS, 2010).

In 2006, 2010 and 2013 rounds of the survey, livestock and poultry rearing has, in fact, been included as economic activities, whereas in the 1996 survey, the usual definition (which has been used in data reported in Table 14.6) excluded household economic activities such as care of poultry and livestock, threshing, boiling, drying (paddy), etc. Thus, it is no wonder that LFPR has been low in this round and shows a large increase during the period 1996-2006.

The motivation for better enumeration of women's productive activity may also have resulted in labelling of more women engaged in livestock/poultry raising as labour force in the recent LFS rounds. Whether a better enumeration has contributed to the recent rise of female LFPR can be judged from the discussion of sector and status of employment in the following sections. Moreover, the inclusion of women in such unpaid home-based activities implies that women are engaged for smaller number of hours and face higher underemployment (defined as those working less than standard hours per week). Table 6.2 in chapter 6 shows that underemployment rates among male and female workers were 6.6 and 31.5 per cent respectively in 2010.

14.4.3 Sector of Employment

A discussion of changes in the sectoral pattern of women's employment and its comparison with structure of employment of male labour force is pertinent for an understanding of the dynamism of the female labour market. As has been emphasised in Chapter 6, economic development is expected to result in a structural change in the labour market and a movement of labour force from agriculture to non-agriculture.

The picture of changes in the sectoral structure of employment for the period 1996 to 2013 has been shown in Tables 6.5 and 6.6 (in Chapter 6). Here a summary of the main features of contrasting pattern of sectoral distribution of male and female labour force is presented. Share of male labour force in agriculture has gone through a decline during the 20-year period, from 52.3 per cent in 1990-91 to 40.2 per cent in 2010, indicating that there has been a visible structural change of employment. The share of male labour force in agriculture has declined more rapidly during 2003-2010 and conforms to the conventionally expected accelerated structural change of the labour market.

In contrast, share of female labour force in agriculture has gone through a sharp increase during this period; from 27.8 per cent in 1996 to 46.9 per cent in 2000 and 64.8 per cent in 2010. Rising share of female employment in agriculture stands somewhat contrary to expectation based on conventional dualistic development theories. Moreover, the declining share of agriculture's contribution to GDP goes contrary to the lack of structural change in the female employment pattern. Increase of female labour force in agriculture therefore calls for further investigation.

Table 14.8: Number and Share of Labour Force in Livestock and Poultry Rearing by Sex

Year*	Description	Female	Male
2000	No. (000)	1000	340
	Share of total employment (%)	12.6	1.1
2006	No. (000)	3975	221
	Share of total employment (%)	35.2	0.6
2000-2006	Changes (%) in employment in livestock and poultry	+297.5	-35.0

Note: *The LFS report of 2010 does not provide this data.
Source: BBS, LFS (various years).

Disaggregated data (Table 14.8) of female employment[3] reveal that a dominant share of employed women were engaged in the livestock sub-sector. Thirty-five per cent female and less than one per cent male labour force have been employed in this sub-sector. Growing awareness about the need for recognition of women's economic activity has resulted in enumeration of women engaged in livestock and poultry rearing as agricultural work force. Thus it may be concluded that the recent increase of female LFPR has at least partly resulted from better enumeration of female unpaid workers in the family's livestock unit.

Table 14.9: Average Annual Growth Rate of Sectoral Employment

Industry	2003-2006 (Average Growth Rate) Male	2003-2006 (Average Growth Rate) Female	2006-2010 (Average Growth Rate) Male	2006-2010 (Average Growth Rate) Female
Agriculture, hunting and forestry	-4.2	9.3	1.8	8.4
Manufacturing	14.2	-8.7	5.2	9.6
Wholesale & retail trade; repair of motor vehicles, motor	4.4	23.5	-0.7	23.4
Hotels and restaurants	7.6	15.6	4.0	2.3
Transport, storage and communications	9.4	38.2	-0.8	32.9
Community, social and personal service activities	13.3	-11.8	2.3	11.9

Source: BBS, LFS (various years).

[3] Such data has been presented for 2000 and 2006. For other rounds of the LFS, the disaggregated data has not been made available.

Table 14.9 shows that the highest growth of female employment was in the community and personal services during 2006-2010. Agriculture and manufacturing also experienced a significant growth of female employment during the same period.

14.4.4 Status of Employment

Data on the distribution of women's employment by status (Table 6.9 in Chapter 6) show that 25.1 and 47.5 per cent of Bangladesh's employed women and men are in self-employed category. In rural areas, this category accounts for a larger share (Table 14.10) because family-based subsistence agriculture is the main economic activity. In addition, 56.3 per cent of the employed female labour force are in the category of unpaid family workers. Among male labour force, 7.1 per cent is in this category. Only 8.9 per cent of the female labour force is in regular paid employment and 7.1 per cent women are day labourers or irregular employees (Table 6.9 in Chapter 6).

Table 14.10: Distribution of Employment by Status, Sex and Location, 2010

(Per Cent)

Status of Employment	Urban Female	Urban Male	Rural Female	Rural Male
Self-employed	29.9	45.3	11.5	51.5
Employer	0.1	0.3	0.1	0.3
Employee	33.3	30.5	5.0	9.6
Unpaid family helper	22.3	5.5	71.8	10.9
Day labourer	8.1	16.6	7.8	26.3
Others	6.3	1.8	3.8	1.4
Total	100.0	100.0	100.0	100.0

Source: BBS, LFS (various years).

The contrasting pattern of changes of status of male and female employment has been discussed in Chapter 6 and here the major findings are highlighted. The shares of self-employment in female employment were 26.6 and 25.1 per cent in 2000 and 2010 respectively (Table 6.9 in chapter 6). Shares of women in employee and day labourer groups went through a major decline during the period 2000-2010 (together from 20.3 to 8.9 per cent). The decline in the share of hired employment was greater among female workers compared to male workers. Share of women in self-employment has also shown a small negative change. This has been made up by a large increase in share of women employed as unpaid family helpers. As has been mentioned earlier, the increase of "unpaid family workers" among women is to some extent, a reflection of better enumeration in the recent LFS rounds. It should be emphasised that women's contribution to GDP through such unpaid labour and through domestic work must be adequately recognised.

Women's empowerment is likely to be strengthened by direct income earning and therefore regular employment can be viewed as more empowering. However, during the entire decade, share of women in better quality employment has been on the decline.

14.4.5 Access to Formal Employment

Informality is one of the important disadvantages in the female labour market. Data on the extent of informality and its changes have been presented in Table 14.11. In 2006, about 16 per cent of employed women were in the formal sector. It came down to 7.7 per cent in 2010.

The absolute number of both men and women engaged in formal sector decreased during 2006-2010 and an explanation of the decline is difficult because both industry and service sectors have grown during this period.

Table 14.11: Type of Employment: Distribution of Employed Labour Force by Sex and Formal vs. Informal

Year		Male		Female	
		Number ('000)	Share (%)	Number ('000)	Share (%)
2000	Formal	8420	21.1	1230	15.6
	Informal	22669	78.9	6660	84.4
2006	Formal	8594	23.8	1614	14.3
	Informal	27486	76.2	9663	85.7
2010	Formal	5542	14.6	1244	7.7
	Informal	32391	85.5	14959	92.3

Source: BBS, LFS (various years).

14.4.6 Wage Differential

A number of previous studies demonstrate large gender differences in wage in Bangladesh.

Table 14.12 and Table 14.13 present data on wage differences as obtained from the recent surveys. Data for 2006, quoted from the LFS report, show that female wage was only two-thirds of male wage (Table 14.12). The ratios were similar for rural and urban areas.

Table 14.12: Female and Male Wage by Location

	Female (Tk.)	Male (Tk.)	Female*100 ÷ Male
Urban	69.0	111.0	62.0
Rural	61.0	93.0	66.0
Urban & Rural	63.0	95.0	66.0

Source: LFS.

Table 14.13: Male-Female Difference in Wage and Salary

	Wage (Tk. Per Day)	Salary (Tk. Per Month)
Male	169.3	18154.7
Female	142.9	9762.1
Female/Male (ratio)	0.84	0.54

Source: HIES.

Wage data from the HIES 2010 have been presented in Table 14.17. Data show that the ratio of female wage to male wage was 0.84, which was an improvement compared to the ratio obtained from the LFS 2006 (which was 0.54). The improvement of the ratio of female to male wage reflects a tightening of the casual labour market. HIES data show that female to male ratio for monthly salary (plus other benefits) of regular employees was much lower than the ratio of daily wage.

The LFS 2010 and 2013 data on male-female wage differences have not been quoted here. These data show higher or equal wage of women, which goes contrary to data from other sources published by BBS. For example, male and female wage in agriculture are shown as the same in the LFS 2013, whereas "Monthly Statistical Bulletin" has shown female wage as 20-30 per cent lower. An ongoing study of the author shows even larger wage difference in the rural areas.

Wage inequality between male and female workers can be disaggregated into two components. A part of it is due to unequal endowment of education (and human capital) and the rest are due to pure discrimination.

A paper by Kapsos (2008) uses Bangladesh Occupational Wage dataset to investigate the determinants of wage differential and provides estimates of gender related differential. The study finds that women's earnings are 21 per cent lower than men's, of which pure gender wage gap was 15.9 per cent. The study observes that education reduces wage gap. An obvious policy implication is therefore to improve women's education and encourage educated women's participation in the labour force.

Ahmed and Mitra (2010) also report the presence of gender related wage discrimination. Such discrimination is considerably higher in urban areas compared to rural areas. However, urban wage is usually much higher than rural wage and therefore women can benefit from the expansion of urban employment despite higher discrimination.

However, the fact remains that lower endowment of human capital among female workers is also due to various forms of gender inequality and social biases and thus the artificial disaggregation of wage inequality into two components may lead to underestimation of the disempowerment caused through wage inequality.

14.4.7 Social Factors behind Gender Differential of Wage

Gender differential of wage actually results from three factors: gender segmentation of occupation due to social factors, differences in endowment and pure discrimination which is linked to the social factors and the lower bargaining power of female workers. Elaboration of these factors is pertinent.

In a traditional economy it is difficult to relate wage difference with the productivity difference, because most workers are unskilled and the productivity differences may not be captured by human capital variables. Certain types of unskilled work require simple physical strength. Earth cutting, load carrying, etc. are some examples. In these jobs women have a disadvantage and, therefore, receive a lower wage.

Gender differential of productivity is difficult to estimate even in skilled jobs in the formal sector. For example, how would one measure the difference between productivity of an operator and that of a supervisor in ironing section in a RMG production unit? In RMG enterprises, "cutting" is considered a more skilled/"heavy" work, which is done mainly by male workers. But the workers in this section may sometimes take a few minutes break because this work is outside the "production line." In contrast, the sewing machine operators working in a "line" cannot take time out and they must perform the boring and tedious work continuously. How can one judge which work is heavier? However, the workers in the cutting section, who are mainly male, receive a higher wage.

Pure sex differential of wage resulting from non-economic factors originates in the deeply rooted social, cultural and institutional factors. Such differentials enter through both direct and indirect routes. Society's perception of women's role in the labour market and women's bargaining power both play dominant roles in this context.

An important socio-cultural factor behind the lower wage of women is the perception that women are secondary earners. Such a notion prevails among both employers and female employees and as a result lower wage is offered and accepted respectively. The perception that women are secondary earners also influences the institutional wage setting process. Minimum wage of the sub-sectors with a higher share of female workers is usually lower. The RMG sector in Bangladesh is an example in support of such hypothesis. Minimum wage for the RMG sector is lower than other manufacturing industries dominated by male workers.

Male-female wage difference, which is apparently linked with pure gender bias, may, in fact, reflect the lower bargaining power of women. A number of factors operating at both household level and societal level result in lower bargaining power of female workers who are seeking paid jobs. For example, families' male guardians (especially from low-income groups) sometimes keep a pressure that women accept employment even if the wage is low. Case studies revealed two types of pressures. First, women without male earner in the household are required to earn to ensure survival and second, many women have to earn to save for dowry which they will pay to their husband. Many women in the RMG sector mentioned this as an important reason for taking up employment.

14.5 Determinants of Women's Employment

Discussion of the previous sections shows that women's employment expansion has taken place through changing pattern in terms of sector and type of jobs. At this point, the determinants of women's choice of type of employment can be of interest. In this context, the policy relevant question would be the linkages among households' poverty, women's education and employment. These interrelations can be assessed by probing into the demand factors as well as the supply-side considerations. These linkages have been shown in Figure 14.1.

Figure 14.1: Linkages among Poverty, Education and Female Employment

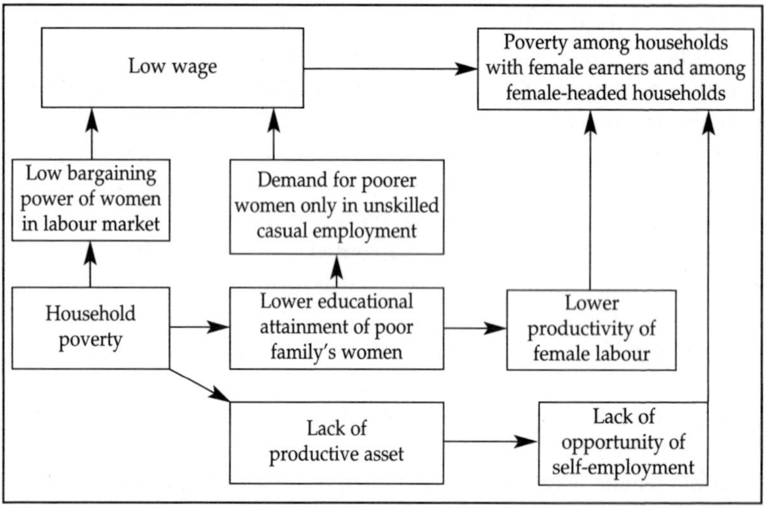

```
                                              Poverty among households
              Low wage ─────────────────────▶ with female earners and among
                 ▲         ▲                  female-headed households
                 │         │                      ▲           ▲
    Low bargaining      Demand for poorer         │           │
    power of women     women only in unskilled    │           │
    in labour market    casual employment         │           │
         ▲                   ▲                    │           │
         │             Lower educational       Lower
    Household  ─────▶  attainment of poor ───▶ productivity of
    poverty            family's women          female labour
         │                                        ▲
         │              Lack of                Lack of
         └──────────▶  productive asset ─────▶ opportunity of
                                               self-employment
```

In the female labour market, poverty is likely to act as a push factor creating a positive relationship between poverty and female participation in employment. Even though social attitude is an important impediment to female participation in income earning work, the poorer women may be in a desperate situation and would be willing to break the social barriers. In contrast, women from richer households may face more stringent social barriers which discourage seeking outside employment. Of course, the demand-side forces may take place through employers' preference and counteract the push factor.

Qualifications required for salaried employment in the formal sector also act as a constraint. These jobs need minimum education levels while women from poorer households usually enter labour market without any school education and may not be qualified for such jobs. Therefore, poorer women are likely to resort only to inferior types of employment, including casual work in the informal sectors. In fact, the relationship between poverty and type of female employment usually reinforces each other and the causality flows in both directions, as shown in Figure 14.1.

Women from poorer households are likely to have higher participation in inferior types of employment. Poverty can also act as a negative force on wage and women's earnings. As discussed above, this can be attributed to lower productivity and lower bargaining power of the poor women, which leads to casual employment and less days of employment, lower wage and thus lower earning.

Empirical findings on the relationship between poverty, education and female labour force participation based on the LFS 2010 data have been presented below. LFS does not collect expenditure data and so the poverty groups cannot be based on usual poverty line cut off. A proxy indicator of poverty based on a combination of landownership and non-land asset has been used in the present discussion.

Participation rates of women in paid and self-employment by asset groups have been shown in Table 14.14. The relationship is negative in the case of paid employment, especially in irregular/casual types, which is in conformity with the hypotheses. Rahman et al. (2013) use logit regression analysis and established that the relationship is significant.

In contrast, family employment requires family's possession of productive resources (like land, livestock, etc.) and poorer households usually possess less of these assets. As a result, the relationship between family employment and poverty is observed to be negative.[4]

Table 14.14: Female Participation Rate in Family Employment and Paid Employment

Asset Group	% of Women (15 + Years Aged) Participating in		
	Salaried Employment	Daily Casual Employment	Self + Unpaid Family Employment
No asset, no land	4.0	14.8	15.1
Non-land asset, but no land	9.0	5.9	18.7
.01 to .49	2.7	3.8	21.1
.50 to .99	1.6	1.6	34.1
1.00 to 2.49	1.6	1.2	40.6
2.50 to 4.99	1.8	0.6	39.5
5.00 +	2.5	1.1	35.6

Source: Estimated from the LFS 2010 data.

---

[4] A study on this relationship was conducted on the basis of HIES data of Bangladesh. It obtained a positive relationship between LFPR and poverty (Bridges, Lawson and Begum, 2011). However, the result is due to the fact that HIES defines LFPR in a narrower sense, with a much smaller share of women in self/family employment and the participation in paid work dominates the link with poverty.

The other aspect of the determinants of female employment/LFPR that has received attention of researchers and policy makers is the role of education. Prevailing hypotheses expect a positive impact of education on female labour force participation, especially in developing countries where education is expected to result in change of individual's attitude as well as the society's attitude. An educated society has a more liberal view about women's employment, thus creating a positive supply-side force. Female education raises their employability in sectors using modern technology. Higher earnings prospect in such sectors creates a supply-side impetus. Structural factors work on the demand side and the impact of education on female labour supply depends on the balance of the two forces.

Quality of education can be important when demand side is being considered. If girls (and boys) with more years of education do not possess significantly higher level of learning than the primary educated ones, the employers will prefer the latter since younger workers with less schooling may be paid lower wage. As the share of educated labour force rises, modern sectors may make use of such labour only if they make sufficient investment in higher technology processes. The uncertain quality of education may discourage such investment.

Table 14.15: Female Participation in Paid and Self-employment by Education

(Per Cent)

Education	% of Women (15 + Years Aged) Participating in		
	Salaried	Daily/Casual/ Servant, Etc.	Self & Unpaid Family Worker
No education	1.3	4.7	24.8
Class I-V	2.4	2.7	31.3
Class VI-IX	4.2	1.7	32.5
Class IX-X	1.8	1.3	30.1
SSC/equivalent	3.8	1.0	26.5
HSC/Degree	10.9	0.7	17.5
Masters/Medical/Engineer	26.2	0.0	15.0
Technical/others	15.4	0.0	51.3
Total	2.7	3.1	27.5

Source: Estimated from the LFS 2010 data.

Empirical results presented in Table 14.15 show that the employment rate of women in salaried jobs rises with education almost continuously. Years of schooling has a positive correlation with asset ownership as well. Access to schooling and its quality is positively associated with economic strength of households. Therefore, the effect of education is similar to that of asset. In addition, household's asset base raises the scope of self-employment of women. So the positive association between education and female employment actually reflects an indirect outcome of positive links between asset and self-employment and between asset and education. In contrast, participation of women in casual work (which is poor women's work) varies inversely with education levels.

The processes and determinants of women's employment discussed above reveal that the linkages operate in a manner which is not conducive for economic empowerment of women from poorer households.

14.6 Prospects of Employment of Women from Poorer Households

14.6.1 Scope of Self-employment of Poor Rural Women[5]

During the last two decades, generation of self-employment has featured as an important strategy for improvement of the situation of poor women. It is essential that the villagers' perceptions about the prospect of self and wage employment of women are properly understood. Therefore, qualitative data have been collected to throw light on these issues. Data based on FGD sessions and case studies depict the views of poor women on the preference and prospect of type of employment.

In the FGD sessions,[6] women were asked about who are the poorest among them and why do they not take microcredit and start self-employment. Some of them have said that they are poor because they do not have a husband. They were once members of an NGO but did not actually take any loan. One of them depends mainly on her son's earnings. She also makes handicraft items with jute and sells them to buyers from an NGO and earns a small amount from this source.

When asked about the reasons for not taking loans, she has replied, "I do not have the courage." NGO credit comes to the doorstep. There are no complex forms to fill in; no waiting at offices and the loan can be repaid in instalments. Her fear is about the repayment in instalments. If she buys a small cow and sells it after a year, she may make a profit of about taka 5,000 to taka 7,000, which would be about 50 per cent of

---

[5] This section draws from Rahman (2007).
[6] Conducted in 2004 in Gazipur district and the taka amounts are at 2004 prices.

total investment. "Where do I get the money for paying monthly instalments?" was her question. Moreover, there are the risks that the cow (or poultry) may die. If an earning husband is there to provide support and money for repaying the loan in instalments, it works well. Thus, the problem is about finding activities where she can generate instant return to repay the loan. For female workers in a village, there are not many activities with such features. In some villages women take up two types of processing activities: paddy processing and food processing (making puffed rice, preparing "pitha" or sweetmeat, etc.). These activities bring low hourly returns. Moreover, hard physical labour-intensive activities like paddy processing cannot be pursued for long hours a day and therefore these activities cannot generate sufficient income for the survival of a family.

Box 14.1: Prospects of Self-employment of Rural Women: Observations Based on FGD among Women

- Women from households with farming activity are seasonally busy with crop processing and cannot take up any other employment on a regular basis.
- Women from non-farm households sometimes have scope for contributing labour to non-farm activity of households, for example in poultry, weaving, etc., where both men and women are engaged. Depending on availability of grazing land, rural families keep livestock and women spend a few hours a week in the care of livestock. Most women undertaking this activity are underemployed.
- Those between age 20 and age 40 usually have small children. These women are busy with household chores. Most women with children referred to burden of housework as the major reason for not taking up income earning work. Rural women who are currently housewives aged 25 and above are mostly without education/literacy. Therefore, they do not want to learn new activities or cannot think of undertaking a business. As we talked to them, it became quite apparent that it will be difficult to give them managerial skill. When probing was done about what type of economic activity they could take up, no specific suggestions came from this group.
- Young unmarried girls have much less burden of domestic work compared to housewives. Both the school going and dropouts are equally enthusiastic about any prospect of income-earning activities. But this group is more interested in regular paid employment. The contrast between the women with children and the young unmarried ones is glaring and makes it clear that all efforts should be made to utilise the latter group in the growing sectors of the economy. In fact, if rural enterprises can create demand for skilled labour, these young women may be easily trained. Some of them are interested in self-employment and may be provided with a combination of skill training and management training so that they may take up self-employment. It should be emphasised that lack of employment opportunity will push this group into the situation of the "disinterested" older group, carrying only the burden of household activities.

Another woman without a male earner in the family obtained regular wage employment in a road maintenance project. This project came to an end. She does not want to take loan from NGOs. She prefers regular wage employment, even if she has to dig earth and work on the roadside as she used to do during the project employment.

Women who are in desperate need to generate an income and the young school dropout girls showed their eagerness to do any work in which they may get a regular salary at a level of lowest wage that prevails in the casual labour market. It is unfortunate that there is not sufficient growth of large-scale secondary and tertiary sector activities to absorb such a willing labour force that can provide cheap supply of labour.

Insights obtained from FGD sessions with women have been listed in Box 14.1.

From the discussion with women it appeared that in many cases they do not contribute labour to the enterprises taken up by men. The reasons have been discussed with male owners of various enterprises. Those engaged in rice trading, transport sector work (owns and drives baby taxi), grocery or other trading activities did not see much scope of involving women. Two of these enterprise owners were crossed with a long series of questions on how women may be involved in these activities. Box 14.2 provides these responses.

Box 14.2: Case Studies on Women's Lack of Access to Family Employment

Women's Indoor Work for Husband's Shop

A grocery shop owner obtains credit from a local NGO. His shop is in the market place and therefore his wife cannot do any work for the shop. And there is scope for employment of only one person. He did not mention that he sold snacks at his shop and his wife helped him prepare those. When we requested him to give the full account of the activity, he said, "Oh! it is only during "Ramadan" that I sell snacks in the afternoon where she can do some work." Then it was revealed that he continued it during other months as well and sold snacks every afternoon. His wife helped him in preparing the snacks, even though her time input was small.

Carpentry is not Women's Work

A carpenter who makes furniture, doors, etc., has been asked why his wife cannot do some of the work, since this can be done within the homestead area. He is against this because this is man's job and as long as "I am healthy and able to support my family, why should the family's women work with those tools." We tried to argue, "say if you are sick and cannot work for a few months, then your wife may run the business if you train her." Then he finds other arguments: she has to take care of children. He thinks that women should find something else.

These case studies demonstrate that it is not only a matter of creating employment for women but also recognising what they are currently doing. The strong stigma against women's involvement in non-conventional work (or in men's work) also becomes clear.

14.6.2 Role of Wage Employment of Rural Women

Through FGD sessions and cross-sectional discussions, an attempt was made to examine the prospects of women's full time wage employment. A set of villages in a poor district (Gaibandha) and a set of not-so-poor villages in the district Mymensingh were covered. The latter set is made up of relatively prosperous villages close to the district headquarter.

In the former areas winter paddy is the main economic activity. There is hardly any industrial or non-farm activity in the area. Many of the poor male wage labourers of this area migrate to other areas during the months of November, January, February and May. The families are often left behind with inadequate means of survival. Women therefore seek employment and themselves approach the prospective employers begging for work. They engage in field work for agriculture where they get only two thirds of male wage.

In the villages in Mymensingh, two sectors dominate as sources of employment for women—rice mills and domestic service. In some of the remote villages in Char (sandbar island) areas, women are employed in agriculture. But only two activities of crop cultivation use female labourers—processing paddy and picking chilli. Chilli is extensively cultivated in these villages and a tedious activity like picking chilli can be done only by women. Women's wage rates in crop activity and in rice mills are almost the same. Women receive 60-70 per cent of men's wage. Employment in crop activity lasts only for a few weeks a year. Work in rice mills is a physically demanding task. Those unable or unwilling to take up such a job may find work as domestic help in the city area. These women get food and clothing along with a small cash payment. Total value of cash and food is equivalent to about taka 30-40 per day.

Women who are currently engaged in wage employment or are seeking work were asked about their preference of activity. Most of them prefer employment in non-farm activities to crop employment mainly because the former gives regular year-round employment.

Some employers have been directly asked about the reasons why they do not employ women in crop agriculture. They resort to the argument that women are physically weak, and cannot carry heavy loads of paddy. They cannot do the heavy work of crushing of the bundles of paddy. But why women do not get employment in activities like transplanting or weeding of paddy or other field crops? Here comes the question of social acceptability and employers expressed the view that "women should not work in open fields, if an employer offers such employment, he will be socially condemned," etc.

In fact, this question has been asked to employers during the field work of the author's ongoing study (conducted in June 2015). Responses obtained are very similar to the responses given in earlier FGDs.

Differences between the "char" areas and the mainland villages to some extent corroborate this view. The customs in the char land are somewhat different and there women are employed in field activities of crop. Demand resulting from special crops like chilli may have contributed to the difference. Labour input in tedious activities like chilli picking can be contributed only by women and children. Since children are these days unavailable because of the increased school enrolment, women get employment. Char lands grow more "chilli" compared to the other villages and the total demand for hired female labour is higher.

Summing up the views, it can be said that women are ready to work in any sector, at about 60 per cent of male wage rate but prefer regular employment with assured earnings. Employers care about social stigma and would not hire female workers for field activities of crop cultivation. But inter-village differences show that with the increase in demand and tightening of the male labour market, social customs and prejudices may give way to economic incentives. Society's preferences, of course, are more stringent when it comes to the question of who is absorbed first. Therefore, an overall growth of employment is required to ensure more employment opportunities for both men and women.

Another important factor creating job segmentation, especially in the rural areas of Bangladesh, is the relatively greater weight attached to women's domestic activities compared to market activities. These social forces creating gender differentials are based on the age old tradition of patriarchal norm prevailing in most parts of Bangladesh (except in some pockets in the north and in the southeast). The patriarchal practices dictate that adult male members of a household are treated as bread earners and should seek employment before family's women do so. Only if there is a need for supplementing their earnings, the female members of a family would consider participating in economic activities. Domestic work and reproductive role are considered as supreme for women and thus women's status is relegated to that of "secondary earners."

An important implication of the traditional attitude is that only limited types of jobs are considered as "women's job." Women are expected to work in locations close to the homestead. This is especially true in the rural areas.[7]

14.7 Women's Role in Decision-Making

Gender disparity is embedded in the social and cultural values of the society and strict adherence to the prevailing norms is hailed by not only men who are the beneficiaries, but also by women. Male dominance is likely to be manifested in lack of decision making power among women in male-headed households.

Table 14.16 presents national level data on women's control over their earnings. Data show that in 33.6 per cent cases it is mainly a self decision. In 8.1 per cent cases the decision is taken mainly by husband. However, comparable data on control of male earnings is not available from this source.

Table 14.16: Women's Control over Decision about Spending Cash Earning by Education and Asset

Characteristics		Per Cent where Decision is	
		Mainly by Self	Mainly by Husband
Education	None	25.4	8.5
	Less than primary	30.3	8.8
	Primary	36.3	11.8
	Less than secondary	39.5	7.9
	Secondary & above	39.6	5.2
Asset	Lowest	29.7	10.4
	2nd	24.1	10.8
	3rd	34.7	10.8
	4th	37.3	7.2
	Highest	38.9	3.4
	All	33.6	8.1

Source: BDHS, 2011.

---

[7] They prefer jobs close to home even in the urban areas because women's access to urban transport system is limited, and therefore transport cost may be very high if the location of job is far from home.

Data from a sample survey (Rahman, 1998) can be used to provide a comparison of decision making by male and female earners in the same type of family and questions are mainly related to decision about spending own income. Since a comparison of male and female decision making role in this context was targeted, the information has been generated from male head and their spouse in the MHH.

An indicator of control over monetary transactions can be obtained by probing into the control over expenditure of one's own income. This question was asked to all respondents with own income. Table 14.17 presents data on this. The results reveal a glaring difference in the control over income by the male earner and his spouse or other female earners in the family. In 61.7 per cent cases in the rural area and 54.9 per cent cases in the urban area, male head of the household spends income according to his own decision. In 36.7 and 39.2 per cent cases, in the urban and rural areas respectively, they consider the opinion of the spouse though their own opinion plays the major role. In contrast, when the (women) spouse of the male head of the family earns an income, only in a small percentage of cases (7 per cent and 17 per cent in the rural and urban areas respectively) women themselves decide about the spending and in a large percentage of cases, husband or other male members have the main control over the spending of income (72.1 and 16.7 per cent cases in the rural and urban areas respectively). Thus in the urban area women have better control over their income, which is still less than male earners.

Table 14.17: Male and Female Earner's Role in Decision Making about Spending Own Income

(Per Cent)

Who Decides	Rural Income of			Urban Income of		
	Male Head	Spouse	Other Women	Male Head	Spouse	Other Women
Self	61.7	7.0	66.7	54.9	16.7	50.0
Mainly self	36.7	20.9	-	39.2	63.9	-
Mainly spouse	-	72.1	33.3	5.9	16.7	-
Mainly other male relatives	1.7	-	-	-	-	25.0
Mainly female relatives	-	-	-	-	-	25.0
Other female members of the family	-	-	-	-	2.8	-
Total	100.0	100.0	100.0	100.0	100.0	100.0

Source: Rahman (1998a).

14.8 Policy Suggestion for Economic Empowerment of Women

The present study shows that effective FHHs in Bangladesh live in a deplorable condition and are faced with constraints of economic opportunities. The urgencies of improving their situation need not be overemphasised. Moreover, the effective FHH and residential FHH differ considerably both in terms of current income and fixed assets. FHHs are poorer than not only the poor MHHs but also compared to residential FHHs.

Male-female disparity is glaring when it comes to the ownership of assets. The disparity in ownership of assets is much larger than the disparity in current earning. Lack of asset has been, to some extent, responsible for low earnings of women. In fact, lack of asset among women pushes them to wage employment whenever they are in need for generating an income.

A direct redistribution of asset is not a practical policy option at present. Even a modification of the laws of inheritance will be difficult and will not bear fruit in the short term. Better implementation of the laws of inheritance can improve women's access to assets.

Policy of distribution of khas land by government should attach priority to poor women. Land title may be given to FHHs or jointly to husband and wife in poor households.

In urban areas, housing is an acute problem for the poor households in general and for the FHHs in particular. Slums in urban areas of Bangladesh pose a difficult problem for the government and steps for rehabilitation of slum dwellers need serious attention. The special problems related to housing and child care for young women, who are divorced/separated, should be addressed with due emphasis so that they may take up outside employment.

For the benefit of poorest women, policies should be targeted to effective FHHs who are the poorest category. It will be difficult to reach the FHHs with the policies of education and employment, because there will be inadequate demand from the FHHs given the age composition of such households. Credit and health care are among the current inputs that can help the FHHs and these are the usual areas of intervention by the government and the NGOs. Quality of such services requires improvement.

Women are getting access to microcredit (MC) through NGOs. Some of the microfinance institutions have special programmes of MC for the poorest and the FHH. This is a step forward. But the MFIs must exercise caution to ensure that women are enabled to utilise the credit for productive purposes.

The most important set of policies for economic empowerment of women, especially poor women, are those related to employment generation and labour market. Detailed suggestions with a focus on the needs of poorer group of women are presented below.

14.8.1 Policies for Women's Employment

In Bangladesh, the mainstream development institutions and private sector growth have evolved around a male dominated clientele and therefore have incorporated deeply rooted prejudices, which have adverse impact on the progress towards gender equity in employment. A determined and deliberate effort to change such environment is a prerequisite for ensuring gender equity in any sphere of the labour market.

A renewed concern about women's employment arises from the data presented so far. To reverse the negative features of women's employment situation and to improve their earnings opportunities, both short-term and long-term interventions are necessary. A number of specific suggestions for women from low-income households have been listed below.

Since underemployment and unemployment rate is much higher among women, policies for poverty alleviation include promotion of labour-intensive industrialisation based on employment of female workers. This option has been mentioned in an earlier chapter as well.

Despite the overwhelming role of private employers in the labour market, public policies can have a significant contribution to the reduction of gender inequity. Government can play important roles in a number of spheres, including both direct and indirect interventions, and developing general guidelines along with specific interventions through various programmes.

An important policy option to improve the employability of women and help raise their wages through higher productivity is to provide appropriate training facilities. Detailed suggestions on this aspect have been provided in an earlier chapter (Chapter 6).

To encourage women's employment in urban industries, government may adopt programmes for provision of services for the female employees (including transport services, health and housing facilities, etc.). Moreover, employment in the export sector implies the possibilities of job loss with the fluctuations in export growth. Programmes must be adopted to minimise the adjustment costs of the workers who lose jobs.

Given the enthusiasm of young girls about engagement in income-earning activities, pilot schemes of special non-conventional employment programmes for young school educated girls may be initiated through the secondary schools. Goods and services to be produced may target local demand and may also be supplied to urban centres. Nursery items, furniture and wood products, services like typing and other non-conventional activities may be encouraged. Such programmes can link formal schooling with development of entrepreneurial skills.

At the end, it should be emphasised that labour standards for female workers and gender equity in employment can be improved only when it is not at the cost of a deterioration of the labour standards provided to the male workers.

14.8.2 Policies for Women from Marginal Poor Groups

Women from marginal poor group are usually allocated with some responsibility of family's economic activity. This group of women can neither venture into full time self-employment nor would they be willing to engage in wage employment. They do not usually possess specific skills and do not possess links with agencies for learning such crafts or marketing of skill-based products. Some of these women may come forward for self-employment and this group can form the typical clientele of NGOs. If NGOs can provide training, loan and inputs, act as social entrepreneurs and take up the responsibility of marketing of output, this group of women may turn into a productive force. NGOs profit in these cases (where new employment for women is generated) may be exempted from tax. Other forms of support to such NGOs may be provided, including subsidised facilities for providing training. Such training and direct income earning self-employment in contrast to "unpaid family employment" can be a step forward for this group of women.

Regionally dispersed industrial growth can take advantage of this source of labour supply. Sub-contracting to female home-based workers can also contribute to enterprise competitiveness. Women willing to engage in subcontracting may be trained by respective employers.

14.8.3 Poorest Women Seeking Wage Employment

In each village, a few women who live in households without male earning members are found to eke out marginal living. Number of such women is much larger in villages at the pockets of severe intensity of poverty, for example, in the north western districts. In these areas, women are desperate to obtain wage employment. Special employment programmes for women should be planned for these areas. Women (or even men) who are prepared to work for wage rate, slightly below the closest available private sector employment, should be given opportunities of such employment guarantee schemes. Safety net type employment for women may be provided for building/maintaining roads and other public facilities. Cleaning market areas, public water bodies, schools, etc. are examples of activities which may be assigned on contract basis to groups of women from low-income households.

Annex

Table 14.1A: Determinants of Rural Household's Income: Results of OLS Regression

Dependent Variable: Log of Total Household Income

Indep. Variables	Standardised Coefficient	t-value	Significance
Constant	-	117.23	.00
Head's education	.114	11.52	.00
Head's sex (Male =1)	.099	9.60	.00
Total land owned	.177	17.87	.00
Education of 15+ non-head earning members	.035	3.32	.00
Does the household have an electricity connection?	.133	13.88	.00
No. of persons 0-14 years in the HH	.091	9.38	.00
Whether foreign remittance dummy (yes=1)	.277	28.57	.00
Barisal dummy	-.061	-6.18	.00
Chittagong dummy	.028	2.60	.02
Khulna dummy	-.077	-7.47	.00
Rajshahi dummy	-.025	-2.41	.00
Rangpur dummy	-.037	-3.65	.00
Sylhet dummy	-.020	-1.98	.07
No. of male earners 15+ age in agri.	.103	9.91	.00
No. of female earners 15+ age in agri.	.100	10.56	.00
No. of male earners 15+ age in non-agri.	.170	16.10	.00
No. of female earners 15+ age in non-agri.	.164	16.31	.00
Total non-earners (male + female) 15+	.268	23.83	.00
Non-agri. Capital	.077	8.56	.00
Value of all agri. equipment	.072	7.90	.00
Head age	.354	6.87	.00
Square of head age	-.428	-8.36	.00
Sample size	7,791		
Value of F	247.53		
Adjusted R-square	0.39		

Source: Estimated from the HIES (2010) data.

CHAPTER 15

Linkages between Population Growth and Socio-economic Factors

15.1 Introduction

The links between food shortage and population growth have received attention since the days of Malthus. Nonetheless, Malthus's prediction that food shortage drives down population growth has been, by and large, proved to be unreal even in the low-income countries. Population growth, however, continues to be viewed as a constraint to growth of per capita income in resource poor countries like Bangladesh. During the last two decades reduction of total fertility rate (TFR) and population growth has contributed to significant poverty reduction in this country. Households with smaller share of young dependents have been successful in moving out of poverty (WB, 2008). Reduction of population growth can be one of the easier and much desired routes for further reduction of poverty in the coming days. Therefore, the links among socio-economic factors, poverty, fertility and choice of number of children require a better understanding. The objective of the present chapter is to provide an in-depth analysis of these linkages.

While existing studies on the subject have emphasised that opting for smaller family norm contributes to lower poverty, the association may also run in the reverse direction and poverty of households may stand on the way to acceptance of smaller family norm. This chapter examines how this can happen. The analysis focuses mainly on the demand side of the choice. Nonetheless, the supply side can also be a relevant force and receives attention.

In fact, Bangladesh has experienced a rapid reduction of population growth associated with a decline of TFR since the mid-1970s when the rate of socio-economic development has not picked up. Theories of demographic transition envision this phase of fertility decline to occur only after a significant achievement of overall social and economic development. The exceptional feature of early reduction of TFR in post independence Bangladesh has therefore received attention of all and a number of studies have examined how the achievement of fertility decline in a situation of poverty could be achieved (Mahmud 2006).[1]

Although Bangladesh has entered the phase of rapid decline of TFR quite early, the pace of decline of TFR has gradually slowed down and in recent years there has been a plateauing or a small rise of population growth. Insights into the factors contributing to this change can contribute to the adoption of policies for sustaining the demographic transition and achieving a replacement level TFR.[2]

The early phase of fertility decline, when poverty rate in Bangladesh has been very high (50 per cent to 60 per cent), implies that even poor households may opt for a reduction of family size if they receive appropriate policy support. Therefore, one must examine why the situation has changed in recent years. It requires attention to the choices of households below and above the poverty threshold. This chapter analyses the difference in the perspectives of socio-economic groups of households in terms of preference of family size, adoption of contraceptives, age of marriage and child bearing. In fact, these issues have relevance not only as determinants of TFR but also have a general relevance for social development, children's and mother's health and women's empowerment.

The chapter begins with (Section 15.2) data on TFR to reveal the differences among socio-economic groups. Section 15.3 discusses the factors contributing to fertility decline during the early years after independence and highlights the importance of the supply-side factors. This is followed by an analysis of the links among poverty, age of marriage and children's health and TFR. These are likely to influence fertility regulation and family size related preferences. The focus is on how the adverse situation faced by children from poor households influences quality-quantity trade-off in the fertility decisions (Section 15.4). It is expected that in the present phase of demographic transition, families are likely to opt for improvement of quality of children through better education and health care services and make a trade-off with the desired number of children. This chapter

---

[1] These studies have inspired the present analysis.

[2] This chapter examines only some limited aspects of population dynamics and focuses mainly on links among changes of TFR and socio-economic factors.

goes deeper into the reasons which stand in the way to effective exercise of these options. The penultimate section looks at the role of supply side of family planning inputs and how these differ among poverty groups. The analyses presented in Sections 15.2 through 15.4 can throw light on whether the process of poverty reduction through fertility regulation can be sustained and this analysis can help formulation of policies for achieving the goal of rapid reduction of population growth. The concluding section discusses the major policy options.

15.2 Pattern of Fertility Decline: Difference among Socio-Economic Groups

Data on TFR show that Bangladesh's demographic transition started quite early (Table 15.1). TFR decreased from 5.9 in 1978 to 4.3 in 1990. The decline of TFR during the 1980s occurred despite lack of acceleration of economic growth and very little progress in social development. During the 1990s social and economic changes accelerated and TFR declined from 4.33 in 1990 to 2.56 in 2002. Subsequent decline (especially after 2008) has been slow and since 2010 TFR has been stagnating. As expected, the decline of TFR was accompanied by a rapid increase of contraceptive prevalence rate (CPR) during the period 1985-1997 (Table 15.2). Then it increased at a slower pace.

Table 15.1: Total Fertility Rate (TFR) in Bangladesh: 1976-2011

Year	TFR Per Woman	Natural Growth Rate of Population (%)
1976	6.34	-
1978	5.93	-
1982	5.21	2.26
1986	4.71	2.25
1990	4.33	2.14
1994	3.58	1.80
1998	2.98	1.51
2002	2.56	1.50
2006	2.39	1.49
2009	2.15	1.36
2010	2.12	1.36
2011	2.11	1.37

Source: MoF (various years); BBS: *Statistical Yearbook of Bangladesh* (various years).

Table 15.2: Adoption of Birth Control: 1975-2011

Year	Source of Data	Adoption Rate among 15-46 Years Old Persons (%)
1975	BFS	7.7
1983	CPS	19.1
1985	CPS	25.3
1989	BFS	30.8
1991	CPS	39.9
1994	BFS	44.6
1997	BFS	49.2
2000	BFS	53.8
2004	BFS	58.1
2007	BFS	55.8
2011	BDHS	61.2

Source: BBS: BDHS, BFS, CPS (various years).

TFR differs among socio-economic groups and the pattern of decline has been uneven among these groups. Table 15.3 shows values of TFR in 2000, 2007 and 2011 by socio-economic groups represented by levels of education. Many studies (including the chapter on education included in this book) show that educational attainment varies positively with household income and those without education are likely to be the poorest and thus education level can serve as a proxy indicator of household poverty.

Table 15.3: TFR by Education and Asset

Characteristics		2011	2007	2000
Education	None	2.9	3.0	4.1
	Less than primary	2.6	2.9	3.3
	Primary	2.3	2.9	3.4
	Less than secondary	2.2	2.5	
	Secondary & above	1.9	2.3	2.4
Asset	Lowest 20%	3.1	3.2	NA
	2nd 20%	2.5	3.1	NA
	3rd 20%	2.2	2.7	NA
	4th 20%	2.1	2.5	NA
	Highest	1.9	2.2	NA

Source: BBS: BDHS (various years).

Data (Table 15.3) show that during the period 2000-2011, fertility decline has taken place among all socio-economic groups. However, the differences between the two periods, 2000-2007 and 2007-2011, are quite glaring. While the lowest education group showed the highest decline of TFR during the period 2000-2007, the same group showed smallest decline of TFR during the later period. For the top two groups, TFR decline has been stable. Thus the poorer groups made a large contribution to fertility decline during the early periods. However, this could not be sustained and the factors contributing to the changing pattern require careful investigation.

To understand the difference in the future role of poor and not-so-poor in reducing population growth, their preferences of number of children and actual adoption of family planning practices require attention. Insights into the factors which influence these preferences can reveal whether these groups can play effective roles in fertility reduction in future. An analysis of these factors can help assess whether the poorer group's objectives behind their choice of fertility regulation have been actually realised and this can shed light on the policy options which may help sustain their choice of lower fertility in future.

15.3 Determinants of Fertility Decline during Early Years

The observed phenomenon of fertility reduction at an early stage of economic development through participation of both poor and non-poor households has been analysed from various angles. Analysis of demographic transition usually attributes fertility reduction to overall social and economic development of a country. Such development leads to decline of infant mortality rate (IMR), which leads to reduction of number of births required to achieve a certain number of surviving children. Moreover, higher level of household income reduces the need for children's earnings.

As Bangladesh's fertility decline has started at an early stage, neither of the above factors has been operating. Therefore, a number of other explanations were offered on the basis of the supply side factors (Sirageldin et al., 1975, Arthur et al., 1978). Such explanations focused on the easy availability and the low cost of family planning services. Soon after the independence of the country, beginning from the mid-1970s, population growth was identified as a major obstacle to raising per capita income and therefore conscious policy efforts and programmes for providing contraceptives and family planning services were adopted. The success of such services led to the conclusion that a latent demand for such services prevailed and the supply side intervention helped satisfy that unmet demand and resulted in rapid fertility reduction.

However, the continuous rise of CPR and decline of TFR during the 1980s, 1990s and early part of the last decade imply that not only prevailing unmet demand has been catered to but also new demand for fertility regulation has been generated. In future, a continuous decline of TFR will require that the growth of demand continues. Therefore, a better understanding of factors generating demand and conscious adoption of birth control methods with a motivation of limiting the number of children is required.

Fertility decline through adoption of family planning involves both direct and indirect costs. Direct cost of adoption of family planning is not high because of Bangladesh government's policy of subsidising the inputs and services. However, there are some hidden costs due to adverse health effects and poor quality of follow up services by government providers of contraceptive services and health care.

15.4 Demand-Side Factors behind Fertility Choice: Difference among Socio-Economic Groups

Whether poor and non-poor households demonstrate differences in the TFR, preferred family size and contraceptive prevalence rate can be seen from actual data presented in Tables 15.3 and 15.4. Such difference is quite large as revealed by data (Tables 15.3 and 15.4). As shown in Table 15.4, in 2011, CPR is the highest among the second lowest quintile group of asset ownership and the assetless households' CPR is the same as highest asset group. Moreover, these two groups have risen to highest adopters rank in 2011 through a sharp increase of adoption rate in the early years (between 2000 and 2007). The difference in adoption rates, between 2007 and 2011, is higher in the lowest asset groups compared to highest asset group. In the highest asset group, the rate has stagnated. These differences are linked to differences in the costs and benefits of children among the socio-economic groups.

Table 15.4: Adoption Rate (among 15-46 years aged women) of Birth Control by Education and Asset

Characteristics		Contraceptive Prevalence Rate (CPR) (%)		
		2000	2007	2011
Education	None	41.0	54.6	61.4
	Less than primary	44.0	57.5	64.2
	Primary	41.0	54.3	59.6
	Less than secondary	47.0	54.2	59.0
	Secondary & above	-	60.3	63.4
Asset	Lowest	-	54.8	61.5
	2nd	-	54.7	62.9
	3rd	-	54.1	61.4
	4th	-	55.2	59.5
	Highest	-	59.9	60.8
All			55.8	61.2

Source: BBS, BDHS (2000, 2007, 2011).

The analysis of demand-side forces involves identification of economic factors in terms of costs and benefits of additional children. Direct costs of having children include costs of their essential consumption, child care expenses and investment on education and health. Earnings foregone during child birth and child raising account for the indirect costs. These costs are higher among women who are engaged in paid employment.

Positive aspects (or economic returns) of having children depend on investment on human capital development among children. Economic return of children depends on overall economic development as well. Such return can come from children's employment and earning, which has to be foregone with increased schooling. The investment on human capital pays off through higher earnings from adult sons and daughters. This can lead to a "trade-off between future quality of children and number of children desired" and the choice may have different implications for poorer and better off households.

Decline of the desired number of children and increased demand for family planning services during the 1980s to 1990s by all economic groups can be explained by looking at some profound changes of the socio-economic structure which affected these costs and benefits. This period has seen a rapid pace of urbanisation and a fall in agriculture's role in income and employment. Family labour-based agriculture has given way to hired labour use in larger share. Therefore, children's importance in family's farming activity has fallen. Employment in non-agriculture requires more specific skills and children may not possess such skills. Conscious policy efforts for elimination of child labour also reduced children's participation in income-earning activities.

Thus children's direct economic contribution has declined, especially in small farms and low asset families who would like to engage their children in paid employment. In contrast, during this period real wage has been stagnant or growing slowly in most sectors. Therefore, the low age dependents' consumption burden became the major consideration behind choosing smaller family norm.

Contrary to the experience of the 1980s and early 1990s, during the later part of the 1990s, real wage growth has accelerated and thus has eased the consumption burden from additional children. Free schooling for boys and girls implies investment required for education has been lowered. This may raise the preferred family size or at least keep it non-declining. This attitude may continue if more scope of investment (on children), in post-secondary education and health of children, which generate higher return, is not opened up. In this context, the choice of poor and non-poor women in terms of quality (health and education) and number of children desired can be quite different, which receives attention in the following analysis.

15.4.1 Poverty and Children's Education and Health

Empirical data of the last two decades can reveal the differences among poor and non-poor women's prospects of benefiting from investment on child quality including educational attainment and health situation. Poorest households are deficient of both areas. Data in Chapter 10 show that children (aged 12 years and above) from households in the lowest quartile have lower school enrolment rate compared to upper quartiles. Young persons in the poorer groups have smaller endowment of secondary and higher education compared to higher income groups. BBS (2015) shows similar difference among asset groups. Adjusted net school attendance ratio (in primary or secondary level) declines from 81.4 per cent in the highest wealth quintile to 64.5 per cent in the lowest wealth group.

Similarly, poorer households are losers in terms of children's health outcomes. The BDHS (2011) and MICS (2013) data show (Table 15.5) that the percentage of children stunted (and wasted) is much higher among the assetless groups, and most alarming is that this deficiency has been increasing. They are the worst performers in terms of other health outcomes as well. It implies that though the poorest groups have made their contribution to fertility decline in the early stage of development, this group could not equally share the benefits of the fertility reduction through improvement in child health.

Table 15.5: Child Health related Outcomes by Asset Group

Asset	Per Cent of 12-23 Months Age Children Receiving			% of Children			
				BDHS (2011)		MICS (2012-13)	
	Infant Mortality	All Basic Vaccines	No Vaccination	Severely Stunted	Severely Under-Weight	Severely Stunted	Severely Under-Weight
Lowest	50	76.8	4.0	24.5	16.6	23.2	12.6
2nd	57	84.9	3.4	16.9	11.3	18.3	10.9
3rd	41	84.9	0.8	14.1	11.5	16.5	9.0
4th	38	89.0	1.8	11.2	6.3	13.2	6.2
Highest	29	63.5	0.0	6.4	3.9	8.7	3.7

Source: BBS, BDHS (2011), BBS, GoB and UNICEF (2015).

Table 15.6: Desired Number of Children Desired by Ever-married Women Aged 15-49 by Asset

Characteristics		Desired Number of Children	
		2007	2011
Asset	Lowest quintile	2.3	2.3
	2nd	2.2	2.4
	3rd	2.2	2.3
	4th	2.2	2.2
	Highest	2.1	2.2

Source: BBS, BDHS (2000, 2007, 2011).

This is not only inequitable but is also standing as an obstacle to further reduction of TFR through increase in contraceptive adoption. These deprivations and the related adverse impacts on prospects of rising above poverty threshold have gradually become clearer to the poorer households who opted for fertility regulation. Such realisation may in future cause a reversal of contraceptive adoption rate among these groups of families. Without realisation of improvements in quality of children (in terms of human capital) and who have prospects of better employment and earnings and thus satisfying parental expectations of old age support, the preference for smaller families cannot be sustained. This has been revealed by Table 15.6, which shows that in the lower quintiles of asset ownership, household's ideal number of children were static or increased during the period 2007-2011 and the values were higher than the two highest quintiles.

It may be noted that the desired number of children also depends on mother's employment situation. The higher cost of having children is linked to their higher rate of participation in paid employment, which would be interrupted by childcare burden. Both the BDHS and LFS show that assetless women have a greater participation in employment. However, during the period 2006-2010, the growth of number of women employed on a regular basis has been rather slow. This not only reduces the cost of having an additional child but also reduces the age of marriage of women.

15.4.2 Age of Marriage, Poverty and TFR

The age of marriage as a factor influencing the population dynamics needs attention. Declining age of first marriage (Table 15.7) and low age of first child bearing (Table 15.8) can have profound influence directly through lengthening the period of child bearing as well as indirectly by reducing women's say in the decision making related to family size norms. The links among poverty, quality of children and age of marriage are shown in Figure 15.1, which is self-explanatory.

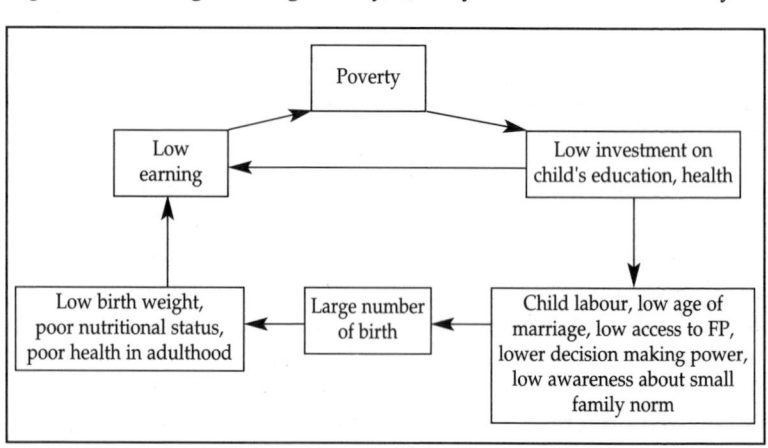

Figure 15.1: Linkages among Poverty, Quality of Children and Fertility

A disturbing feature emerging from data for the last few years is that age at first marriage has been declining (Table 15.7). This is one of the factors responsible for recent plateauing of TFR, despite a rise in the contraceptive use rate. This factor is more damaging for low asset owning households and low educated women for whom age at first marriage and at first child birth (Table 15.8) is lower than the educated women and those from high asset owning families. Figure 15.1, Tables 15.8 and 15.9 vividly show the operation of the vicious cycle of poverty, low age of marriage and weakness in child quality. This aspect needs immediate policy attention not only from the equity point of view but also for sustained success in reducing TFR for the country as a whole.

Table 15.7: Mean Age at Marriage of Women

Year	Age (Years)
2001	20.4
2002	20.6
2003	20.4
2004	19.0
2005	18.0
2006	18.1
2007	18.4
2008	19.1
2009	18.5
2010	18.7
2011	18.6

Source: BBS: Sample Vital Registration System.

Table 15.8: Median Age at First Child Birth and Median Age at First Marriage among Women Aged 20-49 by Education and Asset

Characteristics		Median Age at First Child Birth	Median Age of Marriage
Education	None	17.5	14.8
	Less than primary	17.2	14.9
	Primary	17.7	15.4
	Less than secondary	18.6	16.3
	Secondary & above	NA	19.9
Asset	Lowest	17.6	15.1
	2nd	17.7	15.3
	3rd	17.9	15.5
	4th	18.5	16.0
	Highest	19.8	17.4
All		18.3	15.8

Source: BBS, BDHS (2007).

Table 15.9: Percentage of Currently Married Women Aged 14-49 Who Takes a Decision by Herself or Jointly with Husband by Asset Groups

Characteristics		Type of Decision	
		Women's Own Health Care	Child's Health Care
Asset	Lowest	62.0	65.5
	2nd	61.0	65.1
	3rd	59.9	63.2
	4th	63.2	66.6
	Highest	68.5	72.1

Source: BBS, BDHS (2007).

15.5 Adoption of Family Planning: Link between Poverty and Supply Side of Inputs

Supply of family planning inputs can have important influence on adoption of family planning methods. In fact, analysts have emphasised (Mahmud, 2006, Khan and Khan, 2000) the role of the supply-side factors and consider that the effective steps taken by the government are the major driving forces behind the early reduction of fertility in this country when PCI and level of social development were low.[3]

With the rise of income and education, dissemination of knowledge about family planning practices can increasingly rely on publicity through the media. In fact, during the last one and a half decades, government's policy shift has been reflected in a greater reliance on the media. Programmes of direct intervention have been curtailed and modified. Without going into a detailed analysis of the changes in policies and resource allocations which took place over the years, it is pertinent to mention that the programmes involving frequent household visits by field workers of family planning services have given way to provision of inputs and services through satellite clinics, etc. This change tallies with the position of demographers who consider that the effective route to fertility reduction can be achieved through generating demand by changing the socio-economic and cultural patterns, which requires efforts in directions other than the supply side of family planning.

---

[3] Role of government's family planning programme in early decline of fertility has been recognised by a number of studies (Khan and Khan, 2000, CPD-UNFPA, 2003). Khan's study mentioned that the "shift from outreach domiciliary services to clinic based services provides explanation for recent downslide of programme effectiveness."

The theoretical underpinning behind this position has actually missed the point that the supply-side efforts may actually help break the socio-cultural barriers which stand on the way to fertility reduction, especially among the poorer households. The experiences of supply-side approach adopted during the 1970s support this view. At that time, the focus on contraceptive delivery and lowering of time and monetary cost of contraception played an important role. Nonetheless, this focus also included aggressive motivational campaign and female field workers' home visits, which helped promote a favourable attitude towards two-child family. The programme also helped in overcoming the religious and cultural barriers to legitimise the use of modern methods of family planning. These positive influences were especially useful in the case of poorer households who were more vulnerable to pronatalist and anti-birth control values promoted by richer social classes and religious leaders. Socio-cultural biases impose additional psychological costs on poorer women's adoption of family planning. Preference for male offspring, sanctions against childlessness, and linking of these values with the stability of marriage can act as threats against adoption of birth control by poor women. Moreover, Table 15.9 shows that poor women and for that matter all women have low decision making power even about their own health care matters. A strong family planning programme can prove to be effective in breaking these vicious cycles of socio-cultural norms reinforced by poverty. These roles may continue to be important until the loosening of grips of poverty and social pressure, which can take place through education and employment of women.

Concrete data on poor women's access to family planning related knowledge reaching through modern media can substantiate whether the contention about their exposure to the media is correct or not. Data for 2011 presented in Table 15.10 show that 93 per cent women from poorest (asset) group had no exposure to the media's information on family planning. The percentage with access to none of three (radio, TV and newspaper) is lower among the highest asset group.

In this context, a comparison of the extent of exposure through direct approach of field worker's visit in 2011 and 2007 highlights a drastic decline in this mode. This is a glaring example of lack of attention to the poor women's lack of exposure to the media, as revealed in Table 15.10. With changes in programme focus, the share of women reporting visit by family planning workers has drastically fallen from

19.9 per cent in 2007 to 13 per cent in 2011 among the "no education" group. For more educated women, it is slightly higher. This data obviously points towards a link between poverty, lack of access to knowledge of contraceptives and stagnation of TFR.

Table 15.10: Access to Family Planning Knowledge through Media and Visit by Field Workers: Difference among Asset and Education Groups

Characteristics		1997		2007		2011	
		None of Media Source	FW Visits	None of Media Source	FW Visits	None of Media Source	FW Visits
Education	None	71.8	39.8	78.7	19.9	87.6	13.0
	Less than primary	55.3	37.6	66.8	23.3	80.9	15.2
	Primary	44.6	38.2	63.6	21.1	74.6	16.0
	Less than secondary			45.2	22.5	64.9	16.0
	Secondary & above	25.5	38.1	35.9	19.3	50.5	11.9
Asset	Lowest	NA	NA	85.6	NA	92.9	15.5
	2nd	-	-	76.3	-	86.7	15.9
	3rd	-	-	65.6	-	75.2	17.1
	4th	-	-	45.3	-	61.8	15.6
	Highest	-	-	37.5	-	54.5	9.0

Source: BBS, BDHS (various years).

The foregone opportunity of fertility reduction through motivation and input supply for poorer women can be further emphasised by looking at the "unmet demand" for fertility regulation. According to the BDHS 2011, the unmet demand is the highest in the poorest group and declines for higher asset groups. Although some adverse impacts may result from supply-side policies, there are reasons to argue that altogether reverse policy direction may not be desirable. The poor women are in greater need to reduce family size. But the cost of contraception without government support (both direct monetary cost and indirect cost from social pressure) can be restrictively high for these women.

15.6 Concluding Observations and Policy Implications

Adoption of a balanced population policy is a complex matter. Inability to adopt a balanced approach of population policy may not only result in stalling of fertility decline but may also, in the near future, slow down the rate of poverty reduction associated with poor women's choice of not reducing the number of children (as shown in Figure 15.1). A proper attention to rationale behind the fertility choice of poor couples and especially of women can help policy making. The findings of the present chapter can provide some guidance.

Policy adoption must be based on recognition that the motivation and preferences differ among the asset groups, which, in turn, is due to the difference in social and economic constraints faced by the groups. It has been observed that even after a significant reduction of fertility among all groups, in recent period TFR is higher among the poorer groups. This is associated with higher desired number of children among poorer couples as well as higher unmet demand for family planning. Lower age at marriage and age at first child birth have also contributed to higher TFR among poorer households, especially through current momentum of population growth. Inequality in socio-cultural and economic environment pushes them to these unfavourable circumstances.

If Bangladesh intends to pursue the goal of replacement level TFR within the next ten years or so, it must utilise all possible routes to fertility reduction, of course, without compromising people's right to choice about family size and women's rights of maintaining good health. In this context, short-term strategies should receive adequate attention and medium-term programmes must also be adopted simultaneously even if the results of these efforts are not apparent immediately.

In the short run, one must use the lessons learnt from earlier experience of supply-side interventions which produced visible reduction of TFR even though there have been some excesses due to inflexibility of programmes and unrealistic targets.[4] Supply side efforts can still help because there exists some unmet demand for family planning. Moreover, spread of knowledge through the media appears to be ineffective for poorer households and for a large majority of uneducated women and therefore home visit by family planning and health workers can continue to play a useful role. In fact, visit by programme personnel can also help counter the prevailing negative

---

[4] Studies have highlighted the inadvertent burden resulting from undue female bias in the family planning programmes, inadequate safeguards and health services to reduce morbidity resulting from excess and inappropriate use of contraception and inflexibility of programmes.

forces from family and village leaders. Poor women's fear and vulnerability to these forces can be removed through the physical presence of government/NGO supported persons.

Among the factors behind high population growth, the "current momentum" is a most difficult one to fight through policy intervention. The high fertility in the past has resulted in large cohorts of women in child bearing age. The current momentum of population growth produced by these cohorts can be reduced through raising the age of marriage and age of first child birth. Prevailing average age at marriage is low. In fact, in recent years this has declined or remained static. In poor families, 50 per cent girls are married at age less than 16, which is less than the legal minimum age of marriage. So, an all out effort should be focused on this front. Raising the age of marriage will not only reduce TFR but is also a desirable goal on consideration of women's health and empowerment. Publicity efforts and campaign through home visit by field workers and through the media should be strengthened. The social and religious leaders and teachers can play a role in this campaign if they are properly motivated.

Table 15.11: Policies for Different Routes to Fertility Regulation

Route to Fertility Reduction	Intermediate Impact	Policies
Reduce the desired number of children	a. Improve quality of children	a. Raise demand for better quality of children, remove child labour
	b. Higher income and empowerment of women, awareness raising	b. Education of girls, Employment generation for young (15-30 years) girls
	c. Alternative old age support	c. Safety net and social protection of all low-income households
Reduce current momentum of population growth	Raise age at first child birth	Raise age of marriage through education and awareness
Raise access to family planning inputs and services	Cater to unmet demand, meet new demand and create more demand for family planning	a. Education and awareness raising
		b. Reduce time and financial cost of family planning policy
		c. Improve health services to reduce side effects.

Scope of completion of secondary education and employment outside home can help raise age of marriage. These medium-term policies can play a role in reducing TFR through other routes as well.

Such policies are expected to have positive effects on household income. These changes also raise the cost of having more children, can positively influence new born and infants' health outcomes, and thereby motivate couples for improvement of quality of children through reduction of number of children born. In this context, strengthening of the old age security programmes by the government can play a role.

Policies suggested above for achieving the fertility reduction goal through various routes have been shown concisely in Table 15.11.

The present analysis has demonstrated the negative influence of poverty on fertility regulation as it frustrates women's choices of lower TFR. Therefore, the need for policy emphasis for eliminating poverty through other routes remains valid. In the medium term, success along this route can prove the saying that "Development is the best contraceptive."

References

Ahmed, I. (1981). Farm Size and Labour Use: Some Alternative Explanations. *Oxford Bulletin of Economics and Statistics*, February.

Ahmed, R. & Hossain, M. (1990). Development Impact of Rural Infrastructure in Bangladesh. *Research Report No. 83*. Washington DC: IFPRI.

Ahmed, R. (2001). *Retrospect's and Prospects of the Rice Economy of Bangladesh* Dhaka: UPL.

Ahmed, S. & Mitra, P. (2010). Gender Wage Discrimination in Rural and Urban Labour Market of Bangladesh. *Oxford Development Studies* (Vol. 38, No. 1).

Alam, M. (2007). Bangladesh Education in Transition: Policy Performance and Way Forward. Dhaka: D.Net.

Alamgir, M. & Rahman, A. (1974). Savings in Bangladesh 1959/60-1969/70. *Research Monograph No. 2*. Dhaka: Bangladesh Institute of Development Studies (BIDS).

Arthur, B., and McNicoll, G (1978): "An Analytical Survey of Population and Development in Bangladesh", Population and Development Review, Vol. 4, No. 1.

Asaduzzaman, M. (1979). Adoption of HYV Rice in Bangladesh. *The Bangladesh Development Studies* (Vol. VII, No. 3, Monsoon, pp. 23-52).

Aslam, M. and Kingdom, G. (2005): Gender and Household Education Expenditure in Pakistan, Economics Series Working Paper, GPRG-WPS-025, University of Oxford, Department of Economics.

Barro, R.J. (1991). Economic Growth in a Cross Section of Countries. *The Quarterly Journal of Economics* (Vol. CVI, Issues 2).

Barros, A.R. (1993). Some Implications of New Growth Theory for Economic Development. *Journal of International Development* (Vol. 5, No. 5).

Basu, K. (1999): Child Labour: Causes, Consequences and Cure, with Remarks on International Labour Standards, Journal of Economic Literature, Vol. XXXVII, September.

BBS (Bangladesh Bureau of Statistics). (Various Years). *Report of Census of Manufacturing Industries*.

———, BIDS & UNICEF. (2015). *Ending Child Labour in Bangladesh*.

———, GoB & UNICEF. (2015). Multiple indicator Cluster Survey 2012-13. *Final Report*. Progotir Polhess.

BBS (2010): Sample Vital Registration System (SVRS), Government of Bangladesh.

BBS (CLS) (2003, 1996): Child Labour Survey Report.

BBS, BDHS (2000, 2005, 2011): Bangladesh Demographic and Health Survey, GoB.

BBS, (2005, 2010): Household Income & Expenditure Survey, HIES.

BBS, (1984, 1996, 2008): Report on Bangladesh Census of Agriculture.

——, (LFS 1996, 2000, 2006, 2010, 2013). *Report on Labour Force Survey*. Government of Bangladesh.

——, (Various Years). *Statistical Yearbook of Bangladesh*.

BIDS Survey, SSISP (1992): Small Scale Irrigation Sector Project Report, BIDS.

Bloom, D.E. & Williamson, J.G. (1998). Demographic Dividend and Economic Miracles in Emerging Asia. *World Bank Economic Review*, 12(3).

Boyce, J.K. (1986). Water Control and Agricultural Performance in Bangladesh. *The Bangladesh Development Studies* (Vol. XIV, No. 4).

Bridges, S, Lawson, D & Begum, S. (2011). Labour Market Outcomes in Bangladesh: The Role of Poverty and Gender Norms. In: *European Journal of Development Research* (Vol. 23). www.palgrave-Journals.com.ejdr

Caldwell, J.C., Barkat-e-Khuda, Caldwell, B., Pieris, I. & Caldwell, P. (1999). The Bangladesh Fertility Decline: An Interpretation. *Population and Development Review* (Vol. 25, No. 1).

CAMPE. (1999). *Education Watch: Hope Not Complacency State of Primary Education in Bangladesh 1999*. Dhaka: CAMPE & UPL.

CAMPE. (2001). *A Question of Quality. State of Primary Education in Bangladesh 2000* (Vol. II & III). Dhaka: CAMPE & UPL.

CAMPE. (2005). *Education Watch: The State of Secondary Education Progress and Challenges*. Dhaka: CAMPE & UPL.

CAMPE. (2006). *Education Watch Report 2005: The State of Primary Education: Progress and Challenges*. Dhaka: CAMPE & UPL.

Chandrashekhar, C.P. (1997). The Economic Consequences of the Abolition of Child Labour: An Indian Case Study. *The Journal of Peasant Studies* (Vol. 24, No. 3). London: Frank Cass.

Chowdhury, N. (1987). Household Savings Behaviour in Bangladesh: Issues and Evidences. In: *The Bangladesh Development Studies* (Vol. XV, No. 3).

Clay, E.J. (1978). Environment, Technology and the Seasonal Patterns of Agricultural Employment in Bangladesh. Paper presented at the conference on Seasonal Dimensions to Rural Poverty at the Institute of Development Studies. July (mimeo).

Containing Population Pressure for Accelerating Poverty Reduction in Bangladesh. CPD-UNFPA (2003). Paper Series 25. www.cpd.org.bd/pub-attach.unfpa 25.pdf

CDF (2000): Microfinance Statistics, Vol. 13.

REFERENCES

CPD-UNFPA (2003): Bangladesh's Population Policy: Emerging Issues and Future Agenda, Working Paper 23, Dhaka.

Deninger, K. & Squire, L. (1996). A New Data Set for Measuring Income Inequality. *World Bank Economic Review*, 10(3).

Dollar, D. & Kraay, A. (2002). *Growth is Good for the Poor*. The World Bank: Development Research Group.

Faaland, J. & Parkinson, J.R. (1976). *Bangladesh the Test Case of Development*. London: C. Hurst & Company & Dhaka: UPL.

Fei, J.C.H. & Ranis, G. (1964). *Development of Labour Surplus Economy, Theory and Policy*. Illinois: Irwin Inc.

Frankel, F.R. (1971). *India's Green Revolution Economic Gains and Political Costs*. Princeton.

Ghai, D. (2006). Decent Work: Universality and Diversity. In: D. Ghai (ed.), *Decent Work: Objectives and Strategies*. Geneva: ILO.

Griffin, K. (1974). *The Political Economy of Agrarian Change: An Essays on the Green Revolution*. Cambridge: Harvard University Press.

Hossain, M. & Bayes, A. (2009). *Rural Economy and Livelihoods, Insights from Bangladesh*. Dhaka: A.H. Development Publishing House.

Hossain, M. (1977). Farm Size, Tenancy and Land Productivity: An Analysis of Farm Level Data in Bangladesh Agriculture. *The Bangladesh Development Studies* (Vol. V, No. 3).

Hossain, M. (1984). Credit for the Rural Poor. The Experience of Grameen Bank in Bangladesh. *Research Monograph* (No. 4). Dhaka: BIDS.

Hossain, M. (1986). Irrigation and Agricultural Performance in Bangladesh: Some Further Results. *The Bangladesh Development Studies* (Vol. XIV, No. 4).

Hossain, M. (1988): Nature and Impact of the Green Revolution in Bangladesh. *Research Report* (No. 67). Washington DC: IFPRI.

Hossain, M. (1989). *Green Revolution in Bangladesh, Impact on Growth and Distribution of Income*. Dhaka: UPL.

Hossain, M., Quasem, M.A., Jabbar, M.A. & Akash, M.M. (1994). Production Environment, Modern Variety Adoption and Income Distribution in Bangladesh. In: C.C. David & K. Otsuka (eds.), *Modern Rice Technology and Income Distribution in Asia*. Boulder & London: Lynner Publishers & Manila: IRRI.

Husain, A.M.M. (1998). *Poverty Alleviation and Empowerment. The Second IAS of BRACs Rural Development Programmes*. Dhaka: BRAC.

IIMI. (1995). Study on Privatization of Minor Irrigation in Bangladesh. *Final Report*.

ILO (International Labour Office). (1999). Decent Work. *Report of the Director General*. Geneva: ILO.

Islam, R. & Islam, I. (2015). *Employment and Inclusive Development*. London: Routeledge.

Islam, R. (2004). Labour Market Policies, Economic Growth and Poverty Reduction: Lessons and Non-Lessons from the Comparative Experience of East, South-East and South Asia. In: R. Sobhan (ed.), *Employment and Labour Market Dynamics: A Review of Bangladesh's Development 2002*. Dhaka: CPD and UPL.

Islam, R. (2015). *Unnayan Bhabnae Karmasangsthan O Srambazar*. Dhaka: UPL.

Isvilanonda, S. & Wattanutchariya, S. (1994). Modern Variety Adoption, Factor-price Differential and Income Distribution in Thailand. In: C.C. David & K. Otsuka (eds.), *Modern Rice Technology and Income Distribution in Asia*. London: Lynne Rienner Publishers & Manila: International Rice Research Institute.

Jahan, K. & Hossain, M. (1998). *Nature and Extent of Malnutrition in Bangladesh: Bangladesh National Nutrition Survey, 1995-96*. Dhaka University: Institute of Nutrition and Food Science.

Kaldor, N. (1966). *Causes of Slow Growth in the United Kingdom*. Cambridge: Cambridge University Press.

Kaldor, N. (1967). *Strategic Factors in Economic Development*. Ithaca: Cornell University Press.

Kapsos, S. (2008). The Gender Wage Gap in Bangladesh. *ILO Asia-Pacific Working Paper Series*. Bangkok: ILO.

Khalily, M.A.B. & Rahman, R.I. (2011). *Emerging Issues in Income Growth of Rural Households, Development of Non-Farm Activities and Safety Net Provisions, Background Papers for the Sixth Five Year Plan (2011-2015)*. Dhaka: Bangladesh Institute of Development Studies & General Economics Division, Planning Commission.

Khan, A.A. (2011). *Andhokerer Utso Hote*. Dhaka: Pathak Samabesh.

Khan, A.R. (1995): 'A Quarter Century of Economic Development of Bangladesh: Success and Failures,' Bangladesh Development Studies, Vol. XXIII, Sept-Dec, Nos. 3 & 4.

Khan, A.R. (2016): The Economy of Bangladesh. A Quarter Century of Development, Palgrave Macmillan.

Khan, A.R. & Hossain, M. (1989). *The Strategy of Development in Bangladesh*. [place ???]: Macmillan in association with OECD Development Centre.

Khan, A.R. & Khan, M. (2000). *Population programs in Bangladesh: Problems, Prospects and Policy Issues*. Populationcommunication.com/Medias/popultion-problems-in-Bangladesh.

Khan, A.R. (1972). *The Economy of Bangladesh*. London & Basingstoke: The Macmillan Press Ltd. Reprinted 1973 by The Macmillan. Co of India Ltd.

Khan, A.R., Islam, R. & Haq, M. (1981). *Employment, Income and the Mobilisation of Local Resources: A Study of Two Bangladesh Villages*. Bangkok: ARTEP.

King, M.A. & Knox, R.L. (2002). *Working Children in Bangladesh*. Dhaka: Save the Children.

Krishna, R. (1973). Unemployment in India. *Economic and Political Weekly*, March 3.

Krishnamurty, J. (2008): Indian Antecedent of Disguised Unemployment an Surplus Labour, The Indian Journal of Labour Economics, Vol. 51, No. 1.

Kuznets, S. (1971). *Economic Growth of Nation: Total Output and Production Structure*. Cambridge, USA: Harvard University Press.

Lewis, W.A. (1954). *Economic Development with Unlimited Supplies of Labour*. Manchester School of Economic and Social Studies.

Lipton, M. & Longhurst, R. (1989). *New Seeds and Poor People*. London: Unwin Hyman.

Lipton, M. & Ravallion, M. (1993). Poverty and Policy. *Policy Research Working Papers*. Washington DC: World Bank.

Longhurst, R. & Payne, P. (1977). *Seasonal Aspects of Nutrition: Review of Evidence and Policy Implications, PD 145* (mimeo.). University of Sussex: Institute of Development Studies.

Mahajan, S. (2005). Analysis of Growth Experience, in Transforming Bangladesh into a Middle income Economy. by (ed.) Ahmed, S.. India: Macmillan India Ltd.

Mahmud, S. (2006). Fertility Decline under Poverty. In: S. Ahmed & W. Mahmud (eds.), *Growth and Poverty: The Development Experience of Bangladesh*. Dhaka: UPL.

Mckinsey and Company (2011): Bangladesh's Ready-made Garments Landscape. The Challenge of Growth. Mckinsey and Company, Frankfurt.

Mehra, S. (1976). Surplus Labor in Indian Agriculture. *Indian Economic Review* (Vol. 8, April).

Meier, G.M. (1976). *Leading Issues in Economic Development*. Oxford University Press.

MoF (Ministry of Finance). (Various Years). *Bangladesh Economic Review*, Dhaka: Government of Bangladesh.

MoF. (2015). *Budget Speech FY 2016*. Dhaka: Government of Bangladesh.

Moore, K. (2005): 'Thinking About Youth Poverty through the Lenses of Chronic Poverty. Life-Course Poverty and Intergenerational Poverty.' Working Paper 57, Chronic Poverty Research Centre, University of Manchester.

MRA (2009, 2012): NGO-MFIs in Bangladesh, Vol. 9, 16.

Mukharjee, P.K. (1970). The HYV Programme: Variables that Matter. *Economic and Political Weekly* (Vol. V, No. 13).

Muqtada, M. & Alam, M.M. (1986). Hired Labour and Rural Labour Market in Bangladesh. In: D. Hirashima & M. Muqtada (eds.), *Hired Labour and Rural Labour Market in Asia*. New Delhi: ILO-ARTEP.

Muqtada, M. (1975). The Seed-Fertiliser, Technology and Surplus Labour in Bangladesh Agriculture. *The Bangladesh Development Studies* (Vol. III, No. 4).

Muqtada, M. (1983). Hired Labour and Rural Labour Market in Bangladesh: An Analysis of Farm Level Data. *Asian Employment Programme Working Papers*. Bangkok: ILO-ARTEP.

Osmani, S.R., Ahmed, M., Latif, M.A., Sen, B. (2015). *Poverty and Vulnerability in Rural Bangladesh*. Dhaka: Institute of Microfinance & UPL.

Planning Commission (SFYP) (2011): Sixth Five Year Plan of Bangladesh (2011-2015 SFYP). GoB.

Planning Commission (7FYP) (2011): Seventh Five Year Plan of Bangladesh (2016-2020 7FYP). GoB.

Phang, H.S. (2003). *Rapid Ageing and Changes in Korea*. Paper presented at International Seminar on Low Fertility & Rapid Ageing, organised by Korean National Statistics Office, October 31.

Quasem, M.A. (2011). Conversion of Agricultural Land to Non-agricultural Uses in Bangladesh: Extent and Determinants. *The Bangladesh Development Studies* (Vol. XXXIV, No. 1).

Rahman R.I. (1996b). Impact of Credit for Rural Poor: An Evaluation of Palli Karma-Sahayak Foundation's Credit Programme. *Research Report No. 143*. Dhaka: BIDS.

Rahman, R.I. (1981): Implications of Seasonality of Rural Labour Use Pattern. Evidences from Two Villages in Bangladesh, The Bangladesh Development Studies, Vol. IX, No. 1.

Rahman, R.I. (1993): Determinants of Wage Employment and Labour Supply in Labour Surplus Situation of Rural Bangladesh. The Bangladesh Development Studies, Vol. XXI, No. 2.

Rahman, R.I. (2007): 'Labour Market in Bangladesh: Changes, Inequalities and Challenges', Research Monograph 21, BIDS, 2007.

Rahman, R.I. & Saha, B.K. (1995). Impact of Grameen Krishi Foundation on the Socio Economic Condition of Rural Households in Bangladesh. *Working Paper*. BIDS.

Rahman, R.I. (1983). Adoption of HYV: Role of Availability of Inputs and the Supply Side Problems. *The Bangladesh Development Studies* (Vol. XI, No. 4).

Rahman, R.I. (1986). Impact of Grameen Bank on the Situation of Poor Rural Women. *Report of Grameen Bank Evaluation Project*. Dhaka: BIDS.

Rahman, R.I. (1996a). *Microenterprise Development in Bangladesh*. Paper prepared for Asian Development Bank.

Rahman, R.I. (1998a). *Women in Poverty*. Study Report prepared for UN-ESCAP.

Rahman, R.I. (1998b). Alternative Institutional Forms for Operating Deep Tubewells and the Future of Deep Tubewell Irrigation in Bangladesh. In: *Crisis in Governance*. Dhaka: CPD and UPL.

Rahman, R.I. (2002). Determinants of the use of Modern Agricultural Inputs and Agricultural Productivity in Bangladesh. *The Bangladesh Development Studies* (Nos. 1 & 2).

Rahman, R.I. (2004a). Employment Route to Poverty Reduction in Bangladeshi Role of Self Employment and Wage Employment. *Discussion Paper 17*. Issues in Employment and Poverty. Geneva: ILO.

Rahman, R.I. (2004b). Future Challenges Facing the MFIs of Bangladesh: Choice of Target Groups, Loan sizes and Rate of Interest. In: S. Ahmed & M.A. Hakim (ed.), *Attacking Poverty with Microcredit*. Dhaka: UPL.

Rahman, R.I. (2005). Children in Economic Activity in Bangladesh: Recent Changes and Determinants. *BIDS Research Report No. 180*, December.

Rahman, R.I. (2009). *An Analysis of Real Wage in Bangladesh and Its Implications for Underemployment and Poverty*. Paper presented at the Festschrift Conference in Honour of Professor Azizur Rahman Khan. USA: University of Massachusetts-Amherst.

Rahman, R.I. (2010). *Compatibility of Children's Employment and Schooling in Bangladesh: A Focus on Paid Employment vs. Family Employment*. Paper prepared for ILO, Dhaka.

Rahman, R.I. (2012). *Bangladesher Arthonity O Unnayan: Swadhinatar Por Chollish Bochhor*. Dhaka: Shahitya Prokash.

Rahman, R.I. (2014). Demographic Dividend and Youth Labour Force Participation in Bangladesh. *Research Report 187*, Dhaka: BIDS.

Rahman, R.I. (2015). Situation of Wage Labourers in Bangladesh: A focus on Casual Workers in Agriculture. Abdul Ghafur Memorial Lecture, Dhaka: BIDS.

Rahman, R.I. Begum, A. & Bhuyan, H.R. (2009). *Impact of Paid Employment and Self Employment on Income and Prospects of Food Security*. Final Report of Study Sponsored by National Food Policy Capacity Strengthening Programme. http:www.hfpcsp.org

Rahman, R.I. & Khandker, S. (1994). Role of Targeted Credit Programmes in Promoting Employment and Productivity of the Poor in Bangladesh. *The Bangladesh Development Studies* (Vol, XXII, Nos. 2 & 3).

Rahman, R.I. & Mujeri, M.K. (2000). Savings and Farm Investment in Bangladesh: An Analysis of Rural Households. *Focus Study Series No. 11*. Dhaka: Centre on Integrated Rural Development for Asia and the Pacific.

Rahman, R.I., Mondal, A.H. & Islam, R. (2007). Mapping and Analysis of Growth-Oriented Industrial Sub-sectors and their Skill Requirement in Bangladesh. International Labour Organization and Bangladesh Institute of Development Studies.

Rahman, R.I. and Rashid, L. (2011): 'Microfinance Regulations for Development: Global Experiences', edited by Rushidan Islam Rahman and Lila Rashid, UPL and MRA, May 2011.

Rahman, R.I. and Islam, R. (2013)): Female Labour Force Participation in Bangladesh: Trends, Drivers and Barriers, ILO, New Delhi, Asia-Pacific Working Paper, 2013.

Ramasamy, C.P.P. & Kandaswamy, A. (1994). Irrigation Quality, Modern Variety Adoption and Income Distribution: The case of Tamil Nadu in India. In: C.C. David & K. Otsuka (eds.), *Modern Rice Technology and Income Distribution in Asia*. London: Lynne Rienner Publishers & Manila: International Rice Research Institute.

Rao, C.H.H. (1975). *Technological Change and Distribution of Gains in Indian Agriculture*. Delhi: Institute of Economic Growth.

Robinson, J. (1937): Essays on the Theory of Employment, Mackillan, London.

Rudra, A. (1971). Seasonality of Employment in Agriculture. *Economic and Political Weekly* (Vol. 8, September 29).

Salmon, Claire, (2002): Performance of the Bangladesh Labour Market during the Nineties, Background Paper No. 8, Bangladesh Poverty Assessment, ADB.

Saith, A., Wazir, R. (2010). From Poverty to Well-being: Alternative Approaches to the Recognition of Child Deprivation in India, Institute for Human Development, India, IHD-UNICEF Working Paper Series Children of India: Rights and Opportunities, *Working Paper No. 1*

Sen, A.K. (1962). An Aspect of Indian Agriculture. *Economic Weekly* (Annual Number, February).

Sen, A.K. (1966). Peasant and Dualism with or without Surplus Labour. *Journal of Political Economy* (Vol. 74, No. 5).

Sen, B. (1996). Rural Savings and Investment: Trend and Determinants, in 1987-1994. In: H.Z. Rahman, M. Hossain & B. Sen (eds.), *Dynamics of Rural Poverty in Bangladesh* (Mimeo). Dhaka: BIDS.

Stern, N.H. (2002). *The Investment Climate, Governance and Inclusion in Bangladesh*. Public Lecture at Bangladesh Economic Association, Dhaka.

World Bank (WB 2002): Poverty Assessment in Bangladesh, Dhaka, The World Bank.

World Bank, The. (2005). *Attaining the Millennium Development Goals in Bangladesh*. Human Development Unit, South Asia Region.

World Bank, The. (2007). Bangladesh: Strategy for Sustained Growth. *Bangladesh Development Series* (Paper No. 14).

World Bank, The. (2008). Bangladesh: Poverty assessment for Bangladesh. *Bangladesh Development Series* (Paper No. 26).

World Bank, (Various Years). *World Development Indicators*.

Index

access to education, 173-177, 182, 186, 190, 245, 252
  and employment, 175
  gender gaps in, 187
access to human capital, 254
agricultural GDP, 9-10, 30
  growth of, 29-30
agricultural growth, 10, 12, 24, 29-31, 35, 55, 65, 69, 74, 99, 108, 127, 129, 133, 146, 168
  distributional impact of, 61
  regional aspects of, 55
agricultural production, 24, 37, 56, 62, 122, 168
agricultural productivity, 55, 56, 57, 60, 73
  differenceces in, 57
  district level variation of, 55
agricultural wage, determinants of, 138-139
agriculture, 8-10, 12, 29-31, 38, 49, 55-57, 60, 62, 64, 67, 70, 72-73, 89-90, 92, 97-99, 104, 107-108, 111-114, 116, 118, 120-123, 126, 129, 133-136, 139, 141, 146-147, 157-158, 168, 176, 218, 256, 260-263, 265, 274, 289-290
  GDP growth in, 6, 12, 99
  growth of value added in, 59
  nature of seasonality of labour use in, 108
  pattern of changes of real wage in, 82
  share of male labour force in, 90, 261
availability of arable land, 38
average propensity to save, 204

birth control, adoption rate of, 286, 289

calorie intake, rural-urban differences in, 206-207
capital investment, 24
casual employment, 176, 268, 269
cereal production, 73
Chayanovian hypothesis, 62
child labour, relationship between income and incidence of, 224
children, 154-155, 173, 176-177, 182, 184, 186-190, 193-194, 199, 211-234, 256, 272-273, 275, 283-284, 287-292, 297-299
  economic participation rate of, 215
  formal and informal employment of, 217
  labour force participation rate of, 214-216
children's employment and dropout, 225-226
children's employment impact of family's land ownership and income on, 223-224
  structure of, 217-218

China, 13
consumption, 47, 62, 70, 86, 116, 140, 197-198, 201-203, 205, 207-208, 236, 238, 243, 251, 260, 290
  growth of, 202
  rural urban difference in, 207-208
contraceptive prevalence rate, 285, 288
contract harvesting, 119
corruption, 7
crop agriculture, share of GDP from, 29
crop diversification, 38
crop production, 55-56, 72-73, 108, 110, 130
crop sector, determinants of productivity in, 60
  monthly pattern of labour use in, 109
cropping intensity, 36-38, 45, 51, 60, 62-63, 66-68, 116, 127, 130, 132

decent employment, 93, 105, 169
decision making, 253, 276, 277, 292, 295
  male and female earners role in, 277
  women's role in, 276-277
decision of labour allocation in non-agricultural activities, 107
demographic dividend, 149, 150, 151, 152, 165
demographic transition, 283, 285, 287
development puzzle, 7
disguised unemployment, 85

economic empowerment of women, major components of, 257
educated unemployment, 83, 103
education, 26, 42, 44-45, 137, 141, 145, 150, 156, 159-162, 164, 166, 173-176, 179-190, 194, 201, 222-224, 227-228, 231-232, 253-254, 265-272, 278, 282, 284, 286-287, 289-290, 292, 294-296, 298
  inequality in access to, 156, 174-175, 181
  intergenerational impact of, 182, 187
effective female headed households, income, asset and human capital of, 254
employed workforce, women's share in, 257-258
employment, 14, 21-22, 25, 27, 31, 34, 42, 62, 81-82, 84-96, 98-105, 107-109, 111-114, 116-118, 120-127, 129-130, 132-137, 141-144, 146, 149, 153, 155, 157, 159, 161-164, 166-173, 175-176, 184, 188-190, 211-213, 217-225, 227, 232-235, 237, 240-242, 246-247, 251, 253-254, 256-258, 261-264, 267-275, 278-281, 289, 292, 295, 298
  impact of irrigation on, 136
  sectoral composition of, 90
  share of agriculture in total, 90
  status of, 94, 157-158, 175-176, 213, 217-218, 224, 261
export earning, 21, 100

factors behind, 219
factors productivity, 22
family employment, 84, 88, 95, 136, 149, 157-158, 212-213, 225, 234, 269

family labour based agriculture, 289
family labour based enterprise, 25
family planning, impact of supply of family planning inputs on, 294-295
farm machinery, determinants of the use of, 67
farm size and productivity, relationship between, 57, 74
farm size and rate of HYV adoption, 42, 45, 71
female employment, 90-92, 94, 104, 258, 262-263, 270-271
  in agriculture, 91, 262
  sectoral composition of, 91
female headship and poverty of household, linkage between, 252-253
female labour force participation rate, 27, 88, 102
  impact of education on, 270
  relationship between poverty, education and, 269
female labour market, 91, 252, 261, 264, 268
female poverty, 252, 254
female underemployment, 86
female wage labourer, 241, 242
feminisation of poverty, 252
fertiliser, 44-45, 49-50, 52, 56, 60, 62, 65, 77, 100, 111, 129
fertility choice and demand side factors, 288
fertility decline, 224, 283-284, 287, 291, 297
  determinants of, 287
  factors contributing to, 284, 287
  pattern of, 285

fertility regulation, routes to, 298
food consumption, rural-urban difference in, 207
food insecurity, 107, 122-124, 126-127
  and employment, 123
  monthly employment and, 123
  seasonality of, 122
formal sector, 27, 95-96, 98, 105, 154, 217, 264, 266, 268
  size and share of labour force in, 96
  share of employment in, 95
  women engaged in, 264

gender wage gap, 266
Gross Domestic Product (GDP), 3-15, 19, 24, 28-31, 81, 88-90, 98-99, 258, 262, 264
  growth rate of, 4-5
  growth scenario, 3
  sectoral composition of, 8-9
  share of agriculture in, 9, 30
  share of crop agriculture in, 30
  share of non-agriculture in, 9, 30
  share of small manufacturing in, 19
  structural change of, 8-10
gross national income, 15

high yielding variety cultivation, sources of knowledge of, 44
high yielding variety technology, determinants of the extent of adoption of, 46
hired labour based enterprises, growth of, 27
household food insecurity, 108, 122

household income, 130, 137, 144, 173, 199, 202-204, 222, 224, 236, 249, 286-287, 299
  determinants of, 137, 253
  from agriculture and non-agriculture, 144
household savings rate, 202
human capital development, 152, 174, 211, 224, 232, 289
HYV adoption and farm size, relationship between, 45-47

inclusive growth, 82
income growth, impact of microcredit on, 235
income inequality, 15, 19, 173, 188-190
income poverty reduction, 200
India, 13-15, 21, 61, 85-86, 88, 94, 140, 258, 303-305, 308
Indonesia, 13
industrial growth, constraints to, 23-25
infant mortality rate, 199, 287
informal employment, 82, 105, 217
informal labour market, 84
informal sector, 25, 27-28, 84, 98-99, 189, 213, 217, 233, 268
  size and share of labour force in, 96
  women engaged in, 264
interregional migration of labour, 54
inter-village migration, 112, 127, 134
investment-GDP ratio, 5, 8
irrigated HYV rice, 130
irrigation intensity, 62

irrigation intensive cereal crops, 38
irrigation, 29, 35-39, 41-49, 53-54, 56, 60-63, 65-66, 70, 73, 129-131, 133, 135-139, 144-146
  as the leading input, 65-66
  extent of input use and, 65

jobless growth, 14, 102

Keynesian savings functions, 204

labour allocation, seasonality and, 117
labour constraint, 53-54, 68, 117-118, 127
labour force participation rate, 83, 151-152, 154, 156, 175, 184, 213-214
  age specific, 150, 154
  among youth population, 155
  female and male, 155
  rural and urban, 259
labour intensity, 22, 24
labour intensive industrialisation, 279
labour intensive irrigated crop, 131
labour market information, dissemination of, 172
labour market, 27, 81-84, 88, 91, 95-96, 99, 102-105, 107, 117, 119, 122, 124, 126-127, 129, 135, 141, 149-150, 157, 159-160, 166, 169, 171-172, 175, 184, 186, 188, 212, 220-221, 252-254, 261, 265, 267-268, 273, 275, 279
  impact of education on, 184
  structural change in, 82, 261
labour market, gender inequality in, 257

labour productivity, 22-23, 147, 173
labour supply, 52, 82, 87, 99, 105, 136-137, 140-141, 143-144, 150, 160, 167, 184, 270, 280
  individual decision based model of, 137
labour use, 41, 51-53, 71-72, 87, 107-112, 126-127, 130-133, 137, 221, 290
  impact of irrigated crops on total, 132
  impact of the growth of irrigated agriculture on total, 133
  in crop production, 108, 131-132
  monthly pattern of, 111
  season wise distribution of, 109
land availability for non-farm use, 23
landownership, among male and female headed households, 256
life cycle hypothesis, 205
livestock and poultry rearing, 261-262
  share of labour force in, 262
  women employed in, 262
lost potential, 12-13

Malthus, 283
manual irrigation, 53
manufacturing GDP, 19-21
  share of RMG to, 21
  share of small manufacturing in, 19
manufacturing sector, growth of, 17-19
manufacturing, capital intensity of major subsector of, 22

marginal farmers, 34, 72
marginal propensity to save, 202, 204
mechanised irrigation, 37
medium and large manufacturing, composition of, 20-21
Microcredit Regulatory Authority (MRA), 243-246, 307
microcredit, interest rate of, 243
microfinance institutions, 170, 278
  share of women borrowers in, 246
  sources of funds for, 245
microfinance, 170, 203, 235, 240, 278
micro-financed employment, 235
middle income trap, 14
missing female youth population, 152-153
modern inputs, determinants of the use of, 55
modern irrigation and HYV technology, benefits from, 130
multi-fibre arrangement, 100-102

negative income effect regime, 87
nominal residential female headed households, 254-255
nominal wage index, 97
non-agricultural income, 146
non-boro HYV, 44
non-cereal production, 55
non-crop agriculture, 39, 72
non-farm employment, 136
non-farm sector, 23, 29, 104, 147, 158, 168, 171, 218

non-food consumer goods, 209
non-formal education, 232
Non-governmental organisation (NGOs), 27, 163, 170-171, 232, 243-244, 246-248, 271, 273, 278, 280, 298, 305
non-irrigated crops, 36

on-farm water management, 39
overseas employment, 82, 88, 102-104, 165, 172
  female, 102
  growth of, 100, 102-103
overseas labour market, employment in, 99, 103

paddy processing, 239-242, 256, 272
paddy, 37, 39, 41, 60-61, 63, 65, 67, 71, 130-131, 134, 136, 138-141, 239-242, 256, 261, 272, 274-275
paid employment, 94-95, 161, 168, 213, 218, 224-225, 234, 241, 263, 269, 272, 289-290, 292
  factors affecting children participation in, 222-223
  share of working children engaged in, 218, 223
Pakistan, 13, 14, 15, 17, 101, 180, 301
Palli Karma-Sahayak Foundation (PKSF), 245
piece rate contract, 118
population density, 15, 31, 60, 62, 64

population growth, 26, 33, 149, 151, 283-285, 287, 298
  and socioeconomic factor, 283
  current momentum of, 297, 298
  links between food shortage and, 283
  potential demographic divided, size of, 151
poverty incidence, 98, 116, 127, 197-201, 203, 211, 253, 255
  divisional, 198-199, 209
  regional inequality in, 197
poverty reducing growth, 167
poverty reduction, 3, 14-15, 27, 69, 82, 173, 197-198, 200-201, 203, 209, 236, 283, 285, 297
  change of savings rate and, 197
poverty, 3, 14-15, 25, 27, 64, 69, 82, 98, 107, 114, 116, 127, 129-130, 134, 161, 167-168, 172-173, 175-176, 182, 187-188, 197-201, 203-206, 208-209, 211-212, 219-220, 222-223, 233, 235-236, 244, 251-255, 267-269, 279, 281, 283-286, 291-293, 295-297, 299
  children's health and education and, 290
  impact of microcredit on, 248
  linkages among quality of children and fertility and, 292

Quantum Index of Production, 20

readymade garment, 8, 21, 82, 100, 151
  employment growth in, 99-100
real wage, 28, 82, 96-99, 101, 104-105, 147, 290
  in construction, 98
  in manufacturing, 98

in the informal labour market in agriculture, 98
reduced savings rate, 203
  implications of, 203
  poverty reduction through, 201
regionally balanced growth, 56
regionally dispersed industrialisation strategy, 167
returns to labour and capital of microcredit recipient enterprises, 235, 238-240
rice mill, 241-242, 274

savings functions, 204-205
savings rate, determinants of, 204
savings, as a share of household income, 202
school enrolment, 153, 174, 177-178, 182-183, 186, 188-189, 199, 257, 259-260, 275, 290
  factors affecting, 41, 73, 219
  gender difference in, 178-179
  impact of poverty on, 236
  rate, 153, 174, 178, 189, 199, 259, 290
  regional difference in, 183
schooling, 42, 136, 156, 170, 174, 177, 185, 187-188, 206, 212-213, 219-220, 228-229, 231-232, 234, 270-271, 280, 289
  children employment and its link with, 211
  poor parent's attitude to, 229-230
seasonal food insecurity, link between seasonal unemployment and, 108
seasonal food insecurity, monthly variation of rice price and, 126
seasonal labour use in Bangladesh, 110
seasonal underemployment, implications of, 114-115
seasonal undernourishment, 116
seasonality and labour allocation, 117
sectoral GDP growth, link between real wage growth and, 98
self-employment and return to labour, linkages between, 239
service and industrial sectors, land constraint in, 24-25
share tenancy, impact of, 61
sharecropping, 34, 61, 142
small and tenant farmers, 39
small manufacturing, pattern of growth of, 19
SME refinancing scheme, 20
social development, 3, 15, 23, 199-201, 231, 284-285, 294
Sri Lanka, 13-14
subcontracting to female home based workers, 280
surplus labour economies, 81

technical and vocational education and training, 171
tenancy, and cropping intensity, 63
total fertility rate, 283
  age of marriage, poverty and, 292
  replacement level, 284, 297

underemployment, 27, 81-88, 93, 96, 98-99, 104, 113-114, 120, 126-127, 146, 159, 171, 176, 252,

257, 261, 279
  non-seasonal, 114
  rural and urban, 87
  seasonal, 87, 107, 114, 122, 126-127
unemployment rate in Bangladesh, 83
unpaid family employment, 92-94, 158, 280
urban employment, 266
urban informal sector enterprise, 25
urbanisation, and food habit, 209

very small farms, importance and efficiency of, 69-70
Vietnam, 13-15, 21, 101
vulnerable employment, 92, 104

wage labour based industrialisation, 27
wage labour households, crop income and other income of, 144
wage labour, 27, 62-63, 82, 129-130, 132, 134-136, 142, 145-147, 164, 166, 240-241, 274
wage labourers, impact of irrigation on household income of, 146
wage rate, 9, 116-117, 120-121, 125, 129-130, 134-135, 137, 139, 145-146, 148, 167, 211, 221, 237, 244, 257, 274-275, 281
  impact of irrigation on, 134
  in harvesting season, 119
  monthly fluctuation of, 125
wage, 9, 27-28, 34, 42, 62-63, 82, 87, 96-99, 104-105, 108, 114,
116-118, 120-121, 125-126, 129-130, 132, 134-142, 144-148, 164, 166-168, 175-176, 184, 186, 188, 190, 211, 220-221, 233, 237-238, 240-241, 244, 257, 264-271, 273-275, 278, 280-281
  gender differences in, 264-265
  impact of education on, 186
  non-farm, 147
  ratio of urban and rural, 98
  social factors behind gender differential of, 266-267
women empowerment, gender dimension of, 246
women's employment, determinants of, 267, 271
working children, 189, 211, 213-218, 220-222, 225-227, 229-230, 234
  employed in agriculture, 218
  parents' attitude towards, 222, 225
  sector composition of, 218
working children's education, constrains to, 230-231

youth employment, 150, 154, 158
  in agriculture, 158
  structural change of, 157
youth labour force, 104, 149-152, 154, 156-160, 165-166, 168, 172
  growth of, 150-152
  in non-agriculture, 158
  level of education of, 256
  unemployment rate among, 159
youth unemployment, 150, 159-160

zero opportunity cost of labour, 237